Illustrator:
Howard Chaney

Editor:
Mary Kaye Taggart

Editorial Project Manager:
Karen J. Goldfluss, M.S. Ed.

Editor in Chief:
Sharon Coan, M.S. Ed.

Creative Director:
Elayne Roberts

Associate Designer:
Denise Bauer

Cover Artist:
Chris Macabitas

Product Manager:
Phil Garcia

Imaging:
James Edward Grace

Publishers:
Rachelle Cracchiolo, M.S. Ed.
Mary Dupuy Smith, M.S. Ed.

How to Prepare Your Students for
Standardized Tests

Intermediate

Author:

Julia Jasmine, M.A.

Teacher Created Materials, Inc.
P.O. Box 1040
Huntington Beach, CA 92647
www.teachercreated.com
ISBN 1-1-57690-131-9
©1997 Teacher Created Materials, Inc.
Reprinted, 1999
Made in U.S.A.

Table of Contents

Student Practice Pages

(**NOTE: Boldface** page numbers indicate teacher script pages.)

Language Arts

Table of Contents *(cont.)*

Table of Contents *(cont.)*

Introduction

Traditional standardized tests are back! Returning with them is all of the test anxiety that we thought we had put behind us with the advent of alternative assessment. However, the truth of the matter is that in most cases traditional testing never went away at all. Alternative assessment requirements were simply added to the old methods of assessment. Many school districts continued to use their traditional standardized testing as well as their newer proficiency testing, which they added during the last great assessment upheaval. Teachers and their students felt that they were being "tested to death."

So, if standardized testing never really went away, just what is it that is happening now? It would probably be correct to say that what has returned is the emphasis on standardized testing. National standards are important now, and the states that give the right tests at the right times will receive the most money for education from the federal government.

The most realistic way to look at all of this is that there is not much the individual teacher can do about it either way. It will help our students, however, if we keep in mind that the old objections to standardized testing—the ones that made us seek out alternatives in the first place—are still valid:

- This is a big country with a diverse population, and when tests are "normed," the sample population may not reflect this enormous diversity.

- Students who are not naturally talented in the areas of language and math (who do not excel in what Howard Gardner calls the linguistic and logical/mathematical intelligences in *Frames of Mind: The Theory of Multiple Intelligences,* [Basic Books, 1983]) will not do well on achievement tests, even if these students may be immensely talented in other areas.

- Students who do not speak and read English fluently will not do well on the tests.

- Students who live in poverty will not have the experiential background to understand the questions on the test.

There are many people in education who can help to solve these problems:

- The test makers can help by keeping their assessment tools free from bias and basing their norms on a sample that is as representative of our population as possible.

- Educational administrators can help by interpreting the test results correctly, keeping in mind the student populations that are being tested, and by explaining their interpretations to the public.

- Teachers can help by giving their students the information they need to pass the tests. Some of this information consists of knowledge, but a great deal of it consists of test-taking skills, which are the subject of this book.

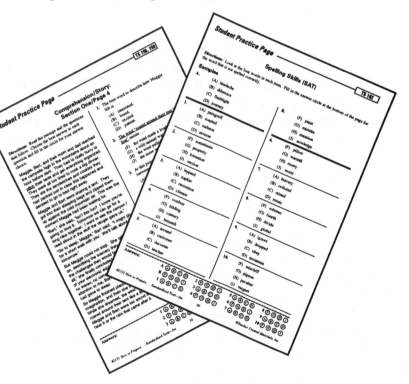

Test Success

At Least Three Requirements

The ability to do well when taking traditional standardized tests requires at least three things:

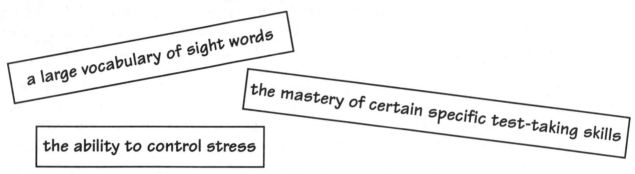

a large vocabulary of sight words

the mastery of certain specific test-taking skills

the ability to control stress

The vocabulary issue is discussed in detail in the section that follows. The test-taking skills, which will be briefly discussed here and reinforced in each relevant practice section, can be taught by teachers, used by students, and have nothing much to do with the stated purpose of the particular test—to determine a student's level in reading or math, for example. Some tools for controlling stress will also be suggested.

Who Needs Test-Taking Skills?

Certainly, all students need test-taking skills, but "good" students may need them most of all. Without test-taking stability, fluent readers may score low on the incremental skills that have been identified as necessary building blocks for beginning readers, for example. (These incremental skills are still included on some of the tests for third through fifth grades.) Fluent readers are well past the place where they labor over, or are even really aware of, beginning sounds, ending sounds, and vowel sounds. They just read. Similarly, students with excellent skills in logic and problem solving may not show much success on problems involving the basic math facts that are often learned by rote. Depending on the test you will be giving, you may need to teach some phonics and math skills almost as separate subjects.

The students who use these incremental skills without really noticing them are, of course, the very students you would like to have excel when they take whatever test your school or district has decided to give. They should be able to carry a record of success with them in their school careers, and you should get credit for teaching them. This is particularly important in an educational climate where school districts, schools, and individual teachers are judged on their students' test results which are often emblazoned across the newspapers to generate public reactions.

What Are These Skills?

The skills students need at all grade levels in order to do well on standardized tests include the ability to follow complicated and often confusing directions, the ability to scale back what they know and focus on just what is asked, the ability to choose among confusing distractors (multiple-choice answers), and the ability to maintain concentration during boring and tedious repetition. Since you have probably spent years perfecting your ability to give clear and easily understood directions, you probably love it when your students bring their existing knowledge to bear on a new problem, you most likely give students clear answer choices from which to choose, and you undoubtedly do not want to change your basic teaching style to one that is boring and repetitious, you will need another approach.

Test Success *(cont.)*

What to Do and How to Do It

You can teach your students to translate the test directions into the words that you use and that they understand. You can show them how to restrict their responses (no application or synthesis). You can turn the tedium into a game. You can teach test-taking skills during a separate segment of your school day and set up some kind of a reward system to help your students stay focused. The material that follows in this book will help you to do all of these things without having a negative impact on your curriculum or individual teaching style.

Inform the Students

Be sure to explain to the students what you are doing and why. Tell them that you will be teaching test-taking skills to them, establishing a room environment much like what they will experience during a real test, and often reading from a script. Assure them that the experience will reduce their stress levels and make them successful test takers. (Assure yourself that the experience will reduce your stress level too and make you look good when the scores are published in your local newspaper or produced as part of your own yearly evaluation.)

Address the Issue of Stress

Give your students some tools for handling the stress that accompanies test taking. Talk about routine habits that they can develop: getting enough sleep, eating a good breakfast, and getting some exercise after school. Even small children know they feel better after they use their large muscles by running, jumping, climbing, and so on. Consider sending home a letter encouraging parents to become part of the testing team by helping their children develop these habits.

Allow self-directed activities and free movement around your classroom when you are not presenting teacher-directed activities. In this way you will prevent the school day from turning into one long paper-and-pencil session.

Tell the students that they can use their imaginations to see themselves doing well on tests. Many athletes use this technique and have written or talked about it at length. They "see" themselves hitting the ball, making the basket, or winning the race. Read to your students some of these accounts and encourage them to see themselves feeling calm, thinking clearly, and marking the correct answers.

Use exercises such as deep breathing and stretching at regular intervals during the day. Try using a "Simon Says" format with younger students. Then, when the test time arrives, your students will be familiar with testing and will not be distracted because of the novelty of the activity.

The Vocabulary Piece

Sight Vocabulary

The size of your students' sight vocabularies will be a deciding factor in how well they score on standardized achievement tests. The term *sight vocabulary* is used here to mean words that students do not have to stop and figure out. There simply will not be time to apply decoding skills, no matter what they happen to be or how well your students can use them, to all of the words in the test. They must know not only the target words in vocabulary questions but also all of the words used in the stories and all of the words used in the distracters (multiple-choice answers). For example, if students cannot correctly read all of the possible answers in a question about spelling words, they will not be able to answer the question.

Depending on the format of the test you are giving, you may be able to encourage your students to answer all of the questions that contain words that they do know and then go back and use their decoding skills to figure out words that they did not recognize. However, because of time constraints, you may not always be able to offer this option to them.

Some Methods to Use

Whatever decoding skills or vocabulary-building skills you are using, consider adding some of these practice methods to increase your students' sight vocabularies. **Flashcards** are a wonderful, if old-fashioned, tool. So is **labeling** everything (a practice in which you write the names of everything in your classroom on cards or sentence strips and actually stick these labels on the objects). **Oral discussion** of words is a handy method that can be used as a part of instruction in any subject matter. Consider posting a list of words to accompany a social studies or science lesson or to provide a recall tool for the words you talked about in an oral discussion. Finally, give your students a **visual context** for as many words as possible. Although some of these skills may be associated with the primary classroom, they are effective at any age and will be particularly appropriate in classrooms where the students speak more than one language.

Flashcards

Gather words for vocabulary flashcards from all of the sources that are available to you. Just write the words on ordinary 3" x 5" or 5" x 7" (7.6 cm x 12.7 cm or 12.7 cm x 17.8 cm) index cards. You can play "Around the World" with these cards as a teacher-directed activity. Or, put packs of the flashcards in your activity centers for your students to use in partner or small group play. Also, you can have classroom aides, volunteers, or cross-age tutors use the flashcards with individuals or small groups.

Depending on how many words you manage to gather, you can pack them according to categories: Basal Reader, Prepositions, Plurals, and so on. (See "Some Sources for Words" starting on page 11.)

The Vocabulary Piece *(cont.)*

Labeling

Sit down with a stack of cards or strips and look around the room. Write a label for everything you see: wall, door, light switch, window, windowsill, teacher's desk, student's desk, table, floor, bookcase, book, pen, pencil, paper, and on and on. You can do this by yourself or you can do it with the students, having them read a word before taping it in the right place. Put loops of tape on the back of each card or strip so that the students can simply press them in place.

Use "reading the room" as a sponge activity when you have a minute or two to fill while waiting to go somewhere, such as an assembly or the computer lab.

Ask your principal if you can label the office, the cafeteria, and/or the multi-purpose room. Then you can "read the school" as you walk to and from lunch and assemblies.

The added benefit of this method is that each word has a concrete object attached to it.

This method will greatly assist those students who are just learning English.

Oral Discussion

This is the easiest of all the methods, requiring no supplies or setup. Just stop and talk about the words you are hearing or reading. (Consider reinforcing this method by jotting the words down on the chalkboard as you talk about them.) For example, if someone reads, hears, or says the word *stream,* you could initiate discussion with the following questions.

What is a stream?

How does a stream compare to a river?

What is a creek?

Who has ever seen a stream, a river, or a creek?

What did it (they) look like?

What are the differences among streams, rivers, creeks, and bodies of water like oceans or lakes?

Who has seen an ocean or a lake?

What did it (they) look like?

The added benefit of this method is that each word automatically has a basic concept attached to it.

The Vocabulary Piece *(cont.)*

Lists

If you had been making a list of the preceding oral discussion, you would have these words:

stream

river

creek

ocean

lake

Depending on the original source of the word *stream*—if it is part of a science lesson about bodies of water, for example—and depending on how many other words you stop to discuss, you might come up with quite an extensive list of words. You might have added pond, bay, sea, canal, gulf, and so on.

List all of these words on a chart titled "Bodies of Water." Post it somewhere in the classroom and review it occasionally.

Visual Context

Provide your students with a visual context for the words that they learn by showing and discussing as many videos and movies as you can fit into your busy day. Show science films, social studies films, math films, and films based on classic or modern stories. In order to make this method work, you will need to look at the movie or video with your class. Make a practice of stopping the projector or VCR to talk about the words. No matter what kind of a film or video you are watching, if your class had participated in the science lesson mentioned above you could stop it and say:

> Look. This is a river. This is what a river looks like in a city (or in a rural setting). I'll rewind the tape so that we can look at it again. Remember, we wrote the word "river" on our chart of "Bodies of Water." (Ask someone go to the chart and point out the written word.)

Try not to be pressured into feeling guilty for showing videos and movies to your students. Some people feel that anything visual is merely entertainment and object to this in the classroom. If you are faced with this kind of criticism, you can counter it by pointing out that you are using the visual experiences as part of your instructional method to maximize your students' success on the upcoming standardized tests by helping them to increase their vocabularies. If necessary, invite your critics to sit in on a lesson in which you do vocabulary exercises, using visual aids.

The Vocabulary Piece *(cont.)*

Some Sources for Words

You can get your words from anywhere and everywhere. For purposes of standardized testing, in addition to what might be called "**grade-level words**," your students will need to know **subject-specific words**, words that may be **outside of their personal experiential backgrounds**, **plural forms of words, words with affixes, compound words, contractions, synonyms and antonyms, words with more than one meaning,** and **prepositions and their meanings**. They will also need a strategy for dealing with a variety of **proper names** and know how the word "**blank**" is used in many standardized test questions.

Grade-Level Words

If you are using a basal reader series, a good source of grade-level words is the word list that usually appears at the back of the book or in the teacher's materials. You should also provide yourself with the word lists from the preceding books in the series. For example, if you are using a fifth grade reader, get the word lists from the third and fourth grade books. If these lists are not provided, call the publisher's customer representative and ask for them.

If you are using other kinds of reading materials—a literature-based program for example—skim through the books and pull the words that you think are the most relevant. Also, get words from other standard lists: contact publishers and ask for the word lists for their basal series; use the Dolch list which you can probably find in a teacher supply store; use the EDL list which contains the words appearing at different grade levels in the most used basal reader series; purchase some of the teacher and/or parent resource books containing basic word lists. Also, if you are fairly new to the field of teaching, talk to teachers on your staff who have been teaching for awhile and who may be willing to share their resources. They probably have word lists tucked away in their files, dating from the last time the educational pendulum swung in the direction of standardized testing.

Subject-Specific Words

Since students understand big words as easily as little ones, use the special vocabularies of the subjects you deal with as you teach. Talk about "numerals" as well as "numbers." Use words like "addend," "sum," "difference," and "product" routinely so that your students will be used to them. Talk about "transportation" and "communication" during social studies. Say that you are going to "observe" or "experiment" when beginning a science activity. Add math words, science words, and social studies words to your flashcards and lists. Most math, science, and social studies texts include glossaries. These are excellent sources for important words.

The Vocabulary Piece *(cont.)*

Words Based on Experiential Backgrounds

Students need to comprehend the meanings of many words that will not be part of their experiential backgrounds. For example, rural students will need some conceptual context for words such as "subway" and "skyscraper." Suburban students may need to recognize the meanings of such words as "apartment" and "taxi." Urban students, especially those who live in the inner city, should be given some idea of what split-level tract houses and suburban shopping malls look like along with the more obviously rural stables and pastures.

Students in many parts of the South and Southwest may need to be given some information about snow. They may know that it is white, but they will not necessarily know that it is cold. Students who live away from the coasts may have no concepts to go with the word "ocean," and students who live on the Great Plains may need to be given some idea of what mountains look like.

Keep in mind that it is always safer to assume that students *do not* have an experiential background than that they *do*. Just because you live only 30 miles from the ocean or the mountains does not mean that your students have ever been to those places.

Lists of words based on experiential background (or the lack of it) will be lists that you develop for your own situation, based on the needs that you identify. The methods described in developing visual contexts for words (see page 10) will be of use here, as will oral discussion. Choose films that will fill in some of your students' blank places. Once you decide on the words you need, you can apply the other methods for reinforcement by making lists and flashcards.

If you are in a situation that allows for field trips, these will help your students develop experiential backgrounds and enrich their vocabularies. When you know where you are going, prepare a list of words that reflect the things that you think you will see and give a copy of the list to each student. Make sure that they can read the words on the list by reviewing and discussing them as often as is necessary. (Add some pictures to help younger students or those who speak little English to remember the words.) Take the lists with you. Have your students look for the things on the list and check off the ones they find. They can also add words to their lists. (Remember to take pencils.) When you get back from the field trip, talk about what all of the words mean and add them to your flashcards and/or make a list titled "Our Field Trip."

Note: On pages 192–201 you will find a list of selected words that may be added to your spelling program throughout the year. Since these words often appear on standardized tests, it would benefit students to become familiar with them prior to taking a test.

The Vocabulary Piece *(cont.)*

Plurals

On standardized tests, students are expected to be able to differentiate between the singular and plural forms of both written words and words given orally and then to use these differences in comprehension questions. Recognition of singular and plural forms of words becomes particularly important in the test section dealing with language usage. In this section students will be expected to identify cases in which subjects and verbs do or do not agree.

When you talk about words, talk about their plurals too. Add plurals to your flashcards and word lists.

Words with Affixes and Inflectional Endings

Students need to be able to read and know the meanings of words with affixes because they will be asked to recognize the **root** word. For example, if the given word is "careful" and two of the distracters are "care" and "car," the student who cannot read the given word with comprehension will not know which answer to choose.

Students also must know the meanings of the suffixes themselves and understand how they affect the meanings of the root words. Remember that the "s" or "es" that forms a plural on the end of a word is sometimes considered a suffix and sometimes an inflectional ending. Teach your students about these two types of endings.

Have your students add prefixes and suffixes to words for practice. Talk about comparatives and superlatives and have the students add "er" and "est" to words that they already know (for example: slow, slower, slowest).

Compound Words

Compound words are made up of two parts that can each stand alone. Students must be able to distinguish compound words from words with prefixes and suffixes. Have your students brainstorm a list of compound words and use them to make lists and packs of flashcards. Help them get started with sports words: baseball, basketball, football, etc.

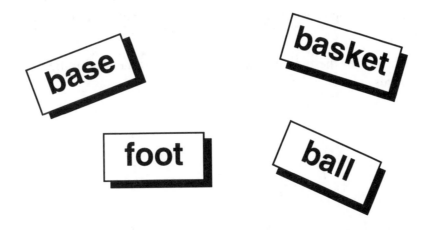

The Vocabulary Piece *(cont.)*

Contractions

The students will be expected to know the words that are represented by common contractions. Do not forget "let's," "I'll," "won't," and "you're." Put a contraction on one side of a flashcard and the words it represents on the other side so that your students can quiz each other.

Synonyms and Antonyms

Both synonyms and antonyms for words can be generated during oral discussions. Make a game of listing them and talk about the fact that synonyms mean the same (or almost the same) as a given word and antonyms mean the opposite.

Words with More Than One Meaning

Words of this type are best demonstrated with an example of a test item.

> Fill in the circle next to the answer that fits best in the blanks in both sentences.
>
> The children _____ into the pool.
>
> The _____ flew into the barn.
>
> ○ bird   ○ jumped
>
> ○ dove   ○ played

Some of the words fit into one sentence or the other, but only one word fits into both sentences.

Prepositions

In order to be successful when taking standardized tests, students need to know (read and understand the meanings of) all of the common prepositions. One easy way to deal with this need is to approach it in terms of opposites: up/down, in/out, over/under, around/through, before/after, to/from, and so on.

If you make flashcards of these words, add a graphic of some kind to help your students remember the words.

The Vocabulary Piece *(cont.)*

Proper Names

Your students will encounter many proper names in sentences and stories, and not all of these will be of the "Dick and Jane" variety. Many unusual names are used as well as many that reflect a range of ethnic diversity. Meeting an unfamiliar proper name, especially as the very first word of a sentence or story, often has the effect of stopping students in their tracks. You can teach them to substitute the word "blank" (see next section) for the names they do not know. You can also make them familiar with the written forms of the names of all of the students in your classroom and point out all of the proper names when you read stories.

Not being able to read proper names *correctly* is a real problem only when the gender of the person named is vital for comprehension. For example: If a statement read, "Bruce and John are smiling," and the pictures show one boy smiling, a boy and a girl smiling, and two boys smiling, it would be imperative that the test taker know that "Bruce" and "John" are both boys' names. There is not much you can do about this except expose your students to a number of proper names. (In addition, you should probably make your students aware of the fact that hair length is usually used to show the difference between boys and girls in the pictures that show only faces on the tests.)

"Blank"

The use of the word "blank" is both a test-taking and a vocabulary issue. Many oral questions are asked using the word "blank," and many written questions are set up with a blank (_____) in them. For example, you might be asked to say, "Read the story and the sentence below it. Choose the words that go in the blank."

Maria went to the store for her mother.

She bought some bread.

When she got back home, her mother made a sandwich for her.

Maria bought _____ for her mother.

○ the store

○ some bread

○ back home

○ a sandwich

The Vocabulary Piece *(cont.)*

Teach your students to read the statement to themselves, using the word "blank":

> Maria bought *blank* for her mother.

Then have them read the statement putting each answer choice in place of the blank:

> Maria bought *the store* for her mother.

> Maria bought *some bread* for her mother.

> Maria bought *back home* for her mother.

> Maria bought *a sandwich* for her mother.

Stress the importance of reading all of the choices in this way and also of checking back in the story before making a decision. The sentence should not only make sense but it should also reflect comprehension of the story.

If your students do not recognize the proper name "Maria," have them read the story to themselves like this:

> *Blank* went to the store for her mother.

Maximizing Vocabulary Results

Send the word lists home with the students:

- Make them part of your homework.
- Use them for spelling words.
- Check out the packs of flashcards to your students in the same way you might check out library books.
- Use the words as the basis for storywriting.

Have contests with prizes (stickers, candy, free time, etc.):

- Who can read a pack of words?
- Who can read the most packs of words?
- Who can tell the meanings of these words?
- Who can add a new word to this list?
- Who can say a synonym word for each of these words?
- Who can write a synonym word for each of these words?

The Vocabulary Piece *(cont.)*

Have the students teach each other:

- As soon as one student has mastered a list or a pack of words, have him or her teach those words to another student.
- As soon as one student has mastered a list or a pack of words, have him or her teach those words to a small group of students.

Have the students play and/or create games:

- Give your students cards to make double sets of word packs. Have them use the double packs to play "Memory."
- Play "20 Questions" with words from your lists. (I'm thinking of a word on our list of math words . . . .)
- Give your students the opportunity to make up word games and to teach them to the class.

Encourage the students to create their own word banks:

- Let the students make dictionaries in three-ring binders. They can add notes, definitions, and pictures to help them remember words. If you want (and if paper is plentiful) let them put only one entry on each page so that they can resort the pages when new words are added to keep their words in alphabetical order.
- Make available file boxes such as those made for recipe cards. Have the students write their words and definitions on index cards and file them in alphabetical order. Add divider cards with tabs showing the letters of the alphabet to help organize this process. Relevant facts can also be added to the definitions to provide context.

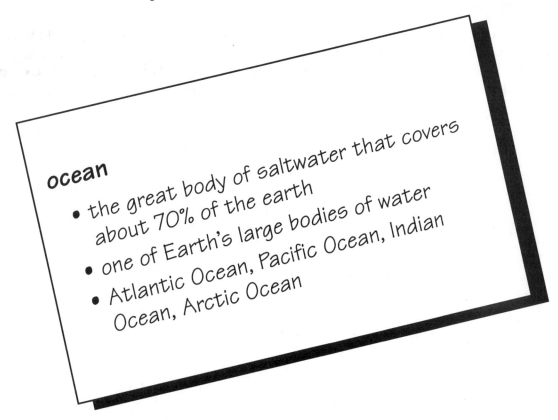

ocean
- the great body of saltwater that covers about 70% of the earth
- one of Earth's large bodies of water
  Atlantic Ocean, Pacific Ocean, Indian Ocean, Arctic Ocean

The Vocabulary Piece *(cont.)*

Have the students use the word lists for writing stories:

- Challenge the students to use as many of the words on a list as they can in a story.

- Tell them to highlight all of the words in a story that are on one or more of the lists in the classroom.

- Let the students use a list of sports words to write a sports story and/or a science list to write a science fiction story.

Tell your students to use the word lists for reading activities:

- Have them read newspaper articles and highlight all of the "list words" they find.

- Divide up a newspaper and have a group search for "list words" to highlight. Count the words and declare the group with the most highlighted words the winner.

An Ongoing Process

Keep in mind that gathering words for your word lists is an ongoing process. Try to add to your list every day and use the various methods suggested in this section. Many of the methods can be approached as sponge activities to make your school day more fun. They will also help your students ease into a richer sight vocabulary that will increase their chances for success on standardized tests.

How to Use This Book

Where to Start

1. Consult the appropriate chart from pages 22–30 for the test you will be giving. (See "Skill Charts" beginning on page 21 for some general information.)

2. Look down the list of skills that appear on that test. You will find page numbers referring you to the Student Practice Pages (SPP) and Teacher Scripts (TS) that address each skill. If you will be giving the CTBS "Book B" test, for example, you will find that the first vocabulary skill listed is synonyms.

3. Identify the pages you will be using.

> **Note:** Abbreviated cross-references have been provided throughout the Student Practice Pages and the Teacher Scripts. To find the teacher page for any Student Practice Page (pages 31–143), see the box at the top of the student page marked TS (Teacher Script). To locate the student page for any Teacher Script (pages 144–189), see the box next to the skill title marked SPP (Student Practice Page).

Making Practice Test Booklets/Scripts/Answer Key

❑ Use the pages you have identified to make a practice test booklet for each of your students.

❑ Put your practice test booklets together by following these steps:

- Make one copy of each of the Student Practice Pages you selected.
- Do not forget to include a cover sheet (page 190).
- Assemble the Student Practice Pages in the order that they appear on the chart.
- Number the pages in the upper right-hand corner.
- If you want your students to stop at the bottom of a page, add a stop sign. If you want them to go ahead, draw an arrow.
- When the pages are arranged and numbered and you have added any symbols you need, make enough copies for your students and staple the pages together in booklet form. Do not forget to make one or two extras for yourself. You will need one for an answer key (see below).

❑ Put your Teacher Script booklet together by following these steps:

- Identify and copy the Teacher Script for each Student Practice Page you selected.
- Several scripts appear on many of the script pages. If you do not need one or more of the scripts on a page you have selected, draw an "X" through the part(s) you will not be using.
- Assemble the script pages in the same order as the Student Practice Pages.
- A Teacher Script cover sheet is provided on page 191.
- Compare your script pages to the student booklet and write the page numbers from the Student Practice Pages onto the appropriate blanks in your script.
- Staple the script pages together in booklet form.

❑ An answer key has been provided on pages 206–224. You may work directly from this answer key or make an answer key for each page by marking the correct answers in one of your extra student practice booklets as you give the test.

How to Use This Book (cont.)

Follow Up

❑ As you use the practice pages, if you come across a skill that is hard for your students, try these ideas:

  • Teach the skill in various ways in your regular curriculum.

  • Create additional supplementary practice pages of your own.

  • Discuss the skill and then retest at a later date, using the practice page in this book.

Teaching the Test-Taking Skills

❑ Set aside a block of time each day to teach test skills, using the booklets you have made.

❑ Provide time for the students to use the restrooms before you start. Anxious students need to use the restrooms more often.

❑ Make your room environment as test-like as possible.

  • If your desks are pushed together in groups, have the students move them apart.

  • Put a "Testing—Do Not Disturb" sign on the door.

  • Explain "test etiquette" to your students:

  -No talking

  -Attentive listening

  -Following directions (such as, "Stop working and put your pencil down")

  • Spend some time explaining the rows of answer circles at the bottom of each practice page. These are designed to approximate the answer sheets the students will be using on the actual tests. Show the students how to keep their places by checking back and forth between the numbers on the practice answer sections and the numbers on the practice pages.

❑ Provide a strip of construction paper for each student to use as a page marker. These can double as bookmarks when your testing practice is finished for the day. Make extras for replacements.

❑ Provide scratch paper and encourage the students to use it. This is really necessary for math questions and comes in handy for some language arts items too.

❑ Establish a routine for replacing broken pencils. Give each student two pencils to start with and have a back-up pencil supply handy. Tell the students that they will need to raise their broken pencils in their hands so that you can give them new ones and take the broken ones without any disturbance. Ask a student or two to take on the job of keeping the pencils sharpened. If your school is short of funds for classroom supplies, send home a letter asking parents to provide pencils. And try to stay calm. Pencils break. Students who are worried about your reaction to their broken pencils will not do as well on the test. You cannot relieve all test anxiety, but you can relieve "pencil anxiety."

❑ Explain to your students that you will be reading from a script and repeating directions and questions in a way that may not sound like your usual teaching style.

Explain typical test symbols such as the arrow that means continue and the stop sign, usually at the bottom of a page, that means do not continue. If applicable to the test pages you are using, explain the answer choice that indicates that the correct answer does not appear. This choice is sometimes found on the math pages. Most importantly, try to get a look at the test you will be giving (or a sample of the test) so that you can tell your students about any differences that they may see in format. Although they may know the skills, format can sometimes be confusing.

Skills Charts

Find the Right Test

Look at the charts on pages 22 through 30 and the headings on the charts themselves to find the type of test (CTBS, ITBS, MAT, etc.) that you will be giving and the edition (Revised Edition, Fourth Edition, etc.).

In General

In general, the older editions of the tests consist of one booklet for grades three through five. This is often called "Book B." The later editions of the tests are often separated and numbered by grade level: Book 3, Book 4, and Book 5. The Texas Assessment of Academic Skills (TAAS) tests at grades three and five.

If you are on the low end of the grade level range for a test (giving any of the older editions in a third grade classroom, for example), prepare your students for the fact that there will be a lot of material that they will not be familiar with and will not be expected to know.

Note that on the charts on pages 21–30 the numbers in parentheses represent the grade levels of the tests.

Test Editions and Levels

CAT	*Third Edition*	*[Level]*		*Fourth Edition*	*[Level]*
	Book B (3–6)	[14,15]		Book 3 (3)	[13]
				Book 4 (4)	[14]
				Book 5 (5)	[15]
CTBS	*Old Edition*	*[Level]*		*Revised Edition*	*[Level]*
	Book B (3–5)	[F]		Book B (3–5)	[13, 14]
ITBS	*Old Edition*	*[Level]*		*Revised Edition*	*[Level]*
	Book B (3–5)	[9, 10, 11]		Book 3 (3)	[9]
				Book 4 (4)	[10]
				Book 5 (5)	[11]
MAT	*Third Edition*	*[Level]*		*Fourth Edition*	*[Level]*
	Book B (3–5)	[Elementary]		Book 3 (3)	[E1]
				Book 4 (4)	[E2]
				Book 5 (5)	[I1]
SAT	Book B (3–5)				
TAAS	Grade 3				
	Grade 5				

A Look at Skills Tested in CAT

Third Edition Book B (3–6)		Fourth Edition Book 3 (3)	
Skill	**Page**	**Skill**	**Page**
Word Analysis		**Word Analysis**	
Consonant Sounds	31–36	Sounds	31–36, 37
Vowel Sounds	35, 37–39	Compounds	40, 41
Root Words	42	Prefixes	42
Affixes	42	Suffixes	42
		Root Words	42
Vocabulary		**Vocabulary**	
Synonyms	44	Synonyms	44
Antonyms	45	Antonyms	45
Multiple Meanings	48, 49	Multiple Meanings	48, 49
Affixes	50	Affixes	50
In Context	51, 52	In Context	51, 52
Comprehension		**Comprehension**	
Selections	54–74	Stories	54–74
Spelling		Critical Reading	75, 76
Spelling Skills	77, 78	**Spelling**	
Language Mechanics		Spelling Skills	77, 78
Capitalization	84	**Language Mechanics**	
Punctuation	87, 88	Capitalization	84
Capitalization and Punctuation	91	Punctuation	87, 88
Language Expression		Capitalization and Punctuation	91
Usage	92, 93	**Language Expression**	
Sentences	96, 97	Usage	92, 93
Sentence Combining	98	Sentences	96, 97
Topic Sentences	99	Paragraphs	100, 101
Sentence Sequence	100	**Math Computation**	
Math Computation		Addition	115–118
Addition	115–118	Subtraction	119–122
Subtraction	119–122	Multiplication	123–125
Multiplication	123–125	Division	126
Division	126	**Math Concepts/Application**	
Math Concepts/Application		Numeration	127, 128
Numeration	127, 128	Geometry	131, 132
Number Sentences	129	Measurement	133–138
Number Theory	130	Problem Solving	140–143
Problem Solving	140–143		
Measurement	133–138		
Geometry	131, 132		
Study Skills			
Library Skills	106		
Parts of a Book	107, 108, 109		
Dictionary Skills	110, 111		

A Look at Skills Tested in CAT

Fourth Edition **Book 4 (4)**		**Fourth Edition** **Book 5 (5)**	
Skill	**Page**	**Skill**	**Page**
Vocabulary		**Vocabulary**	
Synonyms	44	Synonyms	44
Antonyms	45	Antonyms	45
Words in Context	51, 52	Words in Context	51, 52
Derivations	47	Derivations	47
Affix Meanings	50	Affix Meanings	50
Multiple Meanings	48, 49	Multiple Meanings	48, 49
Reading Comprehension		**Reading Comprehension**	
Stories	54–75	Stories	54–74
Spelling		**Spelling**	
Spelling Skills	77, 78	Spelling Skills	77, 78
Language Mechanics		**Language Mechanics**	
Punctuation	87, 88	Punctuation	87, 88
Capitalization and Punctuation	91	Capitalization and Punctuation	91
Language Expression		**Language Expression**	
Usage	92, 93	Usage	92, 93
Sentences	96, 97	Sentences	96, 97
Paragraphs	99, 100	Paragraphs	99, 100
Math Computation		**Math Computation**	
Addition	115–118	Addition	115–118
Subtraction	119–122	Subtraction	119–122
Multiplication	123–125	Multiplication	123–125
Division	126	Division	126
Math Concepts/Applications		**Math Concepts/Applications**	
Numeration	127, 128	Numeration	127, 128
Geometry	131, 132	Geometry	131, 132
Measurement	133–138	Measurement	133–138
Problem Solving	140–143	Problem Solving	140–143
Work-Study Skills		**Work-Study Skills**	
Index	09	Table of Contents	108
Dictionary Skills	110, 111	Dictionary Skills	110, 111
Reference Sources	106	Outlines	112
		Maps and Graphs	113, 114

A Look at Skills Tested in CTBS

Book B (3–5)

Skill	Page
Vocabulary	
Synonyms	44
Affix Meanings	50
Multiple Meanings	48, 49
Words in Context	51, 52
Reading Comprehension	
Stories	54–74
Critical Reading	56, 64, 69, 74, 75
Spelling	
Spelling Skills	77, 78
Language Mechanics	
Capitalization	84
Punctuation	87, 88
Capitalization and Punctuation	91
Language Expression	
Usage	92, 93
Sentences	96, 97
Sentence Combining	98
Paragraphs	99
Organization	100
Math Computation	
Addition	115–118
Subtraction	119–122
Multiplication	123–125
Division	126
Math Concepts/Applications	
Numeration	127, 128
Number Sentences	129
Number Theory	130
Measurement	133–138
Geometry	131, 132
Problem Solving	140–143
Work-Study Skills	
Parts of a Book	107, 108, 109
Dictionary Skills	110, 111

Book B (3–5)–Revised

Skill	Page
Word Analysis	
Sounds	31–36, 37
Compounds	40, 41
Prefixes	42
Suffixes	42
Root Words	42
Vocabulary	
Synonyms	44
Antonyms	45
Multiple Meanings	48, 49
Affix Meanings	50
Words in Context	51, 52
Reading Comprehension	
Stories	54–74
Fact and Opinion	55, 60, 66, 71
Critical Reading	56, 64, 69, 71, 75
Spelling	
Spelling Skills	77, 78
Language Mechanics	
Capitalization	84
Punctuation	87, 88
Capitalization and Punctuation	91
Language Expression	
Usage	92, 93
Sentences	96, 97
Paragraphs	99, 100
Math Computation	
Addition	115–118
Subtraction	119–122
Multiplication	123–125
Division	126
Math Concepts/Applications	
Numeration	127, 128
Geometry	131, 132
Measurement	133–138
Problem Solving	140–143
Work-Study Skills	
Outlines and Schedules	112
Maps and Graphs	113, 114
Catalog Cards	106
Reference Sources	106
Guide Words	111

A Look at Skills Tested in ITBS

Third Edition **Book B (3–5)**		**Fourth Edition** **Book 3 (3)**	
Skill	**Page**	**Skill**	**Page**
Vocabulary		**Vocabulary**	
Synonyms	44	Vocabulary Skills	44–52
Reading Comprehension		**Reading Comprehension**	
Facts	55, 60, 71	Selections	54–74
Inferences	56, 61, 68, 72	**Spelling**	
Generalizations	56, 62, 67, 71	Spelling Skills	79
Spelling		**Language Arts**	
Spelling Skills	79	Capitalization and Punctuation	85, 89, 91
Language Mechanics		Usage and Expression	92, 93
Capitalization	85	Sentences	96, 97
Punctuation	89	Paragraphs	99, 100
Language Expression		**Math Computation**	
Usage	92, 93	Addition	115–118
Correct Words	92, 93	Subtraction	119–122
Sentences	96, 97	Multiplication	123–125
Paragraphs	99, 100	Division	126
Math Computation		**Math Concepts/Applications**	
Addition	115–118	Concepts/Estimation	127–130
Subtraction	119–122	Problem Solving	140–143
Multiplication	123–125	Data Analysis	140–143
Division	126	**Work-Study Skills**	
Fractions/Decimals	115–125	Alphabetizing	110
Math Concepts/Applications		Parts of a Book	107
Numeration	127, 128	Table of Contents	108
Number Sentences	129	Maps	113
Whole Numbers	130		
Fractions/Money	117, 121, 125, 133–135		
Measurement	133–138		
Geometry	131, 132		
Math Problem Solving			
Addition/Subtraction	140–143		
Multiplication/Division	140–143		
Multiple Step Computations	140–143		
Work-Study Skills			
Maps	113		
Graphs and Tables	114		
Dictionary Skills	110, 111		
Table of Contents/Index	108, 109		
Reference Sources	106		

A Look at Skills Tested in ITBS

Fourth Edition Book 4 (4)		**Fourth Edition Book 5 (5)**	
Skill	**Page**	**Skill**	**Page**
Vocabulary		**Vocabulary**	
Vocabulary Skills	44–52	Vocabulary Skills	44–52
Reading Comprehension		**Reading Comprehension**	
Stories	54–74	Stories	54–74
Spelling		**Spelling**	
Spelling Skills	79	Spelling Skills	79
Language Arts		**Language Arts**	
Capitalization and Punctuation	85, 89, 91	Capitalization and Punctuation	85, 89, 91
Usage and Expression	92, 93	Usage and Expression	92, 93
Sentences	96, 97	Sentences	96, 97
Paragraphs	99, 100	Paragraphs	99, 100
Math Computation		**Math Computation**	
Addition	115–118	Addition	115–118
Subtraction	119–123	Subtraction	119–122
Multiplication	123–125	Multiplication	123–125
Division	126	Division	126
Math Concepts/Applications		**Math Concepts/Applications**	
Concepts/Estimation	127–130	Concepts/Estimation	127–130
Problem Solving	140–143	Problem Solving	140–143
Data Analysis	140–143	Data Analysis	140–143
Work-Study Skills		**Work-Study Skills**	
Alphabetizing	110	Alphabetizing	110
Parts of a Book	107	Parts of a Book	107, 108, 109
Table of Contents	108	Maps	113
Maps	113	Reference Sources	106

A Look at Skills Tested in MAT

Third Edition Book B (3–5)		Fourth Edition Book 3 (3)	
Skill	**Page**	**Skill**	**Page**
Vocabulary in Context		**Vocabulary Skills**	
Consonants	31–36	Synonyms	44
Vowels	37–39	Antonyms	45
Word Part Clues	41, 42, 43	Multiple Meanings	48, 49
Reading Comprehension		**Reading Comprehension**	
Stories	54–74	Stories	54–74
Spelling		**Spelling**	
Spelling Skills	82, 83	Spelling Skills	82, 83
Language Mechanics		**Language Mechanics**	
Capitalization	84–86	Capitalization	84–86
Punctuation	87–90	Punctuation	87–90
Capitalization and Punctuation	91	**Language Expression**	
Language Expression		Usage	92, 93
Usage	92, 93	Sentences	96, 97
Grammar and Syntax	94, 95	Paragraphs	99, 100
Math Operations		**Math Computation**	
Addition	115–118	Addition	115–118
Subtraction	119–122	Subtraction	119–122
Multiplication	123–125	Multiplication	123–125
Division	126	Division	126
Math Concepts/Applications		**Math Concepts/Applications**	
Numeration	127, 128	Estimation	140
Measurement	133–138	Problem Solving	141–143
Geometry	131, 132	**Work-Study Skills**	
Problem Solving	140–143		
Work-Study Skills		Parts of a Book	107, 108, 109
Alphabetizing	110	Alphabetizing	110
Dictionary Skills	111	Dictionary Skills	111
		Reference Sources	106

A Look at Skills Tested in MAT

A Look at Skills Tested in SAT/SAT 9

SAT Book B (3–5)		**SAT 9** Primary 3—Intermediate 3 Fall, Grade 4—Spring Grade 6	
Skill	**Page**	**Skill**	**Page**

Word Analysis		**Word Reading**	
Beginning Sounds	31, 33, 34, 36	Sounds and Analysis	31–43
Middle and Ending Sounds	32, 33, 34, 36	**Reading Vocabulary**	44–46, 48, 49, 51, 52
Vowel Sounds	35, 37–39	**Reading Comprehension**	
Syllabication	43	Initial Understanding	54–56, 61
Vocabulary		Interpretation	54, 57, 61, 66, 67, 71
Word Meanings	44–46	Critical Analysis	56, 64, 69, 74–76
Context Clues	51, 52	Reading Strategy	54, 55, 60, 65
Multiple Meanings	48, 49	Listening	53
Reading Comprehension		**Writing Assessment**	
Listening	53	Open-Ended Assessment	101–105
Stories	54–74	**Mathematics**	
Spelling		Problem Solving	140–143
Spelling Skills	80, 81	Procedures	115–130
Language Mechanics		**Spelling**	
Usage	92, 93	Spelling Skills	77–83
Capitalization	86	**Language Mechanics**	
Punctuation	90	Capitalization	84–86
Language Expression		Punctuation	87–91
Sentence Structure	96, 97	Usage	92, 93
Sentence Combining	98	**Study Skills**	
Math Computation		Parts of a Book	107–109
Addition	115–118	Resource Materials	106
Subtraction	119–122	Outlining	112
Multiplication	123–125	**Science**	
Division	126	Cause and Effect	57, 63, 65
Math Concepts/Applications		Estimation	140
Numeration	127, 128	Seeking Patterns	128
Number Theory	129, 130	Reading Instruments	136–138
Geometry	131, 132	Making Calculations	139–141
Measurement	133–138	Drawing Conclusions	57, 62, 67, 71
Problem Solving	140–143	**Social Science**	
Work-Study Skills		Maps	113
Alphabetizing	110	History	70
Reference Skills	106	Geography	71, 60–61
Dictionary Skills	111	Civics	105
Parts of a Book	107, 108, 109		

A Look at Skills Tested in TAAS

Grade 3	Grade 5

Skill	Page	Skill	Page
Language Arts		**Language Arts**	
Sentences	96, 97	Sentences	96, 97
Usage	92, 93	Usage	92, 93
Writing Mechanics	77–91	Writing Mechanics	77–91
Descriptive Writing	101	Descriptive Writing	101
Informative Writing	102	Informative Writing	102
Narrative Writing	103	Narrative Writing	103
		Classificatory Writing	104
		Persuasive Writing	105
Reading Comprehension		**Reading Comprehension**	
Vocabulary	54–74	Vocabulary	54–74
Supporting Ideas	54, 60, 65, 70	Supporting Ideas	54, 60, 65, 70
Main Idea	54, 60, 65, 70	Main Ideas	54, 60, 65, 70
Relationships/		Relationships/	
Outcomes	58, 59, 61, 62, 66, 67, 71, 73	Outcomes	58, 59, 61, 62, 66, 67, 71, 73
Generalizations/Inferences	56, 61, 67, 68, 71	Generalizations/Inferences	56, 61, 67, 68, 71
Reality and Fantasy	56, 64, 69, 74	Evaluation	56, 64, 69, 74
Math Concepts		**Math Concepts**	
Number Concepts	127–129	Number Concepts	127–129
Number Relations	127–129	Number Relations	127–129
Geometry	131, 132	Geometry	131–132
Measurement	133–138	Measurement	133–138
Probability and Statistics	139	Probability and Statistics	139
Math Operations		**Math Operations**	
Addition	115–118	Addition	115–118
Subtraction	119–122	Subtraction	119–122
Multiplication	123–125	Multiplication	123–125
Division	126	Division	126
Problem Solving		**Problem Solving**	
Estimation	140	Estimation	140
Strategies	141	Strategies	141
Problem Solving	142	Problem Solving	142
Reasonable Answers	143	Reasonable Answers	143

Note: Even though the TAAS (Texas Assessment of Academic Skills) Grade 3 Test is often given at the beginning of the third grade as a pre-test to establish a baseline, it is included here because it is designated as a third grade test.

Word Analysis: Consonant Sounds/Beginning

Directions: Read the word with the underlined letter or letters. Decide what sound the letter or letters make. Then fill in the circle for the word that has the same sound.

Samples

A. <u>c</u>all

   (A) take

   (B) cereal

   (C) match

B. <u>tr</u>ip

   (F) part

   (G) extra

   (H) tore

---

1. <u>z</u>ipper

   (A) rosy

   (B) miss

   (C) city

6. <u>ch</u>op

   (F) share

   (G) mash

   (H) picture

2. <u>s</u>upper

   (F) dash

   (G) tack

   (H) race

7. <u>st</u>ool

   (A) pets

   (B) catch

   (C) cost

3. <u>fr</u>own

   (A) wharf

   (B) afraid

   (C) for

8. <u>th</u>ank

   (F) teach

   (G) math

   (H) that

4. <u>j</u>ust

   (F) chip

   (G) page

   (H) rang

9. <u>kn</u>ot

   (A) kite

   (B) in

   (C) beach

5. <u>pl</u>ow

   (A) camp

   (B) replant

   (C) palace

10. <u>sl</u>ip

   (F) walls

   (G) slide

   (H) best

Answers:

A Ⓐ Ⓑ Ⓒ	**2** Ⓕ Ⓖ Ⓗ	**5** Ⓐ Ⓑ Ⓒ	**8** Ⓕ Ⓖ Ⓗ
B Ⓕ Ⓖ Ⓗ	**3** Ⓐ Ⓑ Ⓒ	**6** Ⓕ Ⓖ Ⓗ	**9** Ⓐ Ⓑ Ⓒ
1 Ⓐ Ⓑ Ⓒ	**4** Ⓕ Ⓖ Ⓗ	**7** Ⓐ Ⓑ Ⓒ	**10** Ⓕ Ⓖ Ⓗ

Word Analysis: Consonant Sounds—Middle and Ending

Directions: Read the word with the underlined letter or letters. Decide what sound the letter or letters make. Then fill in the circle for the word that has the same sound.

Samples

A. fa<u>c</u>e

   (A) soup
   (B) king
   (C) chop

B. se<u>nt</u>

   (F) teeth
   (G) pants
   (H) not

1. ba<u>nd</u>

   (A) opened
   (B) bunny
   (C) went

6. ru<u>bb</u>er

   (F) lamp
   (G) tub
   (H) muddle

2. ca<u>ge</u>

   (F) dog
   (G) jelly
   (H) thing

7. ta<u>sk</u>

   (A) scene
   (B) scold
   (C) cost

3. pu<u>ff</u>

   (A) soccer
   (B) with
   (C) elephant

8. di<u>sh</u>

   (F) church
   (G) station
   (H) distant

4. sle<u>pt</u>

   (F) dropped
   (G) patting
   (H) laps

9. ti<u>lt</u>

   (A) little
   (B) felt
   (C) tallest

5. fu<u>nn</u>y

   (A) some
   (B) raft
   (C) know

10. ti<u>g</u>er

   (F) gallop
   (G) general
   (H) ages

Answers:

A (A) (B) (C)   2 (F) (G) (H)   5 (A) (B) (C)   8 (F) (G) (H)

B (F) (G) (H)   3 (A) (B) (C)   6 (F) (G) (H)   9 (A) (B) (C)

1 (A) (B) (C)   4 (F) (G) (H)   7 (A) (B) (C)   10 (F) (G) (H)

Word Analysis: Consonant Sounds—Initial and Final

Directions: Listen to each word that is read aloud. Fill in the circle for the word that begins or ends with the same sound.

Samples

A.
- (A) share
- (B) stop
- (C) tore
- (D) skid

B.
- (E) raft
- (F) horse
- (G) funny
- (H) more

1.
- (A) tune
- (B) then
- (C) nothing
- (D) step

6.
- (E) mile
- (F) what
- (G) after
- (H) game

2.
- (E) send
- (F) never
- (G) either
- (H) upper

7.
- (A) chimp
- (B) for
- (C) shoe
- (D) short

3.
- (A) none
- (B) together
- (C) until
- (D) rat

8.
- (E) call
- (F) made
- (G) look
- (H) thing

4.
- (E) good
- (F) glide
- (G) blow
- (H) flood

9.
- (A) ding
- (B) must
- (C) word
- (D) glue

5.
- (A) open
- (B) Saturday
- (C) swing
- (D) step

10.
- (E) lean
- (F) read
- (G) queen
- (H) many

Answers:

A (A) (B) (C) (D)   2 (E) (F) (G) (H)   5 (A) (B) (C) (D)   8 (E) (F) (G) (H)

B (E) (F) (G) (H)   3 (A) (B) (C) (D)   6 (E) (F) (G) (H)   9 (A) (B) (C) (D)

1 (A) (B) (C) (D)   4 (E) (F) (G) (H)   7 (A) (B) (C) (D)   10 (E) (F) (G) (H)

Word Analysis: Consonant Sounds—Initial and Final

Directions: Listen to each word. Fill in the answer circle for the word that begins or ends with the same sound.

Samples

A.	t<u>h</u>en (A)	<u>tr</u>uck (B)	s<u>t</u>uck (C)
B.	ti<u>lt</u> (F)	sa<u>nd</u> (G)	four<u>th</u> (H)

1.	<u>sm</u>ell (A)	<u>sw</u>allow (B)	<u>str</u>ing (C)
2.	<u>br</u>ought (F)	<u>cr</u>ayon (G)	<u>tr</u>uck (H)
3.	<u>cr</u>uel (A)	<u>dr</u>op (B)	<u>pl</u>ow (C)
4.	<u>sl</u>ow (F)	<u>sh</u>out (G)	<u>st</u>op (H)
5.	stro<u>ng</u> (A)	be<u>nd</u> (B)	te<u>nt</u> (C)
6.	du<u>mp</u> (F)	plan<u>t</u> (G)	wi<u>th</u> (H)
7.	a<u>ct</u> (A)	tou<u>ch</u> (B)	ma<u>k</u>e (C)
8.	sa<u>ck</u> (F)	pu<u>sh</u> (G)	mat<u>ch</u> (H)

Answers:

A	Ⓐ Ⓑ Ⓒ	**2**	Ⓕ Ⓖ Ⓗ	**5**	Ⓐ Ⓑ Ⓒ	**8**	Ⓕ Ⓖ Ⓗ
B	Ⓕ Ⓖ Ⓗ	**3**	Ⓐ Ⓑ Ⓒ	**6**	Ⓕ Ⓖ Ⓗ		
1	Ⓐ Ⓑ Ⓒ	**4**	Ⓕ Ⓖ Ⓗ	**7**	Ⓐ Ⓑ Ⓒ		

Word Analysis: Consonant Sounds/Vowel Sounds

Directions: Listen to each word. Fill in the answer circle for the word that begins or ends with the same sound.

Samples

A. <u>th</u>en   <u>tr</u>uck   <u>st</u>uck
      (A)   (B)   (C)

B. c<u>o</u>ne   r<u>oa</u>m   sp<u>o</u>t   b<u>o</u>ttle   m<u>o</u>ney
       (D)   (E)   (F)   (G)

1.   <u>w</u>ell   <u>h</u>ow   <u>p</u>ull
       (A)   (B)   (C)

2.   <u>cr</u>ash   <u>p</u>al   <u>cl</u>oud
       (D)   (E)   (F)

3.   mi<u>nt</u>   ha<u>nd</u>   cl<u>am</u>
       (A)   (B)   (C)

4.   ha<u>rd</u>   ca<u>rt</u>   si<u>ft</u>
       (D)   (E)   (F)

5.   r<u>ea</u>l   fell   feel   rake   money
       (A)   (B)   (C)   (D)

6.   n<u>o</u>d   toad   stop   spoke   boy
       (E)   (F)   (G)   (H)

7.   sp<u>oi</u>l   boy   clown   sport   spot
       (A)   (B)   (C)   (D)

8.   b<u>e</u>nd   bean   friend   funny   see
       (E)   (F)   (G)   (H)

- -

Answers: **A** Ⓐ Ⓑ Ⓒ   **2** Ⓓ Ⓔ Ⓕ   **5** Ⓐ Ⓑ Ⓒ Ⓓ   **8** Ⓔ Ⓕ Ⓖ Ⓗ

                B Ⓓ Ⓔ Ⓕ Ⓖ   **3** Ⓐ Ⓑ Ⓒ   **6** Ⓔ Ⓕ Ⓖ Ⓗ

                1 Ⓐ Ⓑ Ⓒ   **4** Ⓓ Ⓔ Ⓕ   **7** Ⓐ Ⓑ Ⓒ Ⓓ

Word Analysis: Consonant Sounds

Directions: Read the first word. Look for the word that does not have the same sound as the underlined part of the first word. Fill in the answer circle for your choice.

Samples

A. j<u>e</u>lly	gentle (A)	jam (B)	gas (C)	germ (D)
B. brea<u>the</u>	either (F)	through (G)	though (H)	the (J)
1. fi<u>sh</u>	nation (A)	fracture (B)	press (C)	wishes (D)
2. <u>z</u>ero	roses (F)	verse (G)	please (H)	hours (J)
3. <u>k</u>ing	castle (A)	crayon (B)	kiss (C)	know (D)
4. <u>ch</u>air	chemist (F)	match (G)	nature (H)	chimp (J)
5. si<u>x</u>ty	tricks (A)	extra (B)	express (C)	exam (D)
6. <u>wh</u>ale	who (F)	well (G)	whether (H)	waffle (J)
7. <u>th</u>ere	father (A)	north (B)	weather (C)	them (D)
8. dwar<u>f</u>	lives (F)	phone (G)	elephant (H)	funny (J)

Answers:

A (A) (B) (C) (D)	**2** (F) (G) (H) (J)	**5** (A) (B) (C) (D)	**8** (F) (G) (H) (J)
B (F) (G) (H) (J)	**3** (A) (B) (C) (D)	**6** (F) (G) (H) (J)	
1 (A) (B) (C) (D)	**4** (F) (G) (H) (J)	**7** (A) (B) (C) (D)	

Word Analysis: Vowel Sounds

Directions: Read the word with the underlined letter or letters. Decide what vowel sound the letter or letters make. Then fill in the circle for the word that has the same vowel sound.

Samples

A. sk<u>i</u>p
(A) smile
(B) bird
(C) fill

B. f<u>oo</u>d
(F) book
(G) growl
(H) moon

1. cr<u>a</u>b
(A) talk
(B) bars
(C) track

2. h<u>i</u>ke
(F) mill
(G) tried
(H) oil

3. f<u>e</u>lt
(A) bread
(B) worker
(C) before

4. c<u>au</u>ght
(F) about
(G) mud
(H) draw

5. r<u>oa</u>d
(A) book
(B) farm
(C) cone

6. s<u>ay</u>
(F) break
(G) pack
(H) yard

7. w<u>or</u>m
(A) bird
(B) born
(C) could

8. cr<u>ow</u>n
(F) blow
(G) cloud
(H) look

9. <u>a</u>head
(A) under
(B) after
(C) able

10. <u>u</u>se
(F) but
(G) cook
(H) cute

Answers:

A	Ⓐ Ⓑ Ⓒ	**2**	Ⓕ Ⓖ Ⓗ	**5**	Ⓐ Ⓑ Ⓒ	**8**	Ⓕ Ⓖ Ⓗ
B	Ⓕ Ⓖ Ⓗ	**3**	Ⓐ Ⓑ Ⓒ	**6**	Ⓕ Ⓖ Ⓗ	**9**	Ⓐ Ⓑ Ⓒ
1	Ⓐ Ⓑ Ⓒ	**4**	Ⓕ Ⓖ Ⓗ	**7**	Ⓐ Ⓑ Ⓒ	**10**	Ⓕ Ⓖ Ⓗ

Word Analysis: Vowel Sounds

Directions: Read the first word. Then read the other words. One of the other words has the same sound as the part that is underlined in the first word. Fill in the answer circle below for that word.

Samples

A.

h<u>a</u>t
- (A) hate
- (B) car
- (C) mail
- (D) clap

B.

r<u>i</u>ce
- (E) rich
- (F) rust
- (G) kind
- (H) field

1.

b<u>a</u>nd
- (A) cake
- (B) trap
- (C) coat
- (D) mail

2.

t<u>e</u>st
- (E) he
- (F) feet
- (G) bed
- (H) break

3.

fl<u>i</u>p
- (A) will
- (B) light
- (C) brain
- (D) like

4.

r<u>o</u>ck
- (E) boot
- (F) four
- (G pot
- (H) look

5.

<u>u</u>nder
- (A) cute
- (B) flour
- (C) round
- (D) puppy

6.

s<u>a</u>ve
- (E) vase
- (F) has
- (G) meat
- (H) grass

7.

c<u>u</u>te
- (A) much
- (B) rub
- (C) cloud
- (D) use

8.

t<u>i</u>tle
- (E) inch
- (F) join
- (G) bike
- (H) kid

9.

t<u>oa</u>st
- (A) town
- (B) bolt
- (C) sock
- (D) coin

10.

c<u>oi</u>n
- (E) cone
- (F) coal
- (G) boys
- (H) rope

Answers:

A Ⓐ Ⓑ Ⓒ Ⓓ   2 Ⓔ Ⓕ Ⓖ Ⓗ   5 Ⓐ Ⓑ Ⓒ Ⓓ   8 Ⓔ Ⓕ Ⓖ Ⓗ
B Ⓔ Ⓕ Ⓖ Ⓗ   3 Ⓐ Ⓑ Ⓒ Ⓓ   6 Ⓔ Ⓕ Ⓖ Ⓗ   9 Ⓐ Ⓑ Ⓒ Ⓓ
1 Ⓐ Ⓑ Ⓒ Ⓓ   4 Ⓔ Ⓕ Ⓖ Ⓗ   7 Ⓐ Ⓑ Ⓒ Ⓓ   10 Ⓔ Ⓕ Ⓖ Ⓗ

Word Analysis: Vowel Sounds

Directions: Look at the word with the underlined part. Fill in the answer circle below for the other word that has the same vowel sound.

Samples

A.	m<u>o</u>le	dash (A)	bear (B)	road (C)	pop (D)
B.	cl<u>o</u>ck	clown (F)	drop (G)	found (H)	poke (J)

1.	b<u>ea</u>n	pill (A)	hen (B)	meet (C)	boot (D)
2.	r<u>ai</u>n	bread (F)	place (G)	bright (H)	stack (J)
3.	st<u>i</u>ll	price (A)	boil (B)	miss (C)	pail (D)
4.	b<u>oo</u>t	true (F)	boat (G)	soil (H)	free (J)
5.	b<u>oi</u>l	couch (A)	some (B)	pile (C)	toy (D)
6.	c<u>ow</u>	calf (F)	sound (G)	watch (H)	open (J)
7.	c<u>a</u>me	face (A)	best (B)	alive (C)	coat (D)
8.	tr<u>i</u>p	climb (F)	fire (G)	print (H)	choice (J)

Answers:

A Ⓐ Ⓑ Ⓒ Ⓓ	2 Ⓕ Ⓖ Ⓗ Ⓙ	5 Ⓐ Ⓑ Ⓒ Ⓓ	8 Ⓕ Ⓖ Ⓗ Ⓙ
B Ⓕ Ⓖ Ⓗ Ⓙ	3 Ⓐ Ⓑ Ⓒ Ⓓ	6 Ⓕ Ⓖ Ⓗ Ⓙ	
1 Ⓐ Ⓑ Ⓒ Ⓓ	4 Ⓕ Ⓖ Ⓗ Ⓙ	7 Ⓐ Ⓑ Ⓒ Ⓓ	

Word Analysis: Compound Words

Directions: Look at each underlined word. Fill in the circle for the other word that can be added to it to make a compound word.

Sample

A.	side	with (A)	bottom (B)	ball (C)	walk (D)

1.	basket	ball (A)	berry (B)	bunny (C)	eggs (D)
2.	under	tent (F)	stand (G)	over (H)	bury (J)
3.	play	game (A)	theater (B)	ground (C)	friend (D)
4.	walk	run (F)	away (G)	slow (H)	way (J)
5.	sun	shine (A)	place (B)	heat (C)	beach (D)
6.	star	wish (F)	fish (G)	point (H)	plane (J)
7.	out	in (A)	above (B)	doors (C)	safe (D)
8.	home	work (F)	house (G)	story (H)	walk (J)
9.	fish	man (A)	bowl (B)	study (C)	lunch (D)

Answers:

A (A) (B) (C) (D)   3 (A) (B) (C) (D)   6 (F) (G) (H) (J)   9 (A) (B) (C) (D)

1 (A) (B) (C) (D)   4 (F) (G) (H) (J)   7 (A) (B) (C) (D)

2 (F) (G) (H) (J)   5 (A) (B) (C) (D)   8 (F) (G) (H) (J)

Word Analysis: Compound Words (MAT)

Directions: Fill in the space for the answer that makes the correct compound word with the underlined part of the sentence.

Sample   A. Stack all of the games on the <u>book</u>   .

> (A) case
> (B) end
> (C) mark
> (D) keeper

---

1. The <u>fire</u>   worked hard to put out the fire.

    (A)   starters
    (B)   fighters
    (C)   places
    (D)   screens

2. Please stay on the <u>side</u>   on your way to school.

    (E)   walk
    (F)   line
    (G)   long
    (H)   show

3. They are returning to their <u>home</u>   for their vacation.

    (A)   work
    (B)   sick
    (C)   spun
    (D)   town

4. They went to school to play <u>basket</u>   .

    (E)   ball
    (F)   work
    (G)   weave
    (H)   bowl

5. I forgot my <u>rain</u>   on the bus.

    (A)   storm
    (B)   bow
    (C)   drop
    (D)   coat

6. Their friendship started with a <u>hand</u>   .

    (E)   spring
    (F)   setting
    (G)   shake
    (H)   ball

7. They got up early to see the <u>sun</u>   .

    (A)   set
    (B)   shade
    (C)   rise
    (D)   stroke

8. They put on their <u>snow</u>   .

    (E)   balls
    (F)   men
    (G)   flakes
    (H)   shoes

- -

Answers: A Ⓐ Ⓑ Ⓒ Ⓓ   3 Ⓐ Ⓑ Ⓒ Ⓓ   6 Ⓔ Ⓕ Ⓖ Ⓗ

               1 Ⓐ Ⓑ Ⓒ Ⓓ   4 Ⓔ Ⓕ Ⓖ Ⓗ   7 Ⓐ Ⓑ Ⓒ Ⓓ

               2 Ⓔ Ⓕ Ⓖ Ⓗ   5 Ⓐ Ⓑ Ⓒ Ⓓ   8 Ⓔ Ⓕ Ⓖ Ⓗ

Word Analysis: Root Words and Affixes

Directions: Read the underlined word. Look for the root word or affix of the word. Mark the answer space for your choice.

Samples

A.	<u>international</u>	in	tern	nation	tion
		(A)	(B)	(C)	(D)
B.	<u>submarine</u>	sub	submar	marine	ine
		(F)	(G)	(H)	(J)
C.	<u>wonderful</u>	won	wonder	derful	ful
		(A)	(B)	(C)	(D)

Look for the root word of the word that is underlined.

1.	<u>longest</u>	gest	est	long	onge
		(A)	(B)	(C)	(D)
2.	<u>bicycle</u>	icy	cycle	bi	cle
		(F)	(G)	(H)	(J)

Look for the prefix of the word that is underlined.

3.	<u>return</u>	ret	turn	urn	re
		(A)	(B)	(C)	(D)
4.	<u>preflight</u>	pre	pref	flight	light
		(F)	(G)	(H)	(J)

Look for the suffix of the word that is underlined.

5.	<u>dreaming</u>	dream	ream	ming	ing
		(A)	(B)	(C)	(D)
6.	<u>darkness</u>	ark	ness	dark	ess
		(F)	(G)	(H)	(J)

Answers:

A (A) (B) (C) (D) 1 (A) (B) (C) (D) 4 (F) (G) (H) (J)
B (F) (G) (H) (J) 2 (F) (G) (H) (J) 5 (A) (B) (C) (D)
C (A) (B) (C) (D) 3 (A) (B) (C) (D) 6 (F) (G) (H) (J)

Word Analysis: Syllabication

Directions: Fill in the answer circle for the correct way to divide the word into syllables.

Samples

A.
- (A) him-self
- (B) hims-elf
- (C) hi-mself

B.
- (F) bec-ause
- (G) be-cause
- (H) becau-se

1.
- (A) si-dewalk
- (B) side-walk
- (C) sid-ewalk

2.
- (F) pe-ople
- (G) peop-le
- (H) peo-ple

3.
- (A) re-turn
- (B) ret-urn
- (C) retu-rn

4.
- (F) slow-ly
- (G) sl-owly
- (H) slowl-y

5.
- (A) slee-ping
- (B) sleep-ing
- (C) sle-eping

6.
- (F) ba-seball
- (G) bas-eball
- (H) base-ball

7.
- (A) pre-pare
- (B) prep-are
- (C) prepa-re

8.
- (F) mo-rning
- (G) mor-ning
- (H) morn-ing

9.
- (A) thou-ghtful
- (B) though-tful
- (C) thought-ful

10.
- (F) mo-ther
- (G) mot-her
- (H) moth-er

11.
- (A) crick-et
- (B) cric-ket
- (C) cri-cket

12.
- (F) afr-aid
- (G) af-raid
- (H) a-fraid

Answers:

A (A) (B) (C)   3 (A) (B) (C)   7 (A) (B) (C)   11 (A) (B) (C)
B (F) (G) (H)   4 (F) (G) (H)   8 (F) (G) (H)   12 (F) (G) (H)
1 (A) (B) (C)   5 (A) (B) (C)   9 (A) (B) (C)
2 (F) (G) (H)   6 (F) (G) (H)   10 (F) (G) (H)

Vocabulary: Synonyms

Directions: Read the phrase. Look for the word that has the same or almost the same meaning as the underlined word. Fill in the answer circle for your choice.

Samples

A. slight change

(A) huge
(B) important
(C) small
(D) slow

B. distant planet

(F) nearby
(G) faraway
(H) small
(J) ringed

1. favorite subject

(A) game
(B) movie
(C) class
(D) hobby

6. courteous reply

(F) rude
(G) quick
(H) thoughtful
(J) polite

2. occupied apartment

(F) lived in
(G) empty
(H) attractive
(J) vacant

7. please cease

(A) comment
(B) stop
(C) continue
(D) stay

3. looked gorgeous

(A) enormous
(B) beautiful
(C) hideous
(D) sincere

8. happy conclusion

(F) celebration
(G) beginning
(H) ending
(J) opening

4. unexpected occurrence

(F) event
(G) present
(H) pleasure
(J) discovery

9. beneficial treatment

(A) harmful
(B) harmless
(C) helpful
(D) useless

5. persistent cough

(A) noisy
(B) long-lasting
(C) occasional
(D) annoying

10. enormous animals

(F) huge
(G) tiny
(H) average
(J) beautiful

Answers:

A (A) (B) (C) (D)   2 (F) (G) (H) (J)   5 (A) (B) (C) (D)   8 (F) (G) (H) (J)

B (F) (G) (H) (J)   3 (A) (B) (C) (D)   6 (F) (G) (H) (J)   9 (A) (B) (C) (D)

1 (A) (B) (C) (D)   4 (F) (G) (H) (J)   7 (A) (B) (C) (D)   10 (F) (G) (H) (J)

Vocabulary: Antonyms

Directions: Read the phrase. Look for the word that has the opposite meaning of the underlined word. Fill in the answer circle for your choice.

Samples

A.   <u>valuable</u> statue

   (A) ancient
   (B) worthless
   (C) beautiful
   (D) modern

B.   <u>obedient</u> child

   (F) friendly
   (G) helpful
   (H) naughty
   (J) well-behaved

1.   <u>accidental</u> result

   (A) chance
   (B) unexpected
   (C) planned
   (D) amusing

6.   <u>depart</u> promptly

   (F) arrange
   (G) inspect
   (H) deliver
   (J) arrive

2.   <u>cheerful</u> voices

   (F) merry
   (G) unhappy
   (H) loud
   (J) shrill

7.   <u>remembered</u> places

   (A) forgotten
   (B) recalled
   (C) exciting
   (D) boring

3.   <u>distribute</u> money

   (A) deliver
   (B) earn
   (C) deposit
   (D) collect

8.   always <u>wasteful</u>

   (F) thrifty
   (G) careless
   (H) thirsty
   (J) untidy

4.   <u>employ</u> them

   (F) utilize
   (G) hire
   (H) dismiss
   (J) enjoy

9.   show <u>cowardice</u>

   (A) fear
   (B) courage
   (C) freedom
   (D) worry

5.   <u>remain</u> here

   (A) leave
   (B) wait
   (C) continue
   (D) stay

10.   <u>create</u> order

   (F) enjoy
   (G) destroy
   (H) design
   (J) plan

Answers:

A (A) (B) (C) (D)   2 (F) (G) (H) (J)   5 (A) (B) (C) (D)   8 (F) (G) (H) (J)
B (F) (G) (H) (J)   3 (A) (B) (C) (D)   6 (F) (G) (H) (J)   9 (A) (B) (C) (D)
1 (A) (B) (C) (D)   4 (F) (G) (H) (J)   7 (A) (B) (C) (D)   10 (F) (G) (H) (J)

Vocabulary: Word Meanings

Directions: Listen carefully as each sentence is read aloud. Then read along in your booklet as the answer choices are read aloud. Fill in the circle for the best answer for each item.

Samples

A.
- (A) old
- (B) new
- (C) ugly
- (D) small

B.
- (F) generous
- (G) helpful
- (H) naughty
- (J) polite

1.
- (A) hard
- (B) soft
- (C) rough
- (D) slippery

6.
- (F) a career
- (G) a clock
- (H) a hobby
- (J) an experience

2.
- (F) jump
- (G) run
- (H) bend
- (J) sleep

7.
- (A) robber
- (B) tool
- (C) police officer
- (D) store

3.
- (A) lose it
- (B) break it
- (C) release it
- (D) protect it

8.
- (F) proceed
- (G) stop
- (H) pass
- (J) finish

4.
- (F) ask
- (G) answer
- (H) reply
- (J) fail

9.
- (A) complain
- (B) whisper
- (C) shout
- (D) rip

5.
- (A) a visit
- (B) a trip
- (C) a diary
- (D) an adventure

10.
- (F) phone
- (G) forget
- (H) discuss
- (J) remember

Answers:

A Ⓐ Ⓑ Ⓒ Ⓓ   2 Ⓕ Ⓖ Ⓗ Ⓙ   5 Ⓐ Ⓑ Ⓒ Ⓓ   8 Ⓕ Ⓖ Ⓗ Ⓙ

B Ⓕ Ⓖ Ⓗ Ⓙ   3 Ⓐ Ⓑ Ⓒ Ⓓ   6 Ⓕ Ⓖ Ⓗ Ⓙ   9 Ⓐ Ⓑ Ⓒ Ⓓ

1 Ⓐ Ⓑ Ⓒ Ⓓ   4 Ⓕ Ⓖ Ⓗ Ⓙ   7 Ⓐ Ⓑ Ⓒ Ⓓ   10 Ⓕ Ⓖ Ⓗ Ⓙ

Vocabulary: Derivations

Directions: Read each question. Fill in the circle for the answer you think is correct.

Samples

A. Which of these words probably comes from the Latin word <u>granum</u> meaning <u>a seed</u>?

   (A) grant

   (B) grain

   (C) groan

   (D) green

B. Which of these words probably comes from the German word <u>schnarren</u> meaning <u>to growl</u>?

   (F) smile

   (G) sneeze

   (H) snore

   (J) snap

1. Which of these words probably comes from the French word <u>femme</u> meaning <u>woman</u>?

   (A) famished

   (B) funny

   (C) fence

   (D) feminine

2. Which of these words probably comes from the German word <u>Gott</u> meaning <u>God</u>?

   (F) Gothic

   (G) gotten

   (H) goddess

   (J) golden

3. Which of these words probably comes from the German word <u>kinder</u> meaning <u>children</u>?

   (A) kind

   (B) kindle

   (C) kindness

   (D) kindergarten

4. Which of these words probably comes from the French word <u>enfant</u> meaning <u>child</u>?

   (F) elephant

   (G) infant

   (H) enforce

   (J) infect

5. Which of these words probably comes from the Italian word <u>cafe</u> meaning <u>coffeehouse</u>?

   (A) cafeteria

   (B) caftan

   (C) cashier

   (D) calf

6. Which of these words probably comes from the German word <u>haus</u> meaning a <u>dwelling place</u>?

   (F) house

   (G) haunt

   (H) hawk

   (J) hound

Answers: A Ⓐ Ⓑ Ⓒ Ⓓ   1 Ⓐ Ⓑ Ⓒ Ⓓ   3 Ⓐ Ⓑ Ⓒ Ⓓ   5 Ⓐ Ⓑ Ⓒ Ⓓ
            B Ⓕ Ⓖ Ⓗ Ⓙ   2 Ⓕ Ⓖ Ⓗ Ⓙ   4 Ⓕ Ⓖ Ⓗ Ⓙ   6 Ⓕ Ⓖ Ⓗ Ⓙ

Vocabulary: Multiple Meanings

Directions: Read the pair of word meanings. Look for the word that fits both meanings. Mark the answer space for your choice.

Samples

A.   a kind of bird and went in head first

   (A) robin   (B) dive   (C) jump   (D) dove

B.   a source of water and a metal coil

   (F) well   (G) spring   (H) faucet   (J) wire

---

1.   something to sleep on and a place flowers grow

   (A) mattress   (B) plot   (C) bed   (D) pillow

2.   to fail to hit and an unmarried woman

   (F) miss   (G) girl   (H) regret   (J) avoid

3.   a written sign and to pay attention to something

   (A) poster   (B) notice   (C) observe   (D) advertisement

4.   to record and a strip of sticky material

   (F) write   (G) photograph   (H) tape   (J) measure

5.   a small timepiece worn on the wrist and to look at

   (A) watch   (B) clock   (C) see   (D) examine

6.   disagreement and the answer to a subtraction problem

   (F) argument   (G) opinion   (H) quarrel   (J) difference

- -

Answers: A (A) (B) (C) (D)   1 (A) (B) (C) (D)   3 (A) (B) (C) (D)   5 (A) (B) (C) (D)

               B (F) (G) (H) (J)   2 (F) (G) (H) (J)   4 (F) (G) (H) (J)   6 (F) (G) (H) (J)

Vocabulary: Multiple Meanings

Directions: Read each pair of sentences. Find the word that fits in both spaces. Fill in the answer circle for your choice.

Samples

A. He left a _____ to let his mother know where he was going.
The musician hit a wrong _____ .

    (A) letter
    (B) tone
    (C) message
    (D) note

B. The _____ was closed for a week after the fire.
I hope I _____ this test.

    (F) road
    (G) pass
    (H) understand
    (J) forest

1. The children were using _____ to build a castle.
The school is seven _____ from here.

    (A) blocks
    (B) sand
    (C) miles
    (D) wood

2. Would you _____ if I use your eraser?
That boy should _____ his mother.

    (F) obey
    (G) object to
    (H) listen to
    (J) mind

3. At the hospital they put a _____ with my name on it around my wrist.
The _____ played a rousing march.

    (A) bracelet
    (B) band
    (C) song
    (D) group

4. Did you remember to _____ your reading time on the chart?
That table was made from a huge _____.

    (F) tree
    (G) record
    (H) log
    (J) plank

5. He tried to do the _____ thing by telling the truth.
Turn _____ at the next corner.

    (A) wrong
    (B) left
    (C) right
    (D) back

6. She gave me a beautiful _____ for my birthday.
When will they _____ the awards?

    (F) present
    (G) gift
    (H) announce
    (J) make

Answers:
A (A) (B) (C) (D)   1 (A) (B) (C) (D)   3 (A) (B) (C) (D)   5 (A) (B) (C) (D)
B (F) (G) (H) (J)   2 (F) (G) (H) (J)   4 (F) (G) (H) (J)   6 (F) (G) (H) (J)

Vocabulary: Affix Meanings

Directions: Read each pair of words. Look for the word or words that best tell the meaning of the underlined affix. Fill in the answer circle for your choice.

Samples

A.   inactive   indirect

(A) too
(B) not
(C) under
(D) between

B.   speechless   worthless

(F) able to
(G) without
(H) in the direction of
(J) one who

---

1.   submarine   subway

(A) under
(B) over
(C) between
(D) across

5.   backward   forward

(A) below
(B) above
(C) in the direction of
(D) opposite from

---

2.   preview   preschool

(F) not
(G) after
(H) before
(J) in place of

6.   worker   builder

(F) able to
(G) unable to
(H) away from
(J) one who

---

3.   superhuman   supermarket

(A) across
(B) under
(C) less
(D) greater

7.   friendly   motherly

(A) in the manner of
(B) in place of
(C) because of
(D) in spite of

---

4.   impatient   impolite

(F) more
(G) less
(H) not
(J) under

8.   babyish   girlish

(F) against
(G) like
(H) with
(J) across

Answers:

A Ⓐ Ⓑ Ⓒ Ⓓ   2 Ⓕ Ⓖ Ⓗ Ⓙ   5 Ⓐ Ⓑ Ⓒ Ⓓ   8 Ⓕ Ⓖ Ⓗ Ⓙ

B Ⓕ Ⓖ Ⓗ Ⓙ   3 Ⓐ Ⓑ Ⓒ Ⓓ   6 Ⓕ Ⓖ Ⓗ Ⓙ

1 Ⓐ Ⓑ Ⓒ Ⓓ   4 Ⓕ Ⓖ Ⓗ Ⓙ   7 Ⓐ Ⓑ Ⓒ Ⓓ

——————————————— TS 155

Vocabulary: Words in Context

Directions: Read each sentence. Find the most appropriate word to fit in the blank or to replace the underlined word. Fill in the answer circle for your choice.

Samples

A. The treasure chest was filled with gold coins and crowns set with sparkling <u>gems</u> of many different colors.

    (A) lights

    (B) jewels

    (C) stars

    (D) drops

B. After two weeks of _____ weather, we were glad when the sun broke through the clouds.

    (F) warm

    (G) gloomy

    (H) fair

    (J) nice

1. Tom was <u>infuriated</u> when some boys knocked him down and ripped his new blue sweatshirt.

    (A) amused

    (B) interested

    (C) angry

    (D) curious

3. The night was dark and stormy and the rain made it hard to see the road, so it was <u>fortunate</u> that we knew the way so well.

    (A) curious

    (B) lucky

    (C) annoying

    (D) serious

2. The desert was hot and <u>arid</u> so we were glad we had several large cans of water packed with our supplies.

    (F) dry

    (G) beautiful

    (H) empty

    (J) silent

4. My mother <u>investigates</u> accidents for an insurance company to try to find out who was at fault.

    (F) settles

    (G) records

    (H) looks into

    (J) photographs

GO→

Answers: A Ⓐ Ⓑ Ⓒ Ⓓ   1 Ⓐ Ⓑ Ⓒ Ⓓ   3 Ⓐ Ⓑ Ⓒ Ⓓ

              B Ⓕ Ⓖ Ⓗ Ⓙ   2 Ⓕ Ⓖ Ⓗ Ⓙ   4 Ⓕ Ⓖ Ⓗ Ⓙ

Vocabulary: Words in Context (cont.)

5. Food is so _____ in that country that mothers and fathers often go to bed hungry so their children can eat.

    (A) plentiful

    (B) delicious

    (C) scarce

    (D) precious

6. Even though Sue had a lot of work to do and there wasn't much time left, she felt _____ that she would finish in time.

    (F) uncertain

    (G) confident

    (H) angry

    (J) upset

7. "I can't wait!" said Margaret, who felt so _____ that she could not even sit still.

    (A) warm

    (B) friendly

    (C) relaxed

    (D) impatient

8. Amanda was more _____ than usual because she had a headache and didn't feel well.

    (F) pleasant

    (G) irritable

    (H) attractive

    (J) friendly

Read the paragraph. Look for the best words to complete the sentences. Fill in the answer circles for your choices.

On rainy mornings in the _____, the cars on the
                          9

street swish through the puddles. The water _____
                                10

people walking on the _____, making them even more
                    11

cold and _____.
      12

9.
    (A) yard
    (B) farm
    (C) city
    (D) desert

10.
    (F) sprays
    (G) paints
    (H) colors
    (J) heats

11.
    (A) buildings
    (B) sidewalks
    (C) cars
    (D) bridges

12.
    (F) warm
    (G) dry
    (H) happy
    (J) wet

STOP

Answers: **5** Ⓐ Ⓑ Ⓒ Ⓓ   **7** Ⓐ Ⓑ Ⓒ Ⓓ   **9** Ⓐ Ⓑ Ⓒ Ⓓ   **11** Ⓐ Ⓑ Ⓒ Ⓓ

                  6 Ⓕ Ⓖ Ⓗ Ⓙ   **8** Ⓕ Ⓖ Ⓗ Ⓙ   **10** Ⓕ Ⓖ Ⓗ Ⓙ   **12** Ⓕ Ⓖ Ⓗ Ⓙ

Reading Comprehension: Listening

Directions: Listen carefully as each story is read to you. Then listen to each question. Read along in your booklet as the answer choices are read aloud. Fill in the circle for the best answer to each item.

Samples

A.
- (A) park
- (B) field
- (C) street
- (D) yard

B.
- (F) breakfast
- (G) lunch
- (H) dinner
- (J) tea

1.
- (A) beggars
- (B) dancers
- (C) tree-climbers
- (D) clowns

6.
- (F) music
- (G) acting
- (H) art
- (J) science

2.
- (F) cubs
- (G) food
- (H) trees
- (J) tricks

7.
- (A) pay a fee
- (B) sign up
- (C) bring a parent
- (D) make a poster

3.
- (A) look around
- (B) climb
- (C) do experiments
- (D) land

8.
- (F) mean
- (G) impatient
- (H) generous
- (J) lazy

4.
- (F) silver
- (G) gray
- (H) blue
- (J) black

9.
- (A) too old
- (B) too dirty
- (C) her sister's
- (D) her favorite

5.
- (A) blood pressure
- (B) pulse
- (C) rocks
- (D) The story does not say.

10.
- (F) dolls
- (G) games
- (H) blocks
- (J) The story does not say.

- -

Answers:

A Ⓐ Ⓑ Ⓒ Ⓓ 2 Ⓕ Ⓖ Ⓗ Ⓙ 5 Ⓐ Ⓑ Ⓒ Ⓓ 8 Ⓕ Ⓖ Ⓗ Ⓙ

B Ⓕ Ⓖ Ⓗ Ⓙ 3 Ⓐ Ⓑ Ⓒ Ⓓ 6 Ⓕ Ⓖ Ⓗ Ⓙ 9 Ⓐ Ⓑ Ⓒ Ⓓ

1 Ⓐ Ⓑ Ⓒ Ⓓ 4 Ⓕ Ⓖ Ⓗ Ⓙ 7 Ⓐ Ⓑ Ⓒ Ⓓ 10 Ⓕ Ⓖ Ⓗ Ⓙ

Reading Comprehension: Stories

Sample

Directions: Read the passage and the questions that follow it. Choose the best answer to each question and fill in the circle for your answer choice.

My brother Jeff is always making big plans. He decided yesterday afternoon that he wants to be an astronaut when he grows up. Last week he wanted to be an actor. Last month he said he wanted to be a detective. Last year it was a doctor. It would not matter to me what he wanted to be or how often he changed his mind if he did not get everyone in the family so <u>involved</u> with his career choices.

When Jeff planned to be a doctor, he carried bandages in his pockets. He learned how to wash off skinned knees and put ice on bumps. He was very kind and helpful, but I always felt that he was glad when someone got hurt so that he could practice.

When Jeff wanted to be a detective, he went around with a notebook and a pencil, writing down everything that was going on. He made notes about what we had for dinner and what clothes each member of the family was wearing. He kept track of what we were wearing in case he had to identify us. I do not know why he wanted to remember what we ate.

When he wanted to be an actor, Jeff put on shows in the living room after dinner. We all had to stop whatever we were doing and sit down and watch. The shows were entertaining, I must admit, but I missed my favorite movie on TV and I did not get much homework done.

This astronaut thing is different though. Right now, Jeff is building a rocket ship out in the garage. He says he will be ready to blast off first thing in the morning. I don't want to go to the moon!

1. This story is mainly about . . .
  - (A) the notes detectives make.
  - (B) Jeff's living room shows.
  - (C) how Jeff's plans affect his family.
  - (D) how Jeff plans to get to the moon.

2. Jeff used a notebook and pencil when he wanted to be . . .
  - (F) an actor.
  - (G) a detective.
  - (H) a doctor.
  - (J) an astronaut.

3. Jeff's brother is worried about the rocket ship being built in the garage because . . .
  - (A) he will miss his brother when he blasts off.
  - (B) he is afraid Jeff will get hurt.
  - (C) he knows Jeff will want him to take part in the project.
  - (D) he thinks the garage might be damaged.

4. Jeff is a person who is always . . .
  - (F) worried about everything.
  - (G) making new plans.
  - (H) bored with life.
  - (J) sad and unhappy.

5. The word <u>involved</u> means . . .
  - (A) mixed up in.
  - (B) upside-down.
  - (C) upset.
  - (D) unhappy.

- -

Answers:

1 (A) (B) (C) (D)　　　　4 (F) (G) (H) (J)

2 (F) (G) (H) (J)　　　　5 (A) (B) (C) (D)

3 (A) (B) (C) (D)

Student Practice Page

Comprehension/Story:
Section One/Page 1

Directions: Read the passage and the questions that follow. Choose the best answer to each question and fill in the circle for your answer choice.

Do you believe in mermaids? <u>Seafarers</u> have believed in them for centuries. According to legend, mermaids, who were also called sirens, were half human and half fish. They sat on the sand or on rocks in the ocean, combing their long golden hair with golden combs. They attracted sailors with their beauty and their splendid singing voices. Some legends tell that they did this to make the sailors crash their ships on the rocks. Other legends tell that they made the sailors their captives by slipping magic caps on their heads. These caps were supposed to allow human beings to breathe under water so they could live in the sea.

<u>The Little Mermaid</u>, a fairy tale by Hans Christian Andersen, is one of the most famous tales ever written about a mermaid. It has been translated into many languages and read all over the world. A statue of Andersen's little mermaid overlooks the harbor in Denmark's capital city of Copenhagen, the home of this famous Danish author.

Disney's movie <u>The Little Mermaid</u> has made this story newly popular. The movie is based on Andersen's tale, although many characters were introduced to add both humor and drama to the story and bring it up to date. Ariel's adventures have brought the story to many people who had never enjoyed it in book form. You may like it better than the original story.

1. This story is mainly about . . .

   (A) Hans Christian Andersen.
   (B) legends of the sea.
   (C) mermaids.
   (D) Disney.

2. Mermaids are also known as . . .

   (F) sirens.
   (G) seafarers.
   (H) sailors.
   (J) singers.

3. Which of these happened first?

   (A) Disney produced the movie, <u>The Little Mermaid</u>.
   (B) Many legends were told about mermaids
   (C) Hans Christian Andersen wrote his story about <u>The Little Mermaid</u>.
   (D) A statue of a mermaid was placed above Copenhagen's harbor.

4. Which sentence from the story is an <u>opinion</u>?

   (F) Some legends tell that they did this to make the sailors crash their ships on the rocks.
   (G) It has been translated into many languages and read all over the world.
   (H) Disney's movie, <u>The Little Mermaid</u>, has made this story newly popular.
   (J) You may like it better than the original story.

5. The word <u>seafarer</u> means . . .

   (A) mermaid.
   (B) siren.
   (C) sailor.
   (D) human.

GO→

Answers:

1 (A) (B) (C) (D)   4 (F) (G) (H) (J)

2 (F) (G) (H) (J)   5 (A) (B) (C) (D)

3 (A) (B) (C) (D)

Comprehension/Story:
Section One/Page 2

Directions: Read the passage and the questions that follow. Choose the best answer to each question and fill in the circle for your answer choice.

Scientists do not believe in mermaids. Most of them think that sailors mistakenly identified sea animals such as the dugong and manatee as mermaids. In fact, they have named the scientific order to which these animals belong *Sirenia* since siren is another name for mermaid.

Sirenians live in the water like seals and walruses. They feed on grasses along the banks of streams or on plants that grow on the floor of the ocean in places where the water is not too deep. They never swim too far out into the ocean but are found in places such as lagoons, swamps, and rivers. They live along the coasts of South America, the West Indies, and Africa in both fresh and salt waters. In the United States, the manatee, known as the Florida sea cow, can be found in the warm waters off the coast of Florida.

The Florida sea cow grows from eight to thirteen feet long and has a blackish-gray skin. It is a clumsy animal with a broad, heavy tail and small front legs that look like flippers. Its upper lip is divided into two parts that work like a scissors to clip off weeds and water grasses.

The sea cow or manatee, like the dugong, is a really ugly animal. It is almost easier to believe in real mermaids than to think that sailors mistook these animals for beautiful girls with long golden hair.

1. A good title for this part of the story might be . . .

   (A) The Florida Sea Cow.
   (B) In the Swamps.
   (C) Real Mermaids?
   (D) The West Indies.

2. This part of the story is about . . .

   (F) real animals.
   (G) make-believe animals.
   (H) fairy tales.
   (J) pretend places.

3. This part of the story was written to . . .

   (A) explain the beginnings of stories about mermaids.
   (B) give information about stories told by sailors.
   (C) convince people that scientists believe in mermaids.
   (D) entertain people with funny stories about mermaids.

4. Stories about mermaids are like stories about . . .

   (F) dinosaurs.
   (G) dragons.
   (H) manatees.
   (J) scientists.

5. The word sirenians means . . .

   (A) all of the mammals that live in the ocean.
   (B) animals belonging to the scientific order called *Sirenia*.
   (C) the scientists who study animals that live in the ocean.
   (D) sailors who tell stories about seeing mermaids.

GO→

Answers:

1 (A) (B) (C) (D)   4 (F) (G) (H) (J)
2 (F) (G) (H) (J)   5 (A) (B) (C) (D)
3 (A) (B) (C) (D)

Comprehension/Story:
Section One/Page 3

Directions: Read the passage and the questions that follow. Choose the best answer to each question and fill in the circle for your answer choice.

"We're going camping!" Maggie sang as she ran upstairs to her bedroom. "We're going camping!" she continued singing as she pulled a duffel bag and a backpack down from the top shelf of her closet. She sat down on the side of her bed and spent a minute thinking about it. Then she started to make piles of jeans and shirts and socks. She found her heavy jacket and her hiking boots. In no time at all, she had finished packing.

"But why do we have to go camping?" whined Bart, Maggie's twin brother. "I want to stay home. I want to watch television. I want to play my stereo. I want to use my computer. I'm not an outdoor person!" He was so slow about packing that Maggie had to help him. She found all of his things and helped him stuff them into a couple of backpacks. "There," Maggie said, "and do try to be cheerful. At least, we will be able to spend some time together."

The car trip seemed <u>interminable.</u> It went on and on and on. Bart put on his earphones and listened to music. Maggie looked at the scenery and talked to their mother and dad. But after a while, Bart ran out of music and started to whine again. Dad looked at Bart in the rear view mirror and said, "Bart, if you can't say something pleasant, don't say anything!" They rode the rest of the way in silence. Mother rolled her eyes and grinned at Maggie and Maggie grinned back.

1. Bart did not want to go camping because . . .

    (A) he did not have the right clothes.
    (B) he does not like his sister, Maggie.
    (C) he is not an outdoor person.
    (D) he has a game on Saturday.

2. Which of these statements is true?

    (F) Bart and Maggie enjoy the same activities.
    (G) Bart and Maggie are both very well-organized.
    (H) Bart likes to stay home and Maggie likes to go camping.
    (J) Maggie likes to stay home and Bart likes to go camping.

3. The setting of the third paragraph is . . .

    (A) Bart's bedroom.
    (B) Maggie's bedroom.
    (C) the campsite.
    (D) inside the car.

4. You can tell from the third paragraph that Maggie and her mother . . .

    (F) often argue.
    (G) understand each other.
    (H) never talk.
    (J) always ignore each other.

5. The word <u>interminable</u> means . . .

    (A) never ending.
    (B) short and sweet.
    (C) hot and stuffy.
    (D) over too quickly.

GO→

- -

Answers:

1 (A) (B) (C) (D)   4 (F) (G) (H) (J)

2 (F) (G) (H) (J)   5 (A) (B) (C) (D)

3 (A) (B) (C) (D)

Comprehension/Story:
Section One/Page 4

Directions: Read the passage and the questions that follow. Choose the best answer to each question and fill in the circle for your answer choice.

Maggie, Bart, and their mom and dad reached the campsite high in the mountains about an hour before dark. They had to really hurry to pitch their tents and get everything organized. They were all too tired to cook a big dinner. They ate the sandwiches and cookies they had packed just in case this happened and decided to go to bed right away.

Maggie and Bart were sharing a tent. They got into their sleeping bags and zipped them up against the cold mountain air. This was the moment Maggie had been waiting for.

"Bart," she said, "isn't this fun? I know you're going to love it. Tomorrow we can go for a long hike together. I want to see the canyon I read about in the stuff the ranger gave us."

"Go to sleep, Maggie," Bart said. "I might go for a short walk with you. We'll talk about it tomorrow."

But Maggie could not stop. She talked on and on, describing the scenery they would see and the challenges they would face. "And best of all," she finally concluded, "you won't have all of your electronic equipment—no television, no stereo, no computer. You'll have to pay attention to me, Bart. Bart? Bart!" But Bart had gone to sleep.

So Maggie finished planning their hike in her imagination, and then she dreamed about it. While she dreamed, the wind came up. It roared around their tent like a lion, but both Maggie and Bart were too sound asleep to hear it or the rain that came after it.

1. The best word to describe how Maggie felt is . . .

   (A) interested.
   (B) bored.
   (C) excited.
   (D) patient.

2. The wind "roared around their tent like a lion" means . . .

   (F) the wind made a loud noise.
   (G) a wild animal was in their camp.
   (H) the wind pulled down the tent.
   (J) the noise was big for a small wind.

3. At this point in the story, the relationship between Maggie and Bart seems . . .

   (A) distant and unfriendly.
   (B) close and friendly on both sides.
   (C) more important to Maggie.
   (D) more important to Bart.

4. Which one of these remarks does not have anything to do with the wind and rain?

   (F) "I don't want to hike in this weather," Bart announced.
   (G) "I'm afraid the trail will be slippery and dangerous," said Dad.
   (H) "I am really excited about going hiking," said Maggie.
   (J) "Do you have your waterproof poncho?" Mom asked.

5. In this part of the story, the word pitch means . . .

   (A) set up.
   (B) throw.
   (C) tilt.
   (D) sap.

GO→

Answers:

1 (A) (B) (C) (D)   4 (F) (G) (H) (J)

2 (F) (G) (H) (J)   5 (A) (B) (C) (D)

3 (A) (B) (C) (D)

Comprehension/Story:
Section One/Page 5

Directions: Read the passage and the questions that follow. Choose the best answer to each question and fill in the circle for your answer choice.

The next morning it was still raining. Dad tuned in the news on the car radio and found out that the storm was probably going to get worse before it was over. "I'm sorry everybody, but I think we'd better pack up and head home."

"Oh no," moaned Maggie. "Please let me go for just one little hike before we leave. I've looked forward to it for so long!"

"Okay, Maggie," said Dad. "Just stay close to the campsite. Don't climb on any rocks."

"Just one hour, Maggie," added Mom. "Do you have your watch on?"

An hour later there was no sign of Maggie. "We'll give her five more minutes and then start to look," Dad said, looking at his watch.

"I know where she went," said Bart. He pulled out the packet of materials that the ranger had given to them and pointed at a place on the map. "She wanted to see this canyon. She talked about it for hours last night."

"You two start looking. I'll drive down to the entrance and get the ranger," Mom said.

Bart had studied the map so he rushed ahead with Dad close behind. The <u>indistinct</u> trail was steep and slippery. Then they heard a voice. "Help!" Maggie called. "I'm over the edge, holding on to a tree trunk."

By the time Mom came back with the ranger, Maggie was safe. Bart had brought a coil of rope, and he used it to pull her to safety. When they all called him a hero, Bart shrugged and said, "Hey, she's my sister."

1. What is the mood at the beginning of this part of the story?
   (A) happiness
   (B) fear
   (C) despair
   (D) disappointment

2. Which is the best summary of this story?
   (F) A family camping trip almost turns to tragedy. However, Bart saves the day by rescuing Maggie in spite of the fact that he does not consider himself an outdoor person.
   (G) Maggie and Bart do not like any of the same things and spoil a family trip by arguing all of the time.
   (H) Mom and Dad have planned a family camping trip even though their children have no interest in it and do not want to go.
   (J) Bart is a whiny, complaining boy who makes his whole family miserable every time they go on a long trip.

3. The words that best describe Bart are . . .
   (A) very athletic.
   (B) extremely funny.
   (C) loyal and dependable.
   (D) sweet and cooperative.

4. Which one of these would probably happen next?
   (F) The trip home would be awful.
   (G) The trip home would be happy.
   (H) Maggie and Bart would argue.
   (J) Mom and Dad would argue.

5. The word <u>indistinct</u> means . . .
   (A) clear.
   (B) rough.
   (C) faint.
   (D) dangerous.

Answers:
1 (A) (B) (C) (D)   4 (F) (G) (H) (J)
2 (F) (G) (H) (J)   5 (A) (B) (C) (D)
3 (A) (B) (C) (D)

Comprehension/Story:
Section Two/Page 1

Directions: Read the passage and the questions that follow. Choose the best answer to each question and fill in the circle for your answer choice.

The Grand Canyon in Arizona is one of the great natural wonders of the world. The rims of the canyon rise up to 9,000 feet above sea level over the Colorado River at the bottom. This river has cut the canyon through the layers of rock that are now exposed to view.

The many layers of rock are of various colors, and each layer has been given a different name by geologists. The layer through which the river now cuts is black and is called "Archean." The second layer of rock, called "Algonkian," is brilliant red. The next layer is brownish lavender. It forms a cliff over the first two layers. Many other layers follow these. The top layer is a plateau of gray limestone about 350 feet thick.

At least 90 different kinds of animals live in or around the Grand Canyon. Among them are mountain lions, deer, porcupines, squirrels, lizards, and snakes. There are also more than 180 different kinds of birds.

Different kinds of plants grow at different levels in the canyon. The rims are covered with thick forests of blue spruce and Douglas fir. Desert cactus grows at the river level. Wildflowers such as delphiniums and poppies grow in other areas.

There are ruins in the Grand Canyon that show Native Americans once lived in this area. In 1540 Spaniards from Francisco Coronado's expedition were the first Europeans to discover the canyon.

1. This story is mainly about . . .
   (A) the history of the Grand Canyon.
   (B) the rocks, animals, and plants of the Grand Canyon.
   (C) Native Americans in the Grand Canyon.
   (D) recreation in the Grand Canyon.

2. The bottom layer of rock in the canyon is . . .
   (F) black.
   (G) red.
   (H) lavender.
   (J) gray.

3. If you started at the bottom of the canyon and followed a trail to the top, the last kind(s) of plants you would find would be . . .
   (A) desert cactus.
   (B) delphinium.
   (C) poppy.
   (D) spruce and fir.

4. Which sentence from the story is an opinion?
   (F) The Grand Canyon in Arizona is one of the great natural wonders of the world.
   (G) The top layer is a plateau of gray limestone about 350 feet thick.
   (H) At least 90 different kinds of animals live in or around the Grand Canyon.
   (J) The rims are covered with thick forests of blue spruce and Douglas fir.

5. The word <u>geologists</u> means . . .
   (A) scientists who study the earth.
   (B) scientists who study the stars.
   (C) scientists who study the oceans.
   (D) scientists who study the weather.

GO→

——

Answers:

1 (A) (B) (C) (D)　　　　4 (F) (G) (H) (J)

2 (F) (G) (H) (J)　　　　5 (A) (B) (C) (D)

3 (A) (B) (C) (D)

Comprehension/Story:
Section Two/Page 2

Directions: Read the passage and the questions that follow. Choose the best answer to each question and fill in the circle for your answer choice.

One hundred five miles of the Grand Canyon are in Grand Canyon National Park. This park covers 673,575 acres in northwestern Arizona. The Grand Canyon was set aside as a national park in 1919.

There are 31 national parks in the United States. National Parks are lands set aside "for the benefit and enjoyment of the people." They are also set aside for the "preservation from injury or spoilation of all timber, mineral deposits, natural curiosities, or wonders" within the parks and "their retention in their natural condition." These words are taken from the Yellowstone Act passed by Congress in 1872 when Yellowstone became the first of our national parks. The National Park Service began later, in 1916, to take care of the parks.

In addition to the national parks which were set aside mostly for their scenic beauty, there are also nine national historical parks. These are places that are being preserved because of the things that happened there. Most of them are associated with either the Revolutionary War or the Civil War. The National Park Service also takes care of eleven national military parks. These are areas where famous battles in American history were fought.

1. A good title for this part of the story might be . . .
   (A) The Grand Canyon.
   (B) Yellowstone.
   (C) Our National Parks.
   (D) Famous Battlefields.

2. Taking care of the scenery in our national parks is like . . .
   (F) locking up money in a bank.
   (G) keeping zoo animals in cages.
   (H) hanging pictures in a museum.
   (J) protecting animals in the wild.

3. Why do you suppose Congress passed the Yellowstone Act?
   (A) There were not many people in that part of the country anyway.
   (B) People planned to cut down trees and dig for minerals in the area.
   (C) They believed tourists would pay to see the natural wonders.
   (D) They planned to let Native Americans use the park.

4. What do you think would happen if there were no national parks?
   (F) People would still make sure that the land would be protected.
   (G) People would use the land for things that would make money.
   (H) People would always remember how beautiful the land was.
   (J) People would send in money to protect the endangered animals.

5. The word retention means being . . .
   (A) improved.
   (B) preserved.
   (C) developed.
   (D) neglected.

GO→

Answers:

1 (A) (B) (C) (D)   4 (F) (G) (H) (J)
2 (F) (G) (H) (J)   5 (A) (B) (C) (D)
3 (A) (B) (C) (D)

Comprehension/Story:
Section Two/Page 3

Directions: Read the passage and the questions that follow. Choose the best answer to each question and fill in the circle for your answer choice.

The old, old house stood alone on the hill by the lake. Its doors <u>creaked</u> on their hinges. Its shutters flapped and banged in the wind. Some of the shingles on its roof were loose, and there was a hole in the front steps. The fireplace and the chimney were still sturdy and strong, but, of course, there was no one there to build a fire.

Most of the people who passed by the old house passed by quickly. The children in the neighborhood ran. Everyone said that the old house was haunted. It was not haunted though. It was just old.

One young woman, Mrs. McCurdy, did not pass by quickly, however. She stopped and looked and then went into town and talked to several people. After awhile she came back with three children. They all stood in front of the house and looked at it.

"Well?" Mrs. McCurdy asked. "What do you think kids? It could be our summer house. Some nails and screws, a few boards, and a lot of paint. And I can get it for a song! Will you help? Are you willing to try?"

It had been a long time since the children had seen their mother so happy. "Sure," said Nell. "Why not?" said Bob. "Cool," said Phyllis.

"Oh, good!" said Mrs. McCurdy. "I knew you three wouldn't let me down. I'm so excited! We'll go to the bank and I'll sign the papers. And tomorrow we can think about getting started and plan what to do first." Mrs. McCurdy hugged all three children at once.

1. What kind of relationship does Mrs. McCurdy have with her children?
   - (A) cool and distant
   - (B) cold and stern
   - (C) warm and friendly
   - (D) chilly and irritable

2. What does Mrs. McCurdy mean when she says, "And I can get it for a song!"?
   - (F) She is a songwriter.
   - (G) She is a professional singer.
   - (H) The property will cost a lot.
   - (J) The property will cost very little.

3. What is the setting of this part of the story?
   - (A) at the house
   - (B) at the bank
   - (C) in a car
   - (D) in town

4. Why do you think the three children were quick to agree to help?
   - (F) Their mother had been unhappy for a long time.
   - (G) Their mother was always happy about everything.
   - (H) They were bored and wanted to have something exciting to do.
   - (J) They were really good at fixing and painting houses.

5. The word <u>creaked</u> means . . .
   - (A) swung easily.
   - (B) made a squeaky noise.
   - (C) hung crookedly.
   - (D) locked tight.

GO→

Answers:
1 (A) (B) (C) (D)   4 (F) (G) (H) (J)
2 (F) (G) (H) (J)   5 (A) (B) (C) (D)
3 (A) (B) (C) (D)

Comprehension/Story:
Section Two/Page 4

Directions: Read the passage and the questions that follow. Choose the best answer to each question and fill in the circle for your answer choice.

Mrs. McCurdy and her children decided to fix the <u>exterior</u> of the house first. The next day they went to the hardware store in town. They bought paint: bluish-gray for the house itself and white for the trim. They bought paintbrushes, screwdrivers, and hammers. They bought screws and nails of different sizes, and they also bought wire brushes and sandpaper. They decided that they needed some help with the hole in the front steps, so they hired a carpenter who agreed to meet them at the house and take a look at it.

While the carpenter fixed the front steps, Mrs. McCurdy and the children used their new wire brushes to take the peeling paint off the outside walls of the house. They worked and worked. "Mom," said Nell. "This is not a one-day job." "This is more like a one-week job," said Bob. "Let's have lunch," said Phyllis.

"Okay," said their mother. "You're not going to be sorry that we are spending your summer vacation doing this, are you? It will be more fun when we can actually start to paint."

"We are having fun now," said Nell. "We love working all summer," said Bob. "Smile!" said Phyllis.

A month later the kids were still working, and they were really tired. The house was painted, inside as well as outside. The furniture was moved in. There were even logs piled in the grate on the hearth, waiting to be burned. But their mother was back in the hospital where she had spent so much time the winter before.

"Don't worry," said Mrs. McCurdy to her children. "Next summer will be better."

1. The kids became really tired because . . .

   (A) they were not used to working.
   (B) they worked for weeks and weeks.
   (C) their mother made them work.
   (D) it was their summer vacation.

2. At the end of this part of the story, Mrs. McCurdy wants her children to feel . . .

   (F) worried.
   (G) sad.
   (H) hopeful.
   (J) curious.

3. What kind of a person is Mrs. McCurdy?

   (A) pessimistic
   (B) optimistic
   (C) contrary
   (D) negative

4. Why did the author end the second part of the story this way?

   (F) to allow the reader to know what will happen next without reading the rest of the story
   (G) to make the reader want to read the next part to find out what is going to happen
   (H) to discourage the reader from reading any farther
   (J) to warn the reader that the story may not have a happy ending

5. The word <u>exterior</u> means . . .

   (A) top.
   (B) bottom.
   (C) inside.
   (D) outside.

GO→

Answers:

1 Ⓐ Ⓑ Ⓒ Ⓓ 4 Ⓕ Ⓖ Ⓗ Ⓙ

2 Ⓕ Ⓖ Ⓗ Ⓙ 5 Ⓐ Ⓑ Ⓒ Ⓓ

3 Ⓐ Ⓑ Ⓒ Ⓓ

Comprehension/Story:
Section Two/Page 5

Directions: Read the passage and the questions that follow. Choose the best answer to each question and fill in the circle for your answer choice.

The children's grandmother came to take care of them while their mother was ill. Every week or so she drove them out to the lake to visit the house and add more finishing touches to their work. Finally, they planted climbing roses. The house was really beautiful, but their mother was not in it. They all cried now and then when they thought no one was watching.

"This is awful," said Nell. "Really, really bad," said Bob. "I hate it!" said Phyllis.

"Now, now, children," said their grandmother. "Cheer up! Everything will be all right. You'll see."

Listening to their grandmother, the children could not help but be cheerful. "It's easy to see who Mother takes after," they said, laughing in spite of themselves.

Then one day in late spring, Mother came home. The doctor said she was much better and a drive out to the lake would do her some good.

"Don't be too excited, Mother," Nell warned from the back seat the next morning. "There is a lot more work to do, you know," Bob agreed. They both <u>nudged</u> Phyllis who looked as if she might burst. In the front seat, Grandmother drove, looking straight ahead. Then, there was the house in front of them, gleaming with paint and blooming with roses. They half carried their mother up the front steps and put her on a sofa in the living room. Then Grandmother lit the fire that had waited so long for all of them to come. It was Mother's turn to cry now, but they were happy tears!

1. The children's mother and grandmother . . .

   (A) had similar attitudes about life.
   (B) had nothing in common at all.
   (C) had different feelings about children.
   (D) had both been very ill in the hospital.

2. The mood at the end of the story is . . .

   (F) sad.
   (G) gloomy.
   (H) happy.
   (J) angry.

3. This story is about . . .

   (A) things that could not happen.
   (B) people who could be real.
   (C) places that could not exist.
   (D) animals acting like people.

4. Which is the best summary of this story?

   (F) A woman with three children buys and remodels a house to surprise their visiting grandmother.
   (G) There is an old house with loose shutters and creaking doors on a hill by the lake.
   (H) Three children learn to use wire brushes to remove old paint from a house before applying fresh paint.
   (J) Three children help remodel a house their mother bought to surprise her when she gets out of the hospital.

5. The word <u>nudged</u> means . . .

   (A) poked.
   (B) patted.
   (C) hugged.
   (D) held.

Answers:

1 (A) (B) (C) (D)   4 (F) (G) (H) (J)

2 (F) (G) (H) (J)   5 (A) (B) (C) (D)

3 (A) (B) (C) (D)

Comprehension/Story:
Section Three/Page 1

Directions: Read the passage and the questions that follow. Choose the best answer to each question and fill in the circle for your answer choice.

The hippopotamus is an animal that lives both in water and on land. It is native to <u>tropical</u> Africa where it lives in swamps, rivers, and marshes. Its name means "river horse," but it is not related to the horse. It is related to the hog.

There are two kinds of hippopotamuses living today, the common hippopotamus and the pygmy hippopotamus. The pygmy variety is the less interesting of the two. It is much smaller than the common hippopotamus. It grows to be about 2 1/2 feet high and about 6 feet long and weighs between 400 and 600 pounds. It spends almost all of its time in the water because its skin cracks when it gets dry.

The common hippopotamus is a huge, thick-skinned animal. It can weigh as much as 8,000 pounds. Its body is shaped like a barrel. Its legs are short and thick. It usually stands a little less than 5 feet high and may be as long as 14 feet, including its tail. Its feet rest flat on the ground and have four toes each. Its head is large and lumpy and so heavy that the animal usually leans its chin on something for support when it comes out of the water. Its eyes and ears are small and pig-like. Its nostrils are set high on its head so that it can raise its head to breathe and still stay safely under water.

The hippopotamus has a really enormous mouth that can spread open 3 or 4 feet. It has powerful teeth and strong tusks which can grow to a length of 4 feet or more. With these tusks and teeth, the hippopotamus can easily root up and chew the toughest grass and stems. A full-grown hippopotamus has a stomach over 10 feet long that can hold 5 to 6 bushels of grass. A bushel is equal to 8 gallons.

1. This story is mainly about . . .

   (A) the common hippopotamus.
   (B) the pygmy hippopotamus.
   (C) tropical Africa.
   (D) pig-like animals.

2. The common hippopotamus can weigh as much as . . .

   (F) 400 pounds.
   (G) 600 pounds.
   (H) 800 pounds.
   (J) 8,000 pounds.

3. When the common hippopotamus comes out of the water, it likes to lean its chin on something because . . .

   (A) its body is shaped like a barrel.
   (B) its head is so large and heavy.
   (C) its eyes and ears are pig-like.
   (D) its nostrils are set high on its head.

4. Which of these statements is true?

   (F) The pygmy hippopotamus is longer than the common hippopotamus.
   (G) The pygmy hippopotamus is much smaller than the common hippopotamus.
   (H) The pygmy hippopotamus spends less time in the water than the common hippopotamus.
   (J) The pygmy hippopotamus has thicker skin than the common hippopotamus.

5. The word <u>tropical</u> means . . .

   (A) hot and wet.
   (B) hot and dry.
   (C) cold and wet.
   (D) cold and dry.

GO→

Answers:

1 (A) (B) (C) (D)   4 (F) (G) (H) (J)
2 (F) (G) (H) (J)   5 (A) (B) (C) (D)
3 (A) (B) (C) (D)

Comprehension/Story:
Section Three/Page 2

Directions: Read the passage and the questions that follow. Choose the best answer to each question and fill in the circle for your answer choice.

Even though the hippopotamus is clumsy on land, it can travel long distances and even gallop with surprising speed. Nevertheless, it is most at home in the water. It may spend days in the water with only its eyes, nostrils, and ears sticking out. It swims and dives well and can remain under the water for as long as five minutes. Some observers claim that individual hippos have stayed submerged for as long as 12 minutes!

It is hard to imagine this huge animal swimming gracefully in the water, and now you don't have to. At the San Diego Zoo in Southern California, there is an attraction called "Hippo Beach." It has a large pool with a glass wall. Through this wall, spectators can watch the hippopotamuses diving and swimming through the water.

There were once many hippopotamuses in Africa. African people used to hunt them both for food and for their hides and tusks. Today, however, hippos are on the list of animals that are in danger of extinction. They are endangered. That means that there are not many of them left. Some of the remaining hippos live in zoos, and some live on game preserves in Africa where they can be protected from hunters.

1. Which of these statements is an opinion?
   (A) Even though the hippopotamus is clumsy on land, it can travel long distances and even gallop with surprising speed.
   (B) It may spend days in the water with only its eyes, nostrils, and ears sticking out.
   (C) It can remain under the water for as long as five minutes.
   (D) Some observers claim that individual hippos have stayed submerged for as long as 12 minutes!

2. What would probably happen if the remaining hippos were not protected?
   (F) They would all live in zoos.
   (G) The hippo population would increase.
   (H) They would become extinct.
   (J) People would not hunt them.

3. Why did the author write this part of the story?
   (A) to give more facts about hippos
   (B) to tell funny stories about hippos
   (C) to help people take care of hippos
   (D) to advertise the San Diego Zoo

4. Looking at swimming hippos through a glass wall is like . . .
   (F) looking at a show on a television set.
   (G) watching ants in an ant farm.
   (H) seeing a movie in a theater.
   (J) going to a game at a stadium.

5. The word spectators means . . .
   (A) hunters.
   (B) scientists.
   (C) surfers.
   (D) onlookers.

GO→

Answers: 1 (A) (B) (C) (D)   4 (F) (G) (H) (J)

2 (F) (G) (H) (J)   5 (A) (B) (C) (D)

3 (A) (B) (C) (D)

Comprehension/Story:
Section Three/Page 3

Directions: Read the passage and the questions that follow. Choose the best answer to each question and fill in the circle for your answer choice.

"And the winner of the essay contest is Fred Foster!" announced Mr. Johnson. The whole school was at the <u>assembly.</u> They all watched as Fred made his way down the aisle and up to the stage. "Congratulations, Fred," Mr. Johnson continued. He handed Fred an envelope and shook his hand. Then he turned back to the assembled students. "All right, let's all give him a hand. Fred will read his essay at our next assembly on Friday."

All of the younger children clapped with enthusiasm as Fred walked back to his seat. The fourth and fifth graders clapped politely. They had all written essays too, and it was hard to be happy for Fred when each of them had been hoping to win.

Fred tried to catch the eyes of his best friends, Andy and Max, but they were looking down at the floor as he passed. Mrs. Merton, Fred's teacher, smiled at him proudly and made room for him to walk by and sit down. The girl he sat next to moved away from him and poked the girl on her other side. "What is going on?" Fred asked himself. He was beginning to feel really uncomfortable.

Andy and Max turned around to look at Fred but quickly looked away when they saw that he had noticed. "I can't believe this," Fred thought. "What is the matter with everybody? Are they all mad at me, or what?"

1. The students were feeling . . .

   (A) happy.
   (B) excited.
   (C) angry.
   (D) jealous.

2. Why is Fred uncomfortable about what is going on?

   (F) He does not think that he deserved to win.
   (G) His teacher is really proud of him.
   (H) His friends are acting strangely.
   (J) His parents were not there at school.

3. What does the expression "Fred tried to catch the eyes of his best friends" mean?

   (A) He reached over and touched their eyes.
   (B) He attempted to get their attention.
   (C) He looked at his friends and looked away.
   (D) He wanted them to ignore him.

4. What conclusion can you come to about Fred's friends?

   (F) They are always mean.
   (G) They are not good students.
   (H) They are usually nice.
   (J) They are not really friends.

5. In this story, the word <u>assembly</u> means . . .

   (A) a gathering of students.
   (B) a teachers' meeting.
   (C) a parents' meeting.
   (D) a musical show.

GO→

Answers:

1 (A) (B) (C) (D)　　　　4 (F) (G) (H) (J)

2 (F) (G) (H) (J)　　　　5 (A) (B) (C) (D)

3 (A) (B) (C) (D)

Comprehension/Story:
Section Three/Page 4

Directions: Read the passage and the questions that follow. Choose the best answer to each question and fill in the circle for your answer choice.

After school Andy and Max pretended not to see Fred when they got on the bus. He waved at them to wait for him, but they ignored him. Fred was so upset that he dropped the envelope Mr. Johnson had given him. Then, when he stopped to pick it up, he dropped his books. Before he could pick them up, the bus pulled away. "This is turning out to be the worst day of my life," Fred thought as he started to trudge home. When Fred got home, the house was empty. He found a note from his mother propped up on the kitchen table. "I'm picking up your sister and taking her to practice," the note read. "Have a snack because dinner will be late. Love, Mom."

Fred threw his books down on the table and himself into a chair. Then he pulled a piece of paper out of his backpack and started to write. He wrote for a long time. When he finished, he folded the piece of paper and put it back in his backpack in a special zipper pocket where it would be safe.

When his mom, dad, and sister came home, he showed them the envelope. The letter inside said that he had won the contest and invited his family to hear him read his essay at the assembly on Friday. They were very happy and excited and began to figure out how they could all be there. Fred was quiet. "I'm not hungry, Mom," he said. "I think I'll go to bed early."

"Oh dear," said his mother feeling his forehead. "You're not getting sick, are you?"

"No," said Fred. "I'm okay."

1. A good title for this part of the story might be . . .

   (A) Fred's Awful Afternoon.
   (B) The Happy Ending.
   (C) The Envelope.
   (D) The Empty House.

2. What happened after Fred dropped his books?

   (F) Andy and Max pretended not to see him.
   (G) Fred waved at Andy and Max.
   (H) Fred dropped the envelope.
   (J) The bus pulled away.

3. In this part of the story, Fred's mood is . . .

   (A) happy.
   (B) gloomy.
   (C) angry.
   (D) excited.

4. What has happened in the story to make Fred's friends act cold to him?

   (F) Fred was mean to them.
   (G) Fred was the teacher's pet.
   (H) Fred won an essay contest.
   (J) Fred missed the school bus.

5. The word ignored means . . .

   (A) did not pay attention to.
   (B) watched carefully.
   (C) shouted loudly at.
   (D) told jokes about.

GO→

Answers:

1 Ⓐ Ⓑ Ⓒ Ⓓ   4 Ⓕ Ⓖ Ⓗ Ⓙ

2 Ⓕ Ⓖ Ⓗ Ⓙ   5 Ⓐ Ⓑ Ⓒ Ⓓ

3 Ⓐ Ⓑ Ⓒ Ⓓ

Comprehension/Story:
Section Three/Page 5

Directions: Read the passage and the questions that follow. Choose the best answer to each question and fill in the circle for your answer choice.

That Friday at the assembly Fred marched up onto the stage. He looked around the large room. His classmates, including Andy and Max, were there. His mother, father, and sister were in the front row with Mrs. Merton, his teacher, and Mr. Johnson, the principal. Fred's face was very pale, but his voice was strong as he began to speak.

"Members of the faculty, honored guests, and fellow students," he said. "Before I read my essay, I want to tell you what it has been like to win this contest. I want to tell you about my week. Since the last assembly when Mr. Johnson announced that I was the winner of the essay contest, I have had a lot of time to think about what I want to say. I have had a lot of time because no one has talked to me, no one has sat by me at lunch, no one has said a single word to me.

"At first I wished that I had never entered the contest, and I wished that I had never written an essay. But then I decided that I wasn't sorry at all. I'm proud of my essay. I'm proud of winning. And I'm proud of having gotten through this week. It has given me a chance to decide that I will be really careful not to be <u>envious</u> of other people and their successes. Thank you for listening. Now I'll read my essay."

When Fred finished reading his essay, the younger students clapped. The older students sat in silence as Mr. Johnson got up to talk. "Girls and boys," he said, "I hope you realize what it took for Fred to share his experience with you. I also hope that you and your teachers will discuss what happened and think of a way to make sure that this does not happen again."

1. Fred could best be described as . . .

   (A) brave.
   (B) whiny.
   (C) scared.
   (D) silly.

2. The setting of this part of the story is . . .

   (F) in Fred's home.
   (G) at the assembly.
   (H) on the school bus.
   (J) in the classroom.

3. Which is the best summary of this story?

   (A) Fred wins an essay contest and feels hurt when his friends are jealous. He decides to share what he has learned.
   (B) There is an essay contest at school, and Fred is surprised to find out that he has won.
   (C) Fred's parents and teacher are very proud of him when he wins the essay contest.
   (D) Fred has an awful day when he wins the essay contest. His friends are mean to him.

4. This story is about . . .

   (F) things that could not happen.
   (G) people who could be real.
   (H) places that could not exist.
   (J) animals that act like people.

5. The word <u>envious</u> means . . .

   (A) generous.
   (B) jealous.
   (C) trusting.
   (D) selfish.

Answers:

1 (A) (B) (C) (D)   4 (F) (G) (H) (J)

2 (F) (G) (H) (J)   5 (A) (B) (C) (D)

3 (A) (B) (C) (D)

Student Practice Page

Comprehension/Story:
Section Four/Page 1

Directions: Read the passage and the questions that follow. Choose the best answer to each question and fill in the circle for your answer choice.

A Spanish explorer named Juan Ponce de Leon was looking for the Fountain of Youth in the early 1500's. In 1513 he landed on the Atlantic coast of Florida between what are now the cities of Jacksonville and St. Augustine and claimed the land for Spain. He named it Florida, a Spanish word that means "flowery" because he saw so many brilliant flowers in bloom.

In 1565 the Spanish founded the city of St. Augustine which is the oldest city established by Europeans in the United States. Jacksonville did not become a city until 1832. It is built on both sides of the Saint Johns River about 20 miles from the Atlantic Ocean.

Florida was passed back and forth between Spain and England for several hundred years. Finally, the Untied States purchased Florida from Spain for $5,000,000 in 1819. It remained a territory until 1845 when it became the 27th state. It was admitted to the Union as a slave state. Iowa was admitted as a free state in 1846 to maintain the balance between slave states and free states. Florida <u>seceded from</u> the United States to join the Confederacy and was then admitted back into the Union in 1868 after the Civil War.

Florida makes up a peninsula that juts out from the southeastern corner of the United States. It has a coastline longer than that of any other state except Alaska. It is bordered on the east by the Atlantic Ocean and on the west and south by the Gulf of Mexico. The highest elevation in the state is only 345 feet above sea level.

1. This story is mostly about . . .

   (A) the fruits grown in Florida.
   (B) the history and geography of Florida.
   (C) Florida's many recreational areas.
   (D) the largest cities in Florida.

2. The city of St. Augustine was founded by the Spanish in . . .

   (F) 1513.
   (G) 1565.
   (H) 1819.
   (J) 1832.

3. What happened to Florida when the Civil War ended?

   (A) It remained a territory until 1845.
   (B) It became the 27th state.
   (C) The United States purchased it from Spain.
   (D) It was admitted back into the Union.

4. Why was Iowa admitted to the Union the year after Florida?

   (F) to make the United States a bigger country
   (G) to fulfill a promise to Spain and England
   (H) to maintain the balance between free and slave states
   (J) to ensure peace at the end of the Civil War

5. The words <u>seceded from</u> mean . . .

   (A) joined.
   (B) left.
   (C) supported.
   (D) helped.

GO→

Answers:

1 Ⓐ Ⓑ Ⓒ Ⓓ   4 Ⓕ Ⓖ Ⓗ Ⓙ

2 Ⓕ Ⓖ Ⓗ Ⓙ   5 Ⓐ Ⓑ Ⓒ Ⓓ

3 Ⓐ Ⓑ Ⓒ Ⓓ

Comprehension/Story:
Section Four/Page 2

Directions: Read the passage and the questions that follow. Choose the best answer to each question and fill in the circle for your answer choice.

Florida has several nicknames. It is called the Peninsula State because it is surrounded by water on three sides and juts out into the sea for more than 400 miles. It is also called the Everglades State. The Everglades are marshy grasslands that lie near the end of the Florida peninsula. Sometimes Florida is called the Sunshine State because the sun shines an average of 220 days a year. Florida is warm and sunny in the winter months when much of the rest of the country is very cold.

Because of its mild climate, Florida has become popular as a vacation spot. Tourism is one of Florida's biggest industries. The beach resorts have been famous for many years. Now, in addition to these areas, the inland region around Orlando is the home to Disney World and Universal Studios and attracts millions of visitors from all over the world.

There are also other unusual attractions. The Ringling Brothers and Barnum & Bailey Circus has its winter quarters in Venice on Florida's Gulf Coast. There, visitors can watch animals being trained and acts being rehearsed in preparation for the next circus season. Cypress Gardens is the place to go for water-skiing exhibitions. These events are often televised too.

In addition to these <u>major</u> tourist attractions, there are national parks, forests, and monuments in Florida as well as many state parks, zoos, gardens, and jungles. Florida is truly a great place to take a vacation!

1. A good title for this part of the story might be . . .

   (A) Down in the Swamps.
   (B) Vacation Land, U. S. A.
   (C) Circus Time.
   (D) Orlando, Florida.

2. Tourist attractions are probably located in Florida because . . .

   (F) it is close to everything.
   (G) it is a peninsula.
   (H) it has such a mild climate.
   (J) it is home to the circus.

3. Which one of these statements is an opinion?

   (A) The Everglades are marshy grasslands that lie near the end of the Florida peninsula.
   (B) The beach resorts have been famous for many years.
   (C) The Ringling Brothers and Barnum & Bailey Circus has its winter quarters in Venice on Florida's Gulf Coast.
   (D) Florida is truly a great place to take a vacation!

4. What will probably happen to Florida in the future?

   (F) People will get tired of going there.
   (G) The climate will change and get cold.
   (H) More and more people will go there.
   (J) It will not be a peninsula any more.

5. In this story the word <u>major</u> means . . .

   (A) big and important.
   (B) small and unimportant.
   (C) military.
   (D) government.

GO→

- -

Answers:

1 Ⓐ Ⓑ Ⓒ Ⓓ
2 Ⓕ Ⓖ Ⓗ Ⓙ
3 Ⓐ Ⓑ Ⓒ Ⓓ

4 Ⓕ Ⓖ Ⓗ Ⓙ
5 Ⓐ Ⓑ Ⓒ Ⓓ

Comprehension/Story:
Section Four/Page 3

Directions: Read the passage and the questions that follow. Choose the best answer to each question and fill in the circle for your answer choice.

"Des," a voice crackled from her wrist phone. "Des, do you have fresh batteries in your rocket booster?"

Des twisted around on the seat of her jet bike, reached back into her space satchel and felt around for the booster. She flipped open the battery compartment and checked. "Yes, Mother," she said into her wrist phone and then silently to herself, "She will never get over the time I forgot to check and she had to call the Space Club!"

Then with a whoosh, Des was off toward the Infocenter. She narrowly missed a little kid on his first space scooter, joined a group of other students on jet bikes, and circled down onto the rooftop parking lot. After locking her bike, Des joined the others on the moving sidewalk. She stepped off at her cubicle, sat down in a thickly padded chair, switched on the screen in front of her, and put on her headphones. For the next two hours there was absolute silence in the Infocenter while Des and all of the other students absorbed information.

At midday, Des removed her headphones and switched off the screen. She stepped out of her cubicle and back onto the moving sidewalk which took her to the dining deck where lunch was being served. "Sit here, Des," her friends called. "Let's talk about our strategy for this afternoon's space hockey game."

1. The Infocenter is evidently a kind of . . .

   (A) store.
   (B) theater.
   (C) school.
   (D) arcade.

2. The author's purpose in this part of the story is to . . .

   (F) set the scene of the story.
   (G) give factual information.
   (H) describe the conflict.
   (J) advertise the Infocenter.

3. In this part of the story, Des appears to be . . .

   (A) a careful person.
   (B) rather careless.
   (C) funny and friendly.
   (D) hard to get along with.

4. The events in this part of the story indicate that it takes place . . .

   (F) in a foreign country.
   (G) in the distant past.
   (H) in a space ship.
   (J) sometime in the future.

5. The word strategy means . . .

   (A) plan of action.
   (B) list of players.
   (C) kind of uniform.
   (D) sports equipment.

GO→

Answers:

1 (A) (B) (C) (D)   4 (F) (G) (H) (J)

2 (F) (G) (H) (J)   5 (A) (B) (C) (D)

3 (A) (B) (C) (D)

Comprehension/Story:
Section Four/Page 4

Directions: Read the passage and the questions that follow. Choose the best answer to each question and fill in the circle for your answer choice.

"We will need to make some really great plans," Des laughed. "Since we haven't practiced, we may just have to face the music!" One of the boys produced some very <u>elaborate</u> diagrams of possible plays, and they discussed them until a bell announced the end of lunch.

Des spent the afternoon in her cubicle, using her computer to review what she had learned that morning. When the session ended, she joined her friends on the rooftop. They all used their rocket boosters to charge their jet bikes, and then they headed for the playing field.

The other team was already there, zooming about on their bikes and practicing their shots. "We don't stand a chance," Des moaned as one of the players whizzed by. "Look how good they are."

The game was a wild one. Everyone wore helmets and pads, but the players who fell off of their bikes into the safety net below still felt shaken up and out of breath by the time they climbed out of the net and restarted their bikes. Des scored once, which was good for her, but the other team won the game.

At the end of the game, they all shook hands. The visiting team boarded their space bus and started for home. Then the coach gave a short pep talk about the importance of coming to practice. The next game was an away game, and he wanted them to be really ready for it.

"I am just exhausted," said Des to no one in particular, "and I know Mother will want me to help her with dinner."

1. The space hockey game seems to be played . . .

   (A) in a pool.
   (B) in midair.
   (C) on the ground.
   (D) on the ice.

2. In the last paragraph of this part of the story, Des feels . . .

   (F) upset.
   (G) angry.
   (H) tired.
   (J) excited.

3. What does Des mean when she says "Since we haven't practiced, we may just have to face the music!"?

   (A) We might have to put up with unpleasant results.
   (B) We may have to play in the school band.
   (C) We must stand when our school song is played.
   (D) We should learn the words of the other team's song.

4. What part does Des play on her school team?

   (F) She assists the coach.
   (G) She is the star of the team.
   (H) She helps coach the team.
   (J) She helps design all of the plays.

5. In this story, the word <u>elaborate</u> means . . .

   (A) plain and simple.
   (B) detailed and fancy.
   (C) clear and serious.
   (D) funny and confused.

GO→

Answers:

1 Ⓐ Ⓑ © Ⓓ   4 Ⓕ Ⓖ Ⓗ Ⓙ

2 Ⓕ Ⓖ Ⓗ Ⓙ   5 Ⓐ Ⓑ © Ⓓ

3 Ⓐ Ⓑ © Ⓓ

Comprehension/Story:
Section Four/Page 5

Directions: Read the passage and the questions that follow. Choose the best answer to each question and fill in the circle for your answer choice.

Des zoomed home, parked her jet bike, and went into the kitchen where her mother stood glaring at the computer oven. "Oh, Des, I'm glad you're here," she said. "Did you have a good day? How was your game?" Without waiting for an answer she rushed on, "Will you choose the dinner and program this thing? I never manage to hit the right buttons, and it sits there just waiting for me to make a mistake!"

Des laughed. "I had a good day," she said. "We lost the game but that's okay. We had fun. And, yes, I will program the oven." Des gave her mother an affectionate hug. "It's just a machine, you know."

Des pushed some buttons on the oven and went to put her things away. By the time she returned to the kitchen, dinner was ready. She helped her mother put the dishes on the table and called for her dad and little brother, Max. They all sat down to eat and talk about the experiences that they had had that day.

"When I flew over to the Space Center this morning, I noticed that there are some new rides at Universe Park," Dad remarked. "Maybe we could go there this weekend."

"That sounds like fun," said Mother. "Do either of you kids have anything else planned?"

Des checked the calendar on the wall. "No games," she reported. "No practices. No reports due. It's all clear for the weekend." She looked at her family and thought, "I'm glad I live on Mars!"

1. This story is about . . .

   (A) things that might be happening right now.
   (B) things that could not currently be happening.
   (C) things that happened last year.
   (D) things that happened long ago.

2. Telling a story about the future is like . . .

   (F) writing a news report of an event.
   (G) writing a report about something.
   (H) telling the story of a movie you saw.
   (J) telling about a dream you had.

3. Which is the best summary of this story?

   (A) A girl has an ordinary day sometime in the future.
   (B) Some students play a game of space hockey and lose.
   (C) A girl spends the day studying hard in school.
   (D) A family has dinner together on Mars.

4. The mood at the end of this story is . . .

   (F) gloomy.
   (G) angry.
   (H) upset.
   (J) happy.

5. In this story, the word glaring means . . .

   (A) smiling.
   (B) staring.
   (C) laughing.
   (D) yawning.

Answers:

1 (A) (B) (C) (D)   4 (F) (G) (H) (J)

2 (F) (G) (H) (J)   5 (A) (B) (C) (D)

3 (A) (B) (C) (D)

Critical Reading: Interpreting Figurative Language

Directions: Read each sentence. Look for the words that have the same or almost the same meaning as the underlined phrase. Fill in the answer circle for your choice.

Samples

A. He <u>ate like a pig</u> at the birthday party.

  (A) ate in the mud

  (B) squealed while he ate

  (C) ate far too much

  (D) ate without a fork

B. The wind <u>roared fiercely</u> through the pine trees.

  (F) blew loudly

  (G) was a lion

  (H) seemed angry

  (J) laughed noisily

1. The street <u>was alive</u> with people.

  (A) was really crowded

  (B) was talking

  (C) came to life

  (D) started to grow

4. She ran <u>like a deer</u>.

  (F) on her hands and feet

  (G) between the trees

  (H) because she was frightened

  (J) with great speed

2. She was so tired that she <u>slept like a log</u>.

  (F) fell asleep on the ground

  (G) slept without moving at all

  (H) took a nap in the forest

  (J) slept with some squirrels

5. She sang <u>like a lark</u>.

  (A) with a beautiful voice

  (B) out in the meadow

  (C) up in a tall tree

  (D) while she built a nest

3. The lake <u>was a mirror for</u> the moon.

  (A) looked at

  (B) looked through

  (C) reflected

  (D) covered up

6. She is <u>a stick figure</u>.

  (F) a cartoon drawing

  (G) very stiff and clumsy

  (H) very thin

  (J) very funny

Answers: A (A) (B) (C) (D) 1 (A) (B) (C) (D) 3 (A) (B) (C) (D) 5 (A) (B) (C) (D)
B (F) (G) (H) (J) 2 (F) (G) (H) (J) 4 (F) (G) (H) (J) 6 (F) (G) (H) (J)

Critical Reading: Recognizing Story Structures

Directions: In each item read the passage and question. Fill in the circle for your answer choice at the bottom of the page.

Sample

A.
This morning the President announced that money has been set aside to help schools buy more computers, printers, and other technical equipment.

This sentence would most likely be found in a . . .

(A) social studies book.
(B) newspaper article.
(C) mystery story.
(D) fairy tale.

1.
The leprechaun buried his pot of gold and hid behind a tree. As the rainbow faded away, he decided that no one was following him after all. His gold was still safe.

This paragraph would most likely be found in a . . .

(A) social studies book.
(B) newspaper article.
(C) mystery story.
(D) fairy tale.

2.
The scout came racing back into the camp. "Circle the wagons!" he cried. Quickly, the covered wagons were pulled into a circle that could be easily defended. The children were hustled inside, and the pioneers loaded their rifles and waited.

In this paragraph from a story about the Westward Movement, which sentence would probably come next?

(F) Danger seemed to lurk behind every bush.
(G) In the meantime, they cooked dinner.
(H) The countryside was beautiful in the moonlight.
(J) There were twelve wagons in the party.

3.
"It's too dark to see anything," Maryanne whispered from the opening of the cave. "I think we should stay here until morning."

"I'm not so sure about that," Donald said in a shaky voice. "Something is rustling around back there. It might be a bear."

This passage would most likely be found in a . . .

(A) social studies book.
(B) newspaper article.
(C) adventure story.
(D) fairy tale.

Answers: A Ⓐ Ⓑ Ⓒ Ⓓ   1 Ⓐ Ⓑ Ⓒ Ⓓ   2 Ⓕ Ⓖ Ⓗ Ⓙ   3 Ⓐ Ⓑ Ⓒ Ⓓ

Spelling Skills (CAT/CTBS)

Directions: Read the sentence. Look for the correct spelling of the word that belongs in the sentence. Fill in the answer circle for your choice.

Samples

A. Look at the _____ and see what today's date is.
- (A) callendar
- (B) calendar
- (C) calender
- (D) collender

B. Did you write down the homework _____?
- (F) asignment
- (G) assinement
- (H) asinement
- (J) assignment

---

1. The birthday cake was _____.
- (A) delicious
- (B) delishus
- (C) delishious
- (D) dalishuss

5. We were snowed in during the _____.
- (A) blizerd
- (B) blizzard
- (C) blisserd
- (D) blizzerd

2. They brought in heavy _____ to fix the street.
- (F) ecwipmunt
- (G) ekwipment
- (H) equipment
- (J) eqwipment

6. We will _____ go to the mountains again next summer.
- (F) probably
- (G) probbly
- (H) probubly
- (J) probabely

3. Valentines Day is always in _____.
- (A) february
- (B) February
- (C) Febuary
- (D) Febbuary

7. They ate in a _____ last night.
- (A) resterant
- (B) restaraunt
- (C) restaurant
- (D) restauraunt

4. We could hear their _____ from the next room.
- (F) lafter
- (G) laffter
- (H) laugher
- (J) laughter

8. Bob and Jeff wanted to wrap the package by _____.
- (F) themselves
- (G) themselfs
- (H) themselfes
- (J) them selves

Answers:

A (A) (B) (C) (D) 2 (F) (G) (H) (J) 5 (A) (B) (C) (D) 8 (F) (G) (H) (J)

B (F) (G) (H) (J) 3 (A) (B) (C) (D) 6 (F) (G) (H) (J)

1 (A) (B) (C) (D) 4 (F) (G) (H) (J) 7 (A) (B) (C) (D)

Spelling Skills (CAT/CTBS)

Directions: Read the phrases in each item. Look for the underlined word that is spelled incorrectly. Fill in the answer circle for your choice.

Samples

A.
- (A) deep <u>canyon</u>
- (B) seven <u>continents</u>
- (C) <u>explane</u> clearly
- (D) <u>highest</u> mountain

B.
- (F) dangerous <u>huricane</u>
- (G) two <u>gallons</u>
- (H) detailed <u>description</u>
- (J) <u>develop</u> pictures

1.
- (A) playful <u>dolphin</u>
- (B) <u>friendly</u> dog
- (C) <u>greatful</u> person
- (D) good <u>humor</u>

6.
- (F) <u>vannila</u> ice cream
- (G) <u>wheat</u> field
- (H) good <u>suggestion</u>
- (J) nice <u>weather</u>

2.
- (F) <u>forward</u> march
- (G) <u>loose</u> tooth
- (H) tropical <u>iland</u>
- (J) sunny <u>morning</u>

7.
- (A) empty <u>bottels</u>
- (B) coin <u>collection</u>
- (C) <u>corner</u> store
- (D) <u>beach</u> house

3.
- (A) beaded <u>mocassins</u>
- (B) <u>original</u> painting
- (C) close <u>relative</u>
- (D) <u>sliced</u> bread

8.
- (F) fried <u>chicken</u>
- (G) <u>cheerfull</u> smile
- (H) <u>garden</u> party
- (J) <u>interesting</u> story

4.
- (F) green <u>spinach</u>
- (G) <u>shadey</u> tree
- (H) <u>plastic</u> toys
- (J) huge <u>rhinoceros</u>

9.
- (A) lost <u>mittens</u>
- (B) <u>phone</u> call
- (C) broken <u>pensil</u>
- (D) spotted <u>leopard</u>

5.
- (A) foreign <u>travel</u>
- (B) <u>yesterday</u> afternoon
- (C) <u>teriffic</u> idea
- (D) favorite <u>uncle</u>

10.
- (F) pleasant <u>memory</u>
- (G) baby <u>powder</u>
- (H) ripe <u>rasberries</u>
- (J) window <u>screen</u>

- -

Answers:

A Ⓐ Ⓑ Ⓒ Ⓓ   2 Ⓕ Ⓖ Ⓗ Ⓙ   5 Ⓐ Ⓑ Ⓒ Ⓓ   8 Ⓕ Ⓖ Ⓗ Ⓙ

B Ⓕ Ⓖ Ⓗ Ⓙ   3 Ⓐ Ⓑ Ⓒ Ⓓ   6 Ⓕ Ⓖ Ⓗ Ⓙ   9 Ⓐ Ⓑ Ⓒ Ⓓ

1 Ⓐ Ⓑ Ⓒ Ⓓ   4 Ⓕ Ⓖ Ⓗ Ⓙ   7 Ⓐ Ⓑ Ⓒ Ⓓ   10 Ⓕ Ⓖ Ⓗ Ⓙ

Spelling Skills (ITBS)

Directions: Read the words in each item and look for a spelling mistake. In the answer rows, fill in the answer circle for the number of the word with the mistake. If you do not find a mistake, fill in answer circle 5.

Samples

A.		B.	
(1) coastal		(1) movement	
(2) anser		(2) kneel	
(3) hunger		(3) magazine	
(4) opinion		(4) sample	
(5) no mistake		(5) no mistake	

1.
(1) statement
(2) quality
(3) serious
(4) sneze
(5) no mistake

6.
(1) company
(2) terminal
(3) twise
(4) Tuesday
(5) no mistake

2.
(1) suspence
(2) visitor
(3) stereo
(4) problem
(5) no mistake

7.
(1) tomorrow
(2) advantage
(3) comfort
(4) signal
(5) no mistake

3.
(1) stranger
(2) wonderful
(3) brisles
(4) nervous
(5) no mistake

8.
(1) important
(2) passage
(3) holliday
(4) echo
(5) no mistake

4.
(1) January
(2) handfull
(3) discovered
(4) imagine
(5) no mistake

9.
(1) familys
(2) harvest
(3) gathered
(4) ground
(5) no mistake

5.
(1) minute
(2) offered
(3) accept
(4) croud
(5) no mistake

10.
(1) hurried
(2) excape
(3) material
(4) notice
(5) no mistake

Answers:

A ① ② ③ ④ ⑤   2 ① ② ③ ④ ⑤   5 ① ② ③ ④ ⑤   8 ① ② ③ ④ ⑤
B ① ② ③ ④ ⑤   3 ① ② ③ ④ ⑤   6 ① ② ③ ④ ⑤   9 ① ② ③ ④ ⑤
1 ① ② ③ ④ ⑤   4 ① ② ③ ④ ⑤   7 ① ② ③ ④ ⑤   10 ① ② ③ ④ ⑤

Spelling Skills (SAT)

Directions: Look at the four words in each item. Fill in the answer circle at the bottom of the page for the word that is not spelled correctly.

Samples

A.
(A) headache
(B) diference
(C) flashlight
(D) journey

B.
(F) paint
(G) mistake
(H) mansion
(J) nowledge

1.
(A) paragraff
(B) roasted
(C) sadness
(D) reverse

6.
(F) pillow
(G) warmth
(H) storey
(J) worst

2.
(F) sometimes
(G) property
(H) kwestion
(J) section

7.
(A) bravery
(B) collored
(C) rained
(D) music

3.
(A) leppard
(B) napkin
(C) recreation
(D) climate

8.
(F) solemm
(G) fourth
(H) divide
(J) global

4.
(F) confuse
(G) bilding
(H) century
(J) beneath

9.
(A) ignore
(B) dropped
(C) obay
(D) mountain

5.
(A) around
(B) customer
(C) decorate
(D) teecher

10.
(F) mischiff
(G) pigeon
(H) peculiar
(J) magnet

Answers:

A Ⓐ Ⓑ Ⓒ Ⓓ 2 Ⓕ Ⓖ Ⓗ Ⓙ 5 Ⓐ Ⓑ Ⓒ Ⓓ 8 Ⓕ Ⓖ Ⓗ Ⓙ
B Ⓕ Ⓖ Ⓗ Ⓙ 3 Ⓐ Ⓑ Ⓒ Ⓓ 6 Ⓕ Ⓖ Ⓗ Ⓙ 9 Ⓐ Ⓑ Ⓒ Ⓓ
1 Ⓐ Ⓑ Ⓒ Ⓓ 4 Ⓕ Ⓖ Ⓗ Ⓙ 7 Ⓐ Ⓑ Ⓒ Ⓓ 10 Ⓕ Ⓖ Ⓗ Ⓙ

Spelling Skills (SAT)

Directions: Read each set of phrases. Look at the word that is underlined in each phrase. One of the underlined words is spelled incorrectly for the way it is used in the phrase. Find the word that is spelled incorrectly. Fill in the circle for your answer choice.

Samples

A.
- (A) a deep whole
- (B) a pair of socks
- (C) the pail of water
- (D) the rows of numbers

B.
- (F) new the answer
- (G) mail the package
- (H) raise the flag
- (J) a clown's red nose

1.
- (A) down the aisle
- (B) sale the boat
- (C) four cute kittens
- (D) bought new clothes

6.
- (F) write a letter
- (G) a Halloween which
- (H) painted wood
- (J) nice weather

2.
- (F) around her waist
- (G) flying in a plane
- (H) tropical isle
- (J) where this shirt

7.
- (A) meet a friend
- (B) a soar throat
- (C) an unpaved road
- (D) tie a knot

3.
- (A) led the way
- (B) once a weak
- (C) their own house
- (D) some good books

8.
- (F) put on the brake
- (G) a big bee
- (H) don't stair
- (J) the brave knight

4.
- (F) the blew sky
- (G) two ripe pears
- (H) don't peek
- (J) threw the ball

9.
- (A) the open sea
- (B) a heard of cows
- (C) an exciting tale
- (D) at low tide

5.
- (A) cost ten cents
- (B) a cinnamon role
- (C) two dollars each
- (D) moan and groan

10.
- (F) burned some would
- (G) through the window
- (H) a red rose
- (J) take a break

Answers:
A Ⓐ Ⓑ ⓒ ⓓ 2 Ⓕ ⓖ ⓗ ⓙ 5 Ⓐ Ⓑ ⓒ ⓓ 8 Ⓕ ⓖ ⓗ ⓙ
B Ⓕ ⓖ ⓗ ⓙ 3 Ⓐ Ⓑ ⓒ ⓓ 6 Ⓕ ⓖ ⓗ ⓙ 9 Ⓐ Ⓑ ⓒ ⓓ
1 Ⓐ Ⓑ ⓒ ⓓ 4 Ⓕ ⓖ ⓗ ⓙ 7 Ⓐ Ⓑ ⓒ ⓓ 10 Ⓕ ⓖ ⓗ ⓙ

Spelling Skills (MAT)

Directions: Read the sentence carefully. Fill in the circle for any word that is misspelled. If all the words are correct, fill in the circle for no mistake.

Samples

A. The <u>race</u> was a <u>chalenge</u> for even the most <u>physically</u> fit students. <u>no mistake</u>
      A   B   C   D

B. <u>Celery</u> and <u>carrots</u> are both <u>vegetables</u>. <u>no mistake</u>
      E   F   G   H

---

1. He will <u>graduate</u> from <u>college</u> next <u>Saterday</u>. <u>no mistake</u>
             A   B   C   D

2. Today in <u>science</u> we <u>disolved</u> <u>sugar</u> in water. <u>no mistake</u>
            E   F   G   H

3. Did you have an <u>opportunity</u> to <u>notice</u> the <u>rhinoceros</u>? <u>no mistake</u>
                A   B   C   D

4. He is <u>suprised</u> that there will be a <u>program</u> in the <u>auditorium</u> today. <u>no mistake</u>
       E   F   G   H

5. We <u>read</u> about the <u>expidition</u> in our <u>history</u> books. <u>no mistake</u>
      A   B   C   D

6. <u>Remember</u> to wax the <u>chrome</u> when you <u>cleen</u> the car. <u>no mistake</u>
      E   F   G   H

7. <u>Frequent</u> storms brought <u>disaster</u> to the <u>communitee</u>. <u>no mistake</u>
    A   B   C   D

8. Our <u>teacher</u> won the <u>basketball</u> <u>tournament</u>. <u>no mistake</u>
      E   F   G   H

Answers:
A Ⓐ Ⓑ Ⓒ Ⓓ 2 Ⓔ Ⓕ Ⓖ Ⓗ 5 Ⓐ Ⓑ Ⓒ Ⓓ 8 Ⓔ Ⓕ Ⓖ Ⓗ
B Ⓔ Ⓕ Ⓖ Ⓗ 3 Ⓐ Ⓑ Ⓒ Ⓓ 6 Ⓔ Ⓕ Ⓖ Ⓗ
1 Ⓐ Ⓑ Ⓒ Ⓓ 4 Ⓔ Ⓕ Ⓖ Ⓗ 7 Ⓐ Ⓑ Ⓒ Ⓓ

Student Practice Page

Spelling Skills (MAT)

Directions: Listen to the words and the sentences that are read aloud. Find the correct ways to spell the words. Fill in the circles for your answer choices at the bottom of the page.

Samples

A.
- (A) happey
- (B) happy
- (C) hapy
- (D) hapey

B.
- (E) baskette
- (F) bascket
- (G) basket
- (H) baskit

1.
- (A) farmer
- (B) farmor
- (C) farmmer
- (D) farmere

6.
- (E) bawght
- (F) bougt
- (G) bought
- (H) baught

2.
- (E) lam
- (F) lamb
- (G) lamm
- (H) lamn

7.
- (A) night
- (B) nit
- (C) niet
- (D) nihgt

3.
- (A) mete
- (B) meit
- (C) meet
- (D) meete

8.
- (E) werst
- (F) woorst
- (G) worst
- (H) worest

4.
- (E) eksept
- (F) eccept
- (G) exsept
- (H) except

9.
- (A) safetey
- (B) safety
- (C) saftey
- (D) saifty

5.
- (A) chapter
- (B) shapter
- (C) chaptere
- (D) chappter

10.
- (E) puppys
- (F) puppeys
- (G) puppies
- (H) puppyes

Answers:

A (A) (B) (C) (D) 2 (F) (G) (H) (J) 5 (A) (B) (C) (D) 8 (F) (G) (H) (J)

B (F) (G) (H) (J) 3 (A) (B) (C) (D) 6 (F) (G) (H) (J) 9 (A) (B) (C) (D)

1 (A) (B) (C) (D) 4 (F) (G) (H) (J) 7 (A) (B) (C) (D) 10 (F) (G) (H) (J)

Language Mechanics: Capitalization (CAT/CTBS)

Directions: Read the sentence. Look for the sentence part that has a word that should begin with a capital letter. Fill in the answer circle for your choice. Fill in the circle for none if no other capital letter is needed.

Samples

A. My aunt | from new York City | used to | live in an apartment.   none
    A   B   C   D   E

B. "Did you ever | make a wish | on a star?" | Janice asked him.   none
    F   G   H   J   K

1. If it is | raining on Saturday | mr. Jones will not | take us sailing.   none
   A   B   C   D   E

2. The state | of texas shares | a border with | Mexico.   none
   F   G   H   J   K

3. We toured | the state capitol | building in | Sacramento, California.   none
   A   B   C   D   E

4. The first score | in the football game | was made | by jason.   none
   F   G   H   J   K

5. Last year | we picked | *Alice in Wonderland* for | our school play.   none
   A   B   C   D   E

6. My sister | Mandy and i | like to look at | cartoons on television.   none
   F   G   H   J   K

7. When I told Jeff | we would be late, | he said, | "oh, no!"   none
   A   B   C   D   E

8. next month | we will take | a trip | to the museum.   none
   F   G   H   J   K

Answers: A Ⓐ Ⓑ Ⓒ Ⓓ Ⓔ   2 Ⓕ Ⓖ Ⓗ Ⓙ Ⓚ   5 Ⓐ Ⓑ Ⓒ Ⓓ Ⓔ   8 Ⓕ Ⓖ Ⓗ Ⓙ Ⓚ
            B Ⓕ Ⓖ Ⓗ Ⓙ Ⓚ   3 Ⓐ Ⓑ Ⓒ Ⓓ Ⓔ   6 Ⓕ Ⓖ Ⓗ Ⓙ Ⓚ
            1 Ⓐ Ⓑ Ⓒ Ⓓ Ⓔ   4 Ⓕ Ⓖ Ⓗ Ⓙ Ⓚ   7 Ⓐ Ⓑ Ⓒ Ⓓ Ⓔ

Language Mechanics: Capitalization (ITBS)

Directions: Read each item and look for a capitalization mistake. In the answer rows below, fill in the circle for the number of the line with the mistake. If you do not find a mistake, fill in circle 4.

Samples

A.
(1)   My brother Carl is learning to
(2)   rollerblade. he practices for one
(3)   half hour every day.
(4)   **no mistakes**

B.
(1)   Melissa Johnson and her mother
(2)   are making plans to visit Europe
(3)   next summer vacation.
(4)   **no mistakes**

1.
(1)   My grandmother and grandfather
(2)   raise horses. They own a big ranch
(3)   in wyoming.
(4)   **no mistakes**

6.
(1)   The moon plays an important
(2)   part in the ceremonies of many
(3)   asian countries.
(4)   **no mistakes**

2.
(1)   Marco is a new member of the
(2)   boy scouts of America. He will
(3)   be a good scout because he is loyal.
(4)   **no mistakes**

7.
(1)   Maria has invited everyone in
(2)   our class to her birthday party on
(3)   october 25th.
(4)   **no mistakes**

3.
(1)   Pham has a big cat named
(2)   tiny that loves to be scratched
(3)   under his chin.
(4)   **no mistakes**

8.
(1)   Our school just received a gift
(2)   of ten apple computers, three printers,
(3)   and some software.
(4)   **no mistakes**

4.
(1)   When we finally got home, we all
(2)   rushed in out of the snow. the
(3)   warmth of the fire felt wonderful.
(4)   **no mistakes**

9.
(1)   My teacher, Miss Taylor, has been
(2)   teaching for twenty-five years. She
(3)   is thinking about retiring.
(4)   **no mistakes**

5.
(1)   On Wednesday afternoon I had to
(2)   miss my piano lesson because i had
(3)   a dentist's appointment.
(4)   **no mistakes**

10.
(1)   My uncle and aunt designed their
(2)   summer cabin together, but the actual
(3)   building was done by uncle Ed.
(4)   **no mistakes**

Answers:

A ① ② ③ ④   2 ① ② ③ ④   5 ① ② ③ ④   8 ① ② ③ ④
B ① ② ③ ④   3 ① ② ③ ④   6 ① ② ③ ④   9 ① ② ③ ④
1 ① ② ③ ④   4 ① ② ③ ④   7 ① ② ③ ④   10 ① ② ③ ④

Language Mechanics: Capitalization (SAT)

Directions: Read each sentence. Choose the correct way to capitalize the word or group of words that go in the blank. Fill in the answer circle for your choice.

Samples

A.   We played a lot of tricks on _____ .

   (A) april fool's Day
   (B) April Fool's Day
   (C) April fool's day
   (D) april Fool's day

B.   Our teacher read to us a story called _____ .

   (F) "the King of Cats"
   (G) "The king of cats"
   (H) "the King of Cats"
   (J) "The King of Cats"

1.   We planted a tree last _____ .

   (A) Arbor Day
   (B) arbor Day
   (C) arbor day
   (D) Arbor day

5.   *Winnie-the-Pooh* was written by _____ .

   (A) A. A. Milne
   (B) A. a. Milne
   (C) a. a. Milne
   (D) a. a. milne

2.   They celebrated the birthday of _____ .

   (F) president Washington
   (G) President washington
   (H) president washington
   (J) President Washington

6.   Jack comes from a _____ .

   (F) city in florida
   (G) city in Florida
   (H) City in Florida
   (J) City in florida

3.   Bolivia is a country in _____ .

   (A) south america
   (B) south America
   (C) South America
   (D) South america

7.   My favorite book is _____ .

   (A) *the Wizard of oz*
   (B) *The wizard of Oz*
   (C) *the wizard of Oz*
   (D) *The Wizard of Oz*

4.   We saw dinosaur bones at the _____ .

   (F) john Smith Museum
   (G) john smith museum
   (H) John Smith museum
   (J) John Smith Museum

8.   There are millions of stars in _____ .

   (F) Outer Space
   (G) outer Space
   (H) Outer space
   (J) outer space

Answers:

A Ⓐ Ⓑ Ⓒ Ⓓ   2 Ⓕ Ⓖ Ⓗ Ⓙ   5 Ⓐ Ⓑ Ⓒ Ⓓ   8 Ⓕ Ⓖ Ⓗ Ⓙ

B Ⓕ Ⓖ Ⓗ Ⓙ   3 Ⓐ Ⓑ Ⓒ Ⓓ   6 Ⓕ Ⓖ Ⓗ Ⓙ

1 Ⓐ Ⓑ Ⓒ Ⓓ   4 Ⓕ Ⓖ Ⓗ Ⓙ   7 Ⓐ Ⓑ Ⓒ Ⓓ

Language Mechanics: Punctuation (CAT/CTBS)

Directions: Read the sentence. Look for the punctuation mark that belongs in the sentence. Fill in the answer circle for your choice. Fill in the circle for none if no other punctuation mark is needed.

Samples

A. There are knives spoons, and forks in the top drawer.

     (A) .   (B) :   (C) ,   (D) "   (E) none

B. "Can you play at my house after school?" Jenny asked Lupe.

     (F) "   (G) ,   (H) .   (J) !   (K) none

---

1. "Please, Grandpa," Susie asked, "will you read a story to me?

     (A) .   (B) :   (C) !   (D) "   (E) none

2. Carlos do you want to have spaghetti or hamburgers for dinner?

     (F) ?   (G) ,   (H) !   (J) .   (K) none

3. When she saw the fire and smoke, Luann yelled, "Help"

     (A) "   (B) ?   (C) !   (D) :   (E) none

4. My sister's new kindergarten teacher is named Ms Watson

     (F) ,   (G) :   (H) .   (J) !   (K) none

5. Madeline Gurney is the head librarian of Davis Middle School.

     (A) :   (B) "   (C) .   (D) ?   (E) none

6. Allied troops landed in France on June 6 1944.

     (F) ,   (G) !   (H) "   (J) :   (K) none

7. When the rain stops, we can look for a rainbow," said Mario.

     (A) !   (B) "   (C) .   (D) ,   (E) none

8. Did you see the pictures of the erupting volcano in the paper

     (F) "   (G) .   (H) ,   (J) ?   (K) none

Answers:

A Ⓐ Ⓑ Ⓒ Ⓓ Ⓔ   2 Ⓕ Ⓖ Ⓗ Ⓙ Ⓚ   5 Ⓐ Ⓑ Ⓒ Ⓓ Ⓔ   8 Ⓕ Ⓖ Ⓗ Ⓙ Ⓚ

B Ⓕ Ⓖ Ⓗ Ⓙ Ⓚ   3 Ⓐ Ⓑ Ⓒ Ⓓ Ⓔ   6 Ⓕ Ⓖ Ⓗ Ⓙ Ⓚ

1 Ⓐ Ⓑ Ⓒ Ⓓ Ⓔ   4 Ⓕ Ⓖ Ⓗ Ⓙ Ⓚ   7 Ⓐ Ⓑ Ⓒ Ⓓ Ⓔ

Language Mechanics: Punctuation (CAT/CTBS)

Directions: Read the sentence. Look for the correct punctuation for the underlined part. Fill in the answer circle for your choice. Fill in the circle for correct as it is if no other punctuation is needed.

Samples

A. The teacher said, "We will leave now to get on <u>the bus</u>"

  (A) the bus.
  (B) the bus."
  (C) the bus,"
  (D) the bus?"
  (E) correct as it is

B. <u>Hooray, our</u> team won the game!

  (F) Hooray our
  (G) Hooray. our
  (H) Hooray our,
  (J) Hooray: our
  (K) correct as it is

1. We saw games of <u>touch football baseball,</u> and soccer in the park.

  (A) touch football, baseball
  (B) touch, football baseball
  (C) touch football, baseball,
  (D) touch, football, baseball,
  (E) correct as it is

4. Have you ever visited Hoover Dam near <u>Las Vegas Nevada</u>?

  (F) Las Vegas Nevada
  (G) Las Vegas: Nevada
  (H) Las Vegas. Nevada?
  (J) Las Vegas, Nevada?
  (K) correct as it is

2. "Can you say," asked Luanna, "the names of all of <u>the continents</u>"

  (F) the continents.
  (G) the continents?
  (H) the continents!"
  (J) the continents?"
  (K) correct as it is

5. <u>E. B White</u> has written many excellent books.

  (A) E B White
  (B) E B. White
  (C) E. B. White
  (D) E, B. White
  (E) correct as it is

3. <u>Mrs. Schultz</u> brought our class a present when she came back from Washington.

  (A) Mrs Schultz
  (B) Mrs, Schultz
  (C) Mrs: Schultz
  (D) Mrs, "Schultz
  (E) correct as it is

6. "Don't forget to add the vanilla <u>extract, Roger</u> reminded me.

  (F) extract" Roger
  (G) extract," Roger
  (H) extract." Roger
  (J) "extract," Roger
  (K) correct as it is

Answers: A (A)(B)(C)(D)(E) 1 (A)(B)(C)(D)(E) 3 (A)(B)(C)(D)(E) 5 (A)(B)(C)(D)(E)
B (F)(G)(H)(J)(K) 2 (F)(G)(H)(J)(K) 4 (F)(G)(H)(J)(K) 6 (F)(G)(H)(J)(K)

Language Mechanics: Punctuation (ITBS)

Directions: Read each item and look for a punctuation mistake. In the answer rows, fill in the answer circle for the number of the line with the mistake. If you do not find a mistake, fill in circle 4.

Samples

A.
(1) Some of the largest amusement
(2) parks in the United States can be
(3) found in Orlando, Florida.
(4) **no mistakes**

B.
(1) Randy said, Let's straighten
(2) the room up quickly and get ready
(3) for our party."
(4) **no mistakes**

1.
(1) Maria and Teresa picked up all of
(2) the puzzles and put them in boxes
(3) Carl put the boxes in the closet.
(4) **no mistakes**

6.
(1) Melissa said to her mother,
(2) "Thank you for packing such a
(3) good lunch for me today.
(4) **no mistakes**

2.
(1) Has anyone seen my notebook?
(2) It has purple, stripes and my name
(3) is on both the front and back.
(4) **no mistakes**

7.
(1) Tornados sometimes cause great
(2) damage These whirling winds have
(3) been clocked at 300 miles per hour.
(4) **no mistakes**

3.
(1) The tallest skyscraper in the
(2) United States can be found in
(3) Chicago, Illinois.
(4) **no mistakes**

8.
(1) On New Year's Day, both the Rose
(2) Parade and the Rose Bowl game take
(3) place in Pasadena California.
(4) **no mistakes**

4.
(1) I wont be at dance practice this
(2) Thursday. We are having a birthday
(3) party for my mother.
(4) **no mistakes**

9.
(1) "Look out!" yelled David. "That
(2) car has no brakes, and it is rolling
(3) backwards down the hill."
(4) **no mistakes**

5.
(1) It is time for our class to have
(2) pictures taken in the cafeteria. Is
(3) everyone ready to go
(4) **no mistakes**

10.
(1) Robert E Lee commanded all of the
(2) Confederate armies during the final
(3) years of the Civil War.
(4) **no mistakes**

Answers:

A ① ② ③ ④   2 ① ② ③ ④   5 ① ② ③ ④   8 ① ② ③ ④
B ① ② ③ ④   3 ① ② ③ ④   6 ① ② ③ ④   9 ① ② ③ ④
1 ① ② ③ ④   4 ① ② ③ ④   7 ① ② ③ ④   10 ① ② ③ ④

Language Mechanics: Punctuation (SAT)

Directions: Read each sentence or question. Find the word or group of words with the correct punctuation. Fill in the answer circle for your choice.

Samples

A. What time will the show _____

    (A) begin.

    (B) begin?

    (C) begin!

    (D) begin

B. Elizabeth comes from _____.

    (F) Des, Moines, Iowa

    (G) Des, Moines Iowa

    (H) Des Moines Iowa

    (J) Des Moines, Iowa

1. Joanie was born on _____ .

    (A) January, 21, 1986

    (B) January 21, 1986

    (C) January 21 1986

    (D) January, 21 1986

5. Which is the correct abbreviation for the word <u>Wednesday</u>?

    (A) Wed

    (B) Wed.

    (C) Wed,

    (D) Wed;

2. My _____ watch is broken.

    (F) mothers's

    (G) mothers'

    (H) mother's

    (J) mothers

6. _____ I didn't hear you.

    (F) No

    (G) No;

    (H) No,

    (J) "No"

3. What a dangerous _____

    (A) stunt.

    (B) stunt?

    (C) stunt!

    (D) stunt

7. Which is the correct way to end a letter?

    (A) Sincerely,

    (B) Sincerely.

    (C) Sincerely

    (D) Sincerely;

4. Which is the correct way to begin a letter?

    (F) Dear Uncle Fred,

    (G) Dear Uncle Fred

    (H) Dear Uncle Fred.

    (J) Dear Uncle Fred;

8. The principal said, _____

    (F) "Please line up.

    (G) Please line up."

    (H) Please line up.

    (J) "Please line up."

- -

Answers:

A Ⓐ Ⓑ Ⓒ Ⓓ   2 Ⓕ Ⓖ Ⓗ Ⓙ   5 Ⓐ Ⓑ Ⓒ Ⓓ   8 Ⓕ Ⓖ Ⓗ Ⓙ

B Ⓕ Ⓖ Ⓗ Ⓙ   3 Ⓐ Ⓑ Ⓒ Ⓓ   6 Ⓕ Ⓖ Ⓗ Ⓙ

1 Ⓐ Ⓑ Ⓒ Ⓓ   4 Ⓕ Ⓖ Ⓗ Ⓙ   7 Ⓐ Ⓑ Ⓒ Ⓓ

Language Mechanics: Capitalization and Punctuation

Directions: Fill in the circle for the answer that shows correct punctuation and capitalization. For sample B and items 4–6 fill in the circle for correct as it is if the underlined part is already correct.

Samples

A.
(A) Please tell Johnny, that his book is here.

(B) Mother there is a package for you at the door.

(C) José, are you on the phone?

(D) Mario, made a home run in today's game.

B. The <u>Empire State Building</u> is in New York.

(F) empire state building

(G) Empire state building

(H) empire State building

(J) correct as it is

1.
(A) The money wasn't in my purse.

(B) I couldnt remember where I might have put it.

(C) My brother and sister didnt' know where it was either.

(D) I really hope I have'nt lost it.

2.
(F) Gerald got a skateboard for his birthday?

(G) He and his friend went to the skateboard park

(H) Gerald wore his helmet and knee pads!

(J) What a terrible fall he took!

3.
(A) my family visited many interesting places on our last vacation.

(B) We enjoyed seeing vancouver, canada.

(C) Salt Lake City was interesting too.

(D) Our last stop was in Portland, oregon.

4. We loaded the car with <u>luggage and</u> we also packed a lunch.

(F) luggage; and

(G) luggage, and

(H) luggage. And

(J) correct as it is

5. He collects <u>stamps, coins, and postcards</u>.

(A) stamps coins, and postcards

(B) stamps, coins and, postcards

(C) stamps coins and postcards

(D) correct as it is

6. "Gather all of your ingredients together before you start <u>to cook advised</u> Mother.

(F) to cook, "advised."

(G) to cook. Advised

(H) to cook," advised

(J) correct as it is

Answers:
A Ⓐ Ⓑ Ⓒ Ⓓ 1 Ⓐ Ⓑ Ⓒ Ⓓ 3 Ⓐ Ⓑ Ⓒ Ⓓ 5 Ⓐ Ⓑ Ⓒ Ⓓ
B Ⓕ Ⓖ Ⓗ Ⓙ 2 Ⓕ Ⓖ Ⓗ Ⓙ 4 Ⓕ Ⓖ Ⓗ Ⓙ 6 Ⓕ Ⓖ Ⓗ Ⓙ

Language Expression: Usage

Directions: Read each item. Choose the word or words to complete the sentence or the pronoun that replaces the underlined words. Fill in the answer circle for your choice.

Samples

A. Bob's sister is _____ than his mother.

   (A) tall
   (B) tallest
   (C) more tall
   (D) taller

B. Jodie and I went to the movies.

   (F) She
   (G) We
   (H) Us
   (J) They

---

1. If you left the packages, you will have to go back for _____ .

   (A) it
   (B) them
   (C) her
   (D) him

5. Let's send a card to Lupe and Rene.

   (A) they
   (B) him
   (C) her
   (D) them

---

2. The _____ shoes are not always the best.

   (F) expensiver
   (G) expensivest
   (H) most expensive
   (J) most expensiver

6. Tell Barbara that her mother is here.

   (F) she
   (G) her
   (H) us
   (J) them

---

3. Todd _____ in a big game next Saturday.

   (A) played
   (B) play
   (C) will play
   (D) playing

7. Marty and Pham gave their reports.

   (A) Them
   (B) They
   (C) We
   (D) Us

---

4. _____ will open the door at 10 o'clock.

   (F) Her
   (G) She
   (H) Hers
   (J) Herself

8. Please read a story to Juan and me.

   (F) him
   (G) them
   (H) we
   (J) us

- -

Answers:

A Ⓐ Ⓑ Ⓒ Ⓓ   2 Ⓕ Ⓖ Ⓗ Ⓙ   5 Ⓐ Ⓑ Ⓒ Ⓓ   8 Ⓕ Ⓖ Ⓗ Ⓙ

B Ⓕ Ⓖ Ⓗ Ⓙ   3 Ⓐ Ⓑ Ⓒ Ⓓ   6 Ⓕ Ⓖ Ⓗ Ⓙ

1 Ⓐ Ⓑ Ⓒ Ⓓ   4 Ⓕ Ⓖ Ⓗ Ⓙ   7 Ⓐ Ⓑ Ⓒ Ⓓ

Language Expression: Usage

Directions: Look for a usage mistake in each item. In the answer rows below, fill in the answer circle for the number of the line with the mistake. If you do not find a mistake, fill in answer circle 4.

Samples

A.
(1) My brother Randy he has always
(2) wanted to take music lessons. He
(3) wants to play the violin.
(4) **no mistakes**

B.
(1) The trees are so beautiful
(2) at this time of the year when their
(3) leaves are turning red and gold.
(4) **no mistakes**

1.
(1) Lupe and I used to live far apart
(2) on different streets. Now we is next
(3) door neighbors.
(4) **no mistakes**

6.
(1) Give them books to Ricardo and I.
(2) We will take them to the library
(3) and return them.
(4) **no mistakes**

2.
(1) Because of the flooded streets, the
(2) school bus was a hour late picking
       us
(3) up after school.
(4) **no mistakes**

7.
(1) The television show had already
       begin
(2) by the time Frank had finished all
(3) of his homework.
(4) **no mistakes**

3.
(1) Mouses are like rats, but they are
(2) smaller. I would like to get one for
(3) a pet, but my mother won't let me.
(4) **no mistakes**

8.
(1) Liz is the smartest student in
(2) our class. She never gets less than
(3) one hundred percent.
(4) **no mistakes**

4.
(1) Jake is building a skateboard ramp.
(2) He says him and me can use it when
(3) it is finished.
(4) **no mistakes**

9.
(1) Rosa said she wanted to solve the
(2) problem all by herself. She didn't
(3) want nobody to help her.
(4) **no mistakes**

5.
(1) Patricia's art class is learning to
(2) sketch with charcoal. Pat has never
(3) drew with charcoal before this.
(4) **no mistakes**

10.
(1) My brother is in first grade. He
(2) hasn't learned to read things that are
(3) wrote in cursive.
(4) **no mistakes**

Answers:

A ① ② ③ ④   2 ① ② ③ ④   5 ① ② ③ ④   8 ① ② ③ ④
B ① ② ③ ④   3 ① ② ③ ④   6 ① ② ③ ④   9 ① ② ③ ④
1 ① ② ③ ④   4 ① ② ③ ④   7 ① ② ③ ④   10 ① ② ③ ④

Language Expression: Grammar and Syntax

Directions: Read the words in each box. Then read each question below the box. Choose the best answers. Fill in the circles for your answer choices.

Samples

```
The kitten is crying for some milk
```

A. These words make . . .
(A) a command
(B) a question
(C) a statement
(D) an incomplete sentence

B. The subject is . . .
(E) the kitten
(F) for some
(G) milk
(H) is crying

```
The nesting bird gathers sticks
```

1. These words make . . .
(A) a question
(B) a command
(C) an incomplete sentence
(D) a statement

2. Which word is used as a singular noun?
(E) sticks
(F) bird
(G) the
(H) nesting

```
Don't let the door slam behind you
```

3. These words make . . .
(A) a command
(B) a statement
(C) a question
(D) an incomplete sentence

4. The predicate is . . .
(E) behind you
(F) Don't let the door slam behind you
(G) Don't let
(H) the door slam

```
Using the last piece of paper
```

5. These words make . . .
(A) a statement
(B) an incomplete sentence
(C) a command
(D) a question

6. Which word is used as a singular noun?
(E) using
(F) the
(G) paper
(H) last

GO→

Answers: A Ⓐ Ⓑ Ⓒ Ⓓ   1 Ⓐ Ⓑ Ⓒ Ⓓ   3 Ⓐ Ⓑ Ⓒ Ⓓ   5 Ⓐ Ⓑ Ⓒ Ⓓ

B Ⓔ Ⓕ Ⓖ Ⓗ   2 Ⓔ Ⓕ Ⓖ Ⓗ   4 Ⓔ Ⓕ Ⓖ Ⓗ   6 Ⓔ Ⓕ Ⓖ Ⓗ

Language Expression: Grammar and Syntax *(cont.)*

Did your mother give you those toys

7. These words make . . .
(A) a command
(B) a statement
(C) a question
(D) an incomplete sentence

8. Which word is used as a plural noun?
(E) your
(F) mother
(G) those
(H) toys

Take this letter to your teacher

9. These words make . . .
(A) a question
(B) a statement
(C) a command
(D) an incomplete sentence

10. The predicate is . . .
(E) to your teacher
(F) this letter
(G) Take this letter to your teacher
(H) Take this letter

Cold rains often fall in the winter

11. These words make . . .
(A) a statement
(B) a question
(C) an incomplete sentence
(D) a command

12. The subject is . . .
(E) cold rains
(F) the winter
(G) often fall
(H) fall in the winter

When did you see the elephants

13. These words make . . .
(A) a question
(B) a statement
(C) a command
(D) an incomplete sentence

14. Which word is used as a plural noun?
(E) when
(F) you
(G) see
(H) elephants

Answers: 7 (A) (B) (C) (D)   9 (A) (B) (C) (D)   11 (A) (B) (C) (D)   13 (A) (B) (C) (D)
8 (E) (F) (G) (H)   10 (E) (F) (G) (H)   12 (E) (F) (G) (H)   14 (E) (F) (G) (H)

Language Expression: Sentences

Directions: Read the sentence or sentences in each item. Look for the simple subject, simple predicate, or complete sentence. Fill in the circle for your answer choice.

Samples

A. Eleven boys played football after school.

     A   B   C   D

B. The plane always lands on that runway.

     F   G   H   J

C.
- (A) The house with the blue roof.
- (B) They decided to paint the roof blue.
- (C) The blue roof they chose for the house.
- (D) They chose a color for their roof it was blue.

Look for the simple subject.

1. The main library is crowded after school.

      A   B   C   D

2. The huge dog stood behind the fence.

      F   G   H   J

3. Lupe handed her homework to the teacher.

     A   B   C   D

Look for the simple predicate.

4. The horses raced around the track.

      F   G   H   J

5. This Halloween mask looks funny on me.

        A   B   C   D

6. Ken polishes his bike after every race.

     F   G   H   J

Look for the complete sentence.

7.
- (A) It was hot we went to the beach.
- (B) Going to the beach when it's hot.
- (C When the hot weather began.
- (D) We went to the beach when it was hot.

8.
- (F) Fran likes tapes Della does too.
- (G) Fran and Della like to listen to tapes.
- (H) Fran and Della listen they listen to tapes.
- (J) Fran and Della listening to tapes.

9.
- (A) The nuts hidden in the pine tree.
- (B) Squirrels hiding nuts in the pine tree.
- (C) The squirrels hid their nuts in the pine tree.
- (D) The squirrels hid nuts they are in the pine tree.

10.
- (F) Mashed potatoes were served with the chicken.
- (G) Mashed potatoes served along with chicken.
- (H) Serving mashed potatoes and chicken.
- (J) We had chicken we had mashed potatoes too.

- -

Answers:

A (A) (B) (C) (D)   **2** (F) (G) (H) (J)   **6** (F) (G) (H) (J)   **10** (F) (G) (H) (J)

B (F) (G) (H) (J)   **3** (A) (B) (C) (D)   **7** (A) (B) (C) (D)

C (A) (B) (C) (D)   **4** (F) (G) (H) (J)   **8** (F) (G) (H) (J)

1 (A) (B) (C) (D)   **5** (A) (B) (C) (D)   **9** (A) (B) (C) (D)

Language Expression: Sentences

Directions: Read each sentence with an underlined part. Find either the complete subject or the complete predicate, depending upon what is asked of you.

Samples

A.
  (A) The dog <u>barked</u> at the moon.

  (B) <u>Her mother</u> builds computers.

  (C) My <u>eraser</u> is worn down.

  (D) <u>That</u> boy fell off of his bike.

B.
  (F) We <u>baked some chocolate cookies</u>.

  (G) <u>Jack painted</u> that for you.

  (H) My new <u>jacket is red</u>.

  (J) Five crayons <u>are missing from this box</u>.

For items 1 through 3, choose the sentence that has the complete subject underlined.

1.
  (A) Lincoln's <u>birthday</u> is in February.

  (B) <u>This glue</u> has dried up.

  (C) <u>The black</u> paper is all gone.

  (D) The winning team <u>was very</u> excited.

2.
  (F) <u>This</u> pizza is too hot.

  (G) <u>Dad and I</u> played baseball.

  (H) A <u>giraffe's</u> neck is very long.

  (J) Someone turned <u>the lights off</u>.

3.
  (A) Tuesday <u>comes after</u> Monday.

  (B) <u>White</u> rattlesnakes are very rare.

  (C) <u>The ice cream man</u> is coming.

  (D) Our <u>television stopped</u> working last night.

For items 4 through 6, choose the sentence that has the complete predicate underlined.

4.
  (F) <u>My aunt has</u> six children.

  (G) <u>The parade</u> came marching by.

  (H) The horse <u>neighed softly</u>.

  (J) San Diego is <u>south of Los Angeles</u>.

5.
  (A) The rain <u>made puddles</u>.

  (B) That boy <u>is too</u> young for school.

  (C) <u>You</u> can do tricks.

  (D) Marco is making <u>a cake</u>.

6.
  (F) The cookies did not <u>turn out well</u>.

  (G) Mother said that <u>dinner is almost</u> ready.

  (H) Frogs <u>sit on the lily pads</u>.

  (J) <u>The swimming pool</u> is closed for the winter.

Answers: A (A) (B) (C) (D)   1 (A) (B) (C) (D)   3 (A) (B) (C) (D)   5 (A) (B) (C) (D)

  B (F) (G) (H) (J)   2 (F) (G) (H) (J)   4 (F) (G) (H) (J)   6 (F) (G) (H) (J)

Language Expression: Sentence Combining

Directions: Read the underlined sentences. Look for the sentence that is the best combination of the underlined sentences. Fill in the answer circle for your choice.

Sample

A. Examples of our work are on the bulletin board.
Examples of our art are on the bulletin board.

   (A) On the bulletin board are examples of our art work.

   (B) Examples of our work and our art are on the bulletin board.

   (C) Examples of our work are on the bulletin board, and examples of our art are on the bulletin board too.

   (D) On the bulletin board are examples of our work, and examples of our art are also on the bulletin board.

———————————————————————————————————

1. Last weekend we cleaned the house.
Last weekend we weeded the garden.

   (A) We cleaned and weeded last weekend.

   (B) Last weekend we cleaned and weeded the garden.

   (C) Last weekend we cleaned the house and weeded the garden.

   (D) We cleaned and weeded the house and the garden last weekend.

2. The children skated on the ice.
The ice was smooth.
The ice was clean.

   (F) Smooth, clean children skated on the ice.

   (G) The children skated on the smooth, clean ice.

   (H) The children were smooth and clean skating on the ice.

   (J) The children skated on the smooth ice, which was clean.

3. Lola turned in her homework.
Travis turned in his homework.

   (A) Lola turned in her homework with Travis.

   (B) Lola and Travis each turned in their homework.

   (C) Lola turned in her homework, and so did Travis turn in his.

   (D) Lola turned in her homework, and Travis turned in his homework.

- -

Answers: A Ⓐ Ⓑ Ⓒ Ⓓ   1 Ⓐ Ⓑ Ⓒ Ⓓ   2 Ⓕ Ⓖ Ⓗ Ⓙ   3 Ⓐ Ⓑ Ⓒ Ⓓ

Language Expression: Paragraphs and Topic Sentences

Directions: Read the paragraph or sentence. Look for the best topic sentence or the sentences that best develop the topic sentence.

Samples

A. _____. He was also a scientist. He developed theories about how the blood circulates and the brain functions. He also predicted modern machines such as the airplane and the submarine. He was truly ahead of his time.

  (A) Leonardo was born in the mountain village of Vinci, near Florence.
  (B) His paintings include the <u>Mona Lisa</u> which hangs in the Louvre Museum.
  (C) Leonardo da Vinci was more than a great artist and sculptor.
  (D) Many books have been written about the life of this great man.

B. On October 4, 1957, the first man-made satellite was rocketed into orbit around the earth by the Soviet Union.

  (F) People have been interested in going into space for thousands of years. Ancient Greek and Roman myths tell of people who tried to reach the sun. The myths of many other civilizations tell similar tales.
  (G) It was called Sputnik 1, meaning "fellow traveler." It weighed 184 pounds and completed a trip around the earth every 96 minutes, traveling at 18,000 miles per hour. It fell to earth on January 4, 1958.
  (H) The ancient Chinese invented gunpowder and used it to launch small rockets. These rockets were used in ceremonies and celebrations and were like the fireworks we use today.
  (J) On July 20, 1969, Apollo II's lunar module landed on the moon. Neil Armstrong, an American astronaut, was the first human to set foot on the moon's surface.

Look for the best topic sentence.

1. _____. This delightful fairyland was introduced in *The Wizard of Oz*, a book by L. Frank Baum. Its quaint characters became even more well known when the movie based on this story was made.

  (A) Fairy tales have always been popular with children from all over the world.
  (B) Ozma of Oz was introduced in one of the later books about Oz.
  (C) L. Frank Baum, who lived in California, wrote many stories for children.
  (D) The land of Oz is one of the most famous places in children's literature.

Look for the sentences that best develop the topic sentence.

2. Bears are dangerous wild animals.

  (F) <u>The Three Bears</u> is a popular children's story. In it, the bears talk and act like people.
  (G) Although they can look cute and friendly in circuses and zoos, they are really huge and have long claws. Rangers in our national parks warn people not to feed the bears.
  (H) Polar bears live in the Arctic. They hunt for seals and other animals. Their white color against the ice and snow helps protect them from enemies.
  (J) Bears can be trained to do many funny tricks. They are natural clowns and are often seen doing tricks in the wild.

Answers: A Ⓐ Ⓑ Ⓒ Ⓓ   1 Ⓐ Ⓑ Ⓒ Ⓓ
                  B Ⓕ Ⓖ Ⓗ Ⓙ   2 Ⓕ Ⓖ Ⓗ Ⓙ

Language Expression: Paragraphs and Sentence Sequence

Directions: Read the paragraph. Look for the correct order for the sentences. Fill in the answer circle for your choice.

Sample

A. 1. Last summer my family took an exciting vacation.

2. While in New York we toured many museums and other places of interest.

3. We began the trip by flying from Los Angeles to New York City.

4. Just before coming home we went to the Statue of Liberty and the Empire State Building.

    (A) 1 - 2 - 3 - 4

    (B) 1 - 3 - 2 - 4

    (C) 3 - 2 - 4 - 1

    (D) 4 - 3 - 1 - 2

1. 1. First we saw how the potatoes are washed, peeled, and sliced.

2. Today our scout troop toured a factory where potato chips are made.

3. The last things we saw were the machines that package the chips.

4. Then we watched the sliced potatoes cook in vats of bubbling oil.

    (A) 1 - 3 - 4 - 2

    (B) 2 - 1 - 4 - 3

    (C) 2 - 4 - 1 - 3

    (D) 4 - 3 - 2 - 1

2. 1. Then the food was delivered to the car on a tray that hooked over the window.

2. People parked and a waiter or waitress came to take their order.

3. Today, however, we do not drive in—we drive through.

4. Drive-in restaurants used to be very popular.

    (F) 1 - 3 - 2 - 4

    (G) 2 - 1 - 4 - 3

    (H) 3 - 4 - 1 - 2

    (J) 4 - 2 - 1 - 3

Answers: A Ⓐ Ⓑ Ⓒ Ⓓ   1 Ⓐ Ⓑ Ⓒ Ⓓ   2 Ⓕ Ⓖ Ⓗ Ⓙ

Language Expression: Descriptive Writing (TAAS)

This picture is about some children having fun at a circus. Look at the picture and write a story about what you see.

Language Expression: Informative Writing (TAAS)

Suppose you are planning to fix dinner for your family. Write a story about what you would have to do. Tell about what you must do first. Then tell about all of the other things you must do.

Language Expression: Narrative Writing (TAAS)

Imagine that you have found a magic ring that will grant three wishes to you. Write a story about what you would wish for and what would happen when you got your wishes.

Language Expression: Classificatory Writing (TAAS)

Being able to predict the future sounds like a great thing at first. However, when you think about it, you might realize that there are good and bad things about knowing what is going to happen. Write a composition about being able to predict the future. Explain what would be good and bad about having this ability.

Language Expression: Persuasive Writing (TAAS)

The high school you will someday attend has the money to buy and equip either a modern gymnasium or a new library, but not both. Which one do you think the high school should build? Decide which one of these ideas is better, building a gymnasium or building a library, and write a letter to the local newspaper explaining why you think this way.

Work-Study Skills: Library Skills (Reference Sources)

Directions: Read the question. Look for the best answer. Fill in the answer circle for your choice.

Samples

A. Where should you look to find the locations of the countries in Asia?

(A) globe

(B) science book

(C) book index

(D) dictionary

B. To find the titles of all of the books by A. A. Milne that are in a library, you should look at . . .

(F) title cards of the card catalog.

(G) subject cards of the card catalog.

(H) author cards of the card catalog.

(J) volume M of an encyclopedia.

---

1. Which is the best place to look for the time a game will be shown on television this weekend?

(A) a catalog

(B) a telephone book

(C) a television guide

(D) a sports magazine

2. To find the most information about the battles of the Civil War, you should look in . . .

(F) a newspaper.

(G) a magazine.

(H) an almanac.

(J) an encyclopedia.

3. Where should you look to find the best way to get to the museum in a big city?

(A) an atlas

(B) a globe

(C) a street map

(D) a world map

4. Which probably best shows the geography of the states around the Great Lakes?

(F) a road map

(G) a travel guide

(H) an atlas

(J) a globe

For items 5 and 6, find the answers by using this library catalog card.

629.1 **Going into Space**
C597
Going into Space, by Arthur Charles Clarke; illus. with photographs and diagrams by Maury Hendrickson and Alice Bentley; New York: Jay Harper and Brothers, 1954.
224 pages; illustrated
1. Space exploration   2. Science

5. The book is about . . .

(A) going into space.

(B) Arthur C. Clarke.

(C) New York.

(D) Jay Harper and Brothers.

6. Who is the author of the book?

(F) Maury Hendrickson

(G) Alice Bentley

(H) Jay Harper

(J) Arthur Charles Clarke

Answers: A Ⓐ Ⓑ Ⓒ Ⓓ 1 Ⓐ Ⓑ Ⓒ Ⓓ 3 Ⓐ Ⓑ Ⓒ Ⓓ 5 Ⓐ Ⓑ Ⓒ Ⓓ

B Ⓕ Ⓖ Ⓗ Ⓙ 2 Ⓕ Ⓖ Ⓗ Ⓙ 4 Ⓕ Ⓖ Ⓗ Ⓙ 6 Ⓕ Ⓖ Ⓗ Ⓙ

Work-Study Skills: Parts of a Book

Directions: Read the question. Look for the best answer. Fill in the answer circle for your choice.

Sample

Contents	
Chapter	**Page**
1- Gold Is Discovered	3
2- Who Were the Forty-Niners?	37
3- Happiness and Hardship	55

A. Which information is probably found in Chapter 2?

(A) the price of food during the Gold Rush

(B) how the discovery of gold came about

(C) where the Forty-Niners came from

(D) living conditions in the gold fields

Use this title page to find the answers to items 1 through 4.

Dragons and Dinosaurs

by Kathy Hofer

Illustrated by Sue Fullam and Blanca Apodaca

Teacher Created Materials, Inc.

Westminster, CA

1. Which best tells what the book is about?

(A) wild animals

(B) fairy tale animals

(C) extinct animals

(D) fairy tale and extinct animals

2. The person who wrote the book is . . .

(F) Kathy Hofer.

(G) Sue Fullam.

(H) Blanca Apodaca.

(J) Teacher Created Materials.

3. The title page of the book tells . . .

(A) the number of pages.

(B) the number of pictures.

(C) the names of the dinosaurs.

(D) the names of the illustrators.

4. Westminster, California, is the place where . . .

(F) Kathy Hofer lives.

(G) the publisher is located.

(H) dinosaur bones were found.

(J) there are dragons.

Answers: A Ⓐ Ⓑ Ⓒ Ⓓ   1 Ⓐ Ⓑ Ⓒ Ⓓ   3 Ⓐ Ⓑ Ⓒ Ⓓ
2 Ⓕ Ⓖ Ⓗ Ⓙ   4 Ⓕ Ⓖ Ⓗ Ⓙ

Word-Study Skills: Table of Contents

Directions: Read the question in each item. Then look at the table of contents and find the best answer. Fill in the answer circle for your choice.

Samples

This is the table of contents from the book *Celebrations Around the World.*

Table of Contents

Chapter	Page
1. Christmas Feasts in France	4
2. New Years Day in Brazil	15
3. ANZAC Day in Australia	26
4. Carnival Dances in Brazil	38
5. Guy Fawkes Day in England	47
6. Sukkot in Israel	60

A. For information about foods served in France at Christmas, you should look in which chapter?

(1) 1   (2) 2   (3) 3   (4) 5

B. In Chapter 5 you might find out . . .

(1) what holidays are celebrated in England.
(2) when Carnival takes place.
(3) who Guy Fawkes was.
(4) what ANZAC means.

This is the table of contents from the book *Up in the Attic*.

Table of Contents

Chapter	Page
1. A Rainy Saturday	3
2. Meg and Barb Explore	12
3. A Mysterious Shadow	20
4. The Locked Chest	29
5. The Key in the Corner	40
6. Grandmother's Treasure	52

1. In which chapter might this sentence appear?

The girls gasped when they saw the shape on the wall.

(1) Chapter 1
(2) Chapter 2
(3) Chapter 3
(4) Chapter 4

2. In which chapter might you find this sentence?

"I hate rainy days because there is nothing at all to do," said Meg.

(1) Chapter 1   (3) Chapter 4
(2) Chapter 2   (4) Chapter 6

3. In which chapter might these sentences appear?

"Oh dear," sighed Barb. "Now we'll never find out what's inside."

(1) Chapter 3   (3) Chapter 5
(2) Chapter 4   (4) Chapter 6

4. In which chapter might you read this?

"Look!" gasped Meg. "It's Grandmother's wedding dress."

(1) Chapter 1   (3) Chapter 4
(2 Chapter 3   (4) Chapter 6

Answers:

A ① ② ③ ④   1 ① ② ③ ④   3 ① ② ③ ④
B ① ② ③ ④   2 ① ② ③ ④   4 ① ② ③ ④

Work-Study Skills: Index

Directions: Read the question in each item. Then look at the index and find the best answer. Fill in the answer circle for your choice.

Samples

This is part of the index from the book *Science in Action.*

> **Index**
>
> Astronomy, 14–20 (see also Telescopes); comets, 45; planets, 95–106; stars, 130–140; sun, 155–157
> Biology, 25–36
> Geology, 60–75
> Geography, physical, 76–80
> Rocks (see Geology)
> Telescopes, 160–165

A. To find out about comets, you should look at which page?

(1) 14   (2) 20   (3) 45   (4) 130

B. On which page should you begin reading to find out about the Hubble telescope?

(1) 14
(2) 25
(3) 76
(4) 160

This is part of the Index from the book *How Things Work.*

> **Index**
>
> Accordion, 139
> Airplane, 168, 269
> Air pressure, 30, 268, 269, 318
> Atom, 183–193, 289
> Automobile (see Car)
> Ax, 224, 241
> Axle, 250, 251, 260, 261
>   car, 301
>   electric motor, 283
> Bell, 91–95
>   clock, 97
>   door-, 5, 18, 19
> Boat, 257, 265–267, 292, 293, 301
> Bulb
>   electric, 201, 205, 208–213
>   flashlight, 185
> Car battery, 189
> Car horn, 102, 103
> Car motor, 189, 280

1. To find out about the axle of an electric motor, you should look at which page?

(1) 250   (2) 251   (3) 283   (4) 301

2. On which page will you find information about a car battery?

(1) 189   (2) 102   (3) 103   (4) 280

3. How many pages of information are provided on the topic of boats?

(1) 6   (2) 7   (3) 257   (4) 5

4. What page might have information about alarm clocks?

(1) 91   (2) 95   (3) 97   (4) 19

Answers: A ① ② ③ ④   1 ① ② ③ ④   3 ① ② ③ ④
          B ① ② ③ ④   2 ① ② ③ ④   4 ① ② ③ ④

Work-Study Skills: Alphabetizing

Directions: Read the directions for each section. Choose the best answer. Mark the answer space for your choice.

Samples

A.
- (A) cowboy
- (B) bench
- (C) story
- (D) lose

B.
- (F) window
- (G) yeast
- (H) zero
- (J) zebra

Which word or name comes first in alphabetical order?

Which word comes last in a dictionary?

1.
- (A) friend
- (B) dairy
- (C) buffalo
- (D) easy

6.
- (F) doctor
- (G) umbrella
- (H) peach
- (J) mother

2.
- (F) great
- (G) journey
- (H) happy
- (J) kangaroo

7.
- (A) elephant
- (B) violin
- (C) queen
- (D) watch

3.
- (A) something
- (B) salad
- (C) steep
- (D) scoop

8.
- (F) yellow
- (G) fancy
- (H) length
- (J) bench

4.
- (F) tree
- (G) trumpet
- (H) truck
- (J) trap

9.
- (A) float
- (B) frog
- (C) fig
- (D) fort

5.
- (A) Jones, Mary
- (B) Jones, Dennis
- (C) Jones, Steve
- (D) Jones, Robert

10.
- (F) apricot
- (G) apple
- (H) appetite
- (J) apron

Answers:

A Ⓐ Ⓑ Ⓒ Ⓓ	2 Ⓕ Ⓖ Ⓗ Ⓙ	5 Ⓐ Ⓑ Ⓒ Ⓓ	8 Ⓕ Ⓖ Ⓗ Ⓙ
B Ⓕ Ⓖ Ⓗ Ⓙ	3 Ⓐ Ⓑ Ⓒ Ⓓ	6 Ⓕ Ⓖ Ⓗ Ⓙ	9 Ⓐ Ⓑ Ⓒ Ⓓ
1 Ⓐ Ⓑ Ⓒ Ⓓ	4 Ⓕ Ⓖ Ⓗ Ⓙ	7 Ⓐ Ⓑ Ⓒ Ⓓ	10 Ⓕ Ⓖ Ⓗ Ⓙ

Work-Study Skills: Dictionary Skills

Directions: Read each question. Find the best answer. Fill in the answer circle for your choice.

Sample

camper (kam´ pər) noun 1. a person who vacations at a camp: *The camper set up his tent.* 2. any of various motor vehicles or trailers equipped for camping out: *They rented a camper for their weekend trip.*

A. What part of speech is the word camper?

(A) verb
(B) noun
(C) adverb
(D) adjective

Use the dictionary entry below to answer questions 1 through 5.

party (par´ tē) noun 1. an organized political group: *He was nominated by the Republican party.* 2. any group of people acting together for some purpose: *The work party left early.* 3. a gathering for pleasure: *We went to a birthday party.* 4. a person who takes part in an action: *He was a party to their plan.*

1. Which answer shows how to pronounce the y in party?

(A) y
(B) e
(C) te
(D) par

2. What part of speech is the word party?

(F) noun
(G) verb
(H) adjective
(J) adverb

3. Which definition of party is used in the sentence "He helped draw up the party platform before the election"?

(A) 1
(B) 2
(C) 3
(D) 4

4. The word party would be found on a dictionary page with which of these guide words?

(F) park—parole
(G) partridge—pass
(H) Pasadena—pass
(J) partake—partner

5. When someone talks about being in the party that decorated the stage for an assembly, which definition of party is he or she using?

(A) 1
(B) 2
(C) 3
(D) 4

Answers: A (A) (B) (C) (D)   2 (F) (G) (H) (J)   4 (F) (G) (H) (J)
            1 (A) (B) (C) (D)   3 (A) (B) (C) (D)   5 (A) (B) (C) (D)

Work-Study Skills: Outlines and Schedules

Directions: Look at the information and read each question. Find the best answer to each item and fill in the circle of your answer choice.

Sample

Swim Team Tryouts

9:00	Sign Up
9:30	Medical Screening
11:00	Stroke Instruction
11:30	Lunch Break
1:00	Warm Up in Pool
1:30	Timed Laps

A. At 1:00, what will the swimmers be doing at the tryouts?

(A) signing up
(B) receiving instructions
(C) warming up
(D) swimming lap

Study this outline for a research paper about communication. Then do items 1 through 3.

Communication Through the Ages

I. Early ways of sending messages

    A. Drums
    B. Smoke signals
    C. _____

II. The beginning of writing

    A. Pictures
    B. Symbols
    C. _____

III. _____

    A. Telegraph
    B. Telephone
    C. Radio
    D. _____

1. Which one of these topics would fit best in space II, C?

(A) Word of mouth
(B) Numbers
(C) Alphabets
(D) Electronic mail

2. What is a good title for section III?

(F) Prehistoric communication
(G) Communication today
(H) Person to person
(J) Cellular phones

3. Which one of these would be a good section to add to the outline?

(A) The future of communication
(B) The history of communication
(C) Communication and transportation
(D) Communication and entertainment

Answers: A Ⓐ Ⓑ Ⓒ Ⓓ 1 Ⓐ Ⓑ Ⓒ Ⓓ 2 Ⓕ Ⓖ Ⓗ Ⓙ 3 Ⓐ Ⓑ Ⓒ Ⓓ

Work-Study Skills: Maps

Directions: Read the question in each item. Then look at the map and find the best answer. Fill in the answer circle for your choice.

Samples

This map shows the streets and buildings in a section of downtown Oakmont.

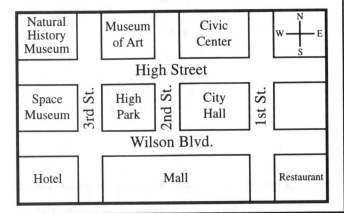

A. Which place is the farthest away from the Natural History Museum?

(1) the hotel   (3) the city hall

(2) the mall   (4) the restaurant

B. A visitor is standing on the southeast corner of Wilson Blvd. and 3rd Street. If she walks north across the street, where will she be?

(1) in the park   (3) at the mall

(2) at the hotel   (4) at the city hall

This map is a section of a road map. The key explains what each symbol on the map means.

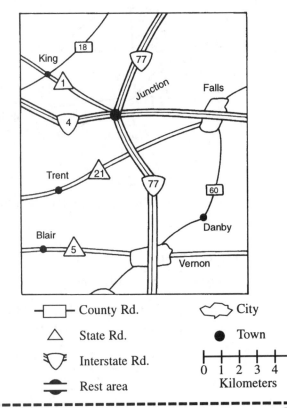

—⊏⊐— County Rd.

△ State Rd.

▽ Interstate Rd.

⩵ Rest area

◇ City

● Town

0 1 2 3 4 5
Kilometers

1. Which roads meet in King?

(1) 4 and 77   (3) 5 and 77

(2) 1 and 18   (4) 21 and 60

2. Between which two towns is a rest area located?

(1) Trent and Falls   (3) Junction and Falls

(2) Vernon and Danby   (4) King and Junction

3. This sign might be in which place?

(1) Junction
(2) Blair
(3) Vernon
(4) Falls

```
↑ Junction    15km
← Blair        8km
```

4. The Moreno family lives in Vernon. To attend a garden show in King, they used interstate 77 and state road 1. About how many kilometers did they drive?

(1) 19   (3) 10

(2) 13   (4) 3

Answers: A ① ② ③ ④   1 ① ② ③ ④   3 ① ② ③ ④

              B ① ② ③ ④   2 ① ② ③ ④   4 ① ② ③ ④

Work-Study Skills: Graphs and Tables

Directions: Read each question. Then look at the graph or table and find the best answer. Fill in the answer circle for your choice.

Samples

Students in National Spelling Bee

Pacific States

Southwestern States

Atlantic States

Southeastern States

Plains States

Each ⬜ stands for 4 students.

A. There were 18 students from which area?

   (1)   Pacific States
   (3)   Atlantic States
   (2)   Southwestern States
   (4)   Plains States

B. How many more students came from the Atlantic States than from the Southwestern States?

   (1) 2   (3) 16
   (2) 8   (4) 24

Advertising Rates for *Daily Bugle*

Number of Days	Size of Ad		
	¼ Page	½ Page	Full Page
1	$100	$250	$500
2	$175	$400	$800
5	$400	$1000	$2000
7	$550	$1500	$3000

1. How much does it cost to run a half-page ad for 5 days?

   (1) $400   (3) $1500
   (2) $1000   (4) $2000

2. Ms. Rogers spent $800 to run a full-page ad. How many days did it run?

   (1) 1   (3) 5
   (2) 2   (4) 7

Valley Farms has a vegetable stand during the summer. This graph shows how many pounds of vegetables the Chan family bought there last August.

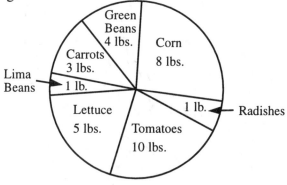

3. Of which vegetable did the Chan family buy 5 pounds?

   (1) green beans   (3) corn
   (2) lettuce   (4) carrots

4. How many pounds of corn and tomatoes did the Chan family buy altogether?

   (1) 7   (3) 15
   (2) 12   (4) 18

Answers:
  A ① ② ③ ④   **1** ① ② ③ ④   **3** ① ② ③ ④
  B ① ② ③ ④   **2** ① ② ③ ④   **4** ① ② ③ ④

Math Computation: Addition—Whole Numbers

Directions: Mark the space for the correct answer to each addition problem. Choose "none of these" if the right answer is not given.

Samples

A.

$$\begin{array}{r} 77 \\ + 13 \\ \hline \end{array}$$

(A) 80
(B) 84
(C) 89
(D) 90
(E) none of these

B.

$448 + 374 =$

(F) 721
(G) 812
(H) 820
(J) 824
(K) none of these

1.

$$\begin{array}{r} 391 \\ + 299 \\ \hline \end{array}$$

(A) 580
(B) 590
(C) 680
(D) 690
(E) none of these

5.

$$\begin{array}{r} 2 \\ 15 \\ 64 \\ + 9 \\ \hline \end{array}$$

(A) 20
(B) 80
(C) 90
(D) 189
(E) none of these

2.

$$\begin{array}{r} 3956 \\ + 5205 \\ \hline \end{array}$$

(F) 8151
(G) 8161
(H) 8751
(J) 9161
(K) none of these

6.

$254 + 60 + 18 =$

(F) 314
(G) 494
(H) 872
(J) 1034
(K) none of these

3.

$$\begin{array}{r} 3728 \\ 604 \\ + 19 \\ \hline \end{array}$$

(A) 4341
(B) 4351
(C) 4522
(D) 11,668
(E) none of these

7.

$$\begin{array}{r} 5841 \\ + 1999 \\ \hline \end{array}$$

(A) 6730
(B) 6740
(C) 7740
(D) 7840
(E) none of these

4.

$5364 + 300 =$

(F) 5664
(G) 5700
(H) 5774
(J) 8664
(K) none of these

8.

$$\begin{array}{r} 2009 \\ + 2009 \\ \hline \end{array}$$

(F) 4008
(G) 4018
(H) 4118
(J) 5008
(K) none of these

Answers:

A (A)(B)(C)(D)(E) 2 (F)(G)(H)(J)(K) 5 (A)(B)(C)(D)(E) 8 (F)(G)(H)(J)(K)

B (F)(G)(H)(J)(K) 3 (A)(B)(C)(D)(E) 6 (F)(G)(H)(J)(K)

1 (A)(B)(C)(D)(E) 4 (F)(G)(H)(J)(K) 7 (A)(B)(C)(D)(E)

Math Computation: Addition—Decimals

Directions: Fill in the circle for the correct answer to each addition problem. Choose none of these if the right answer is not given.

Samples

A.

$$\begin{array}{r} \$7.62 \\ + \ 8.98 \\ \hline \end{array}$$

(A) $15.60
(B) $16.50
(C) $16.60
(D) $16.61
(E) none of these

B.

$3.5 + 9.7 =$

(F) 1.32
(G) 6.2
(H) 12.2
(J) 13.1
(K) none of these

1.

$$\begin{array}{r} \$4.48 \\ + \ 2.16 \\ \hline \end{array}$$

(A) $6.54
(B) $6.62
(C) $6.64
(D) $7.64
(E) none of these

5.

$28.0 + 9.6 =$

(A) 12.4
(B) 21.6
(C) 37.6
(D) 124.0
(E) none of these

2.

$$\begin{array}{r} \$25.98 \\ + \ 17.49 \\ \hline \end{array}$$

(F) $12.57
(G) $32.37
(H) $42.47
(J) $43.47
(K) none of these

6.

$\$10.99 + \$5.03 =$

(F) $15.02
(G) $15.92
(H) $15.96
(J) $16.02
(K) none of these

3.

$28.1 + 7.9 + 6.2 =$

(A) 4.22
(B) 16.91
(C) 42.2
(D) 43.2
(E) none of these

7.

$34.1 + 40.20 =$

(A) 7.430
(B) 43.61
(C) 74.30
(D) 436.1
(E) none of these

4.

$$\begin{array}{r} \$18.99 \\ + \ \ 5.64 \\ \hline \end{array}$$

(F) $13.35
(G) $23.53
(H) $24.63
(J) $33.75
(K) none of these

8.

$$\begin{array}{r} 19.99 \\ + \ \ 9.99 \\ \hline \end{array}$$

(F) $10.00
(G) $18.88
(H) $28.88
(J) $29.99
(K) none of these

Answers:

A Ⓐ Ⓑ Ⓒ Ⓓ Ⓔ 2 Ⓕ Ⓖ Ⓗ Ⓙ Ⓚ 5 Ⓐ Ⓑ Ⓒ Ⓓ Ⓔ 8 Ⓕ Ⓖ Ⓗ Ⓙ Ⓚ

B Ⓕ Ⓖ Ⓗ Ⓙ Ⓚ 3 Ⓐ Ⓑ Ⓒ Ⓓ Ⓔ 6 Ⓕ Ⓖ Ⓗ Ⓙ Ⓚ

1 Ⓐ Ⓑ Ⓒ Ⓓ Ⓔ 4 Ⓕ Ⓖ Ⓗ Ⓙ Ⓚ 7 Ⓐ Ⓑ Ⓒ Ⓓ Ⓔ

Math Computation: Addition—Fractions

Directions: Fill in the circle for the correct answer to each addition problem. Choose none of these if the right answer is not given.

Samples

A.

$$\begin{array}{r} \frac{1}{3} \\ + \frac{1}{3} \\ \hline \end{array}$$

(A) 2/3
(B) 2/6
(C) 1/6
(D) 1
(E) none of these

B.

$$\frac{3}{8} + \frac{2}{8} =$$

(F) 1/8
(G) 5/8
(H) 1/16
(J) 5/16
(K) none of these

1.

$$\begin{array}{r} \frac{1}{7} \\ + \frac{4}{7} \\ \hline \end{array}$$

(A) 3/7
(B) 4/7
(C) 5/7
(D) 5/14
(E) none of these

5.

$$4 + \frac{1}{8} =$$

(A) 5 1/8
(B) 4 1/8
(C) 4
(D) 5/8
(E) none of these

2.

$$\frac{2}{3} + 3 =$$

(F) 5 2/5
(G) 3
(H) 3 2/5
(J) 2 2/5
(K) none of these

6.

$$\begin{array}{r} \frac{3}{8} \\ + \frac{4}{8} \\ \hline \end{array}$$

(F) 1/8
(G) 7/8
(H) 7/16
(J) 7
(K) none of these

3.

$$\begin{array}{r} \frac{1}{9} \\ + \frac{3}{9} \\ \hline \end{array}$$

(A) 4/9
(B) 4/18
(C) 1 3/9
(D) 4
(E) none of these

7.

$$\frac{1}{2} + \frac{1}{2} =$$

(A) 1/4
(B) 2/4
(C) 3/4
(D) 1
(E) none of these

4.

$$\frac{3}{5} + \frac{1}{5} =$$

(F) 1/5
(G) 3/5
(H) 4/5
(J) 4/10
(K) none of these

8.

$$\begin{array}{r} \frac{2}{11} \\ + \frac{3}{11} \\ \hline \end{array}$$

(F) 5/11
(G) 1/11
(H) 13/14
(J) 5/22
(K) none of these

- -

Answers:

A Ⓐ Ⓑ Ⓒ Ⓓ Ⓔ 2 Ⓕ Ⓖ Ⓗ Ⓙ Ⓚ 5 Ⓐ Ⓑ Ⓒ Ⓓ Ⓔ 8 Ⓕ Ⓖ Ⓗ Ⓙ Ⓚ

B Ⓕ Ⓖ Ⓗ Ⓙ Ⓚ 3 Ⓐ Ⓑ Ⓒ Ⓓ Ⓔ 6 Ⓕ Ⓖ Ⓗ Ⓙ Ⓚ

1 Ⓐ Ⓑ Ⓒ Ⓓ Ⓔ 4 Ⓕ Ⓖ Ⓗ Ⓙ Ⓚ 7 Ⓐ Ⓑ Ⓒ Ⓓ Ⓔ

Math Computation: Addition—Mixed Numbers

Directions: Fill in the circle for the correct answer to each addition problem. Choose none of these if the right answer is not given.

Samples

A.

$$2\frac{2}{4}$$
$$+\ 1\frac{1}{4}$$
$$\overline{}$$

(A) 3 3/4
(B) 3 2/4
(C) 3 3/8
(D) 3 3/16
(E) none of these

B.

$$5\frac{2}{5} + 10\frac{2}{5} =$$

(F) 15 2/5
(G) 15 4/5
(H) 15 4/10
(J) 15
(K) none of these

1.

$$3\frac{3}{4}$$
$$+2$$
$$\overline{}$$

(A) 1 3/4
(B) 5 3/4
(C) 6 3/4
(D) 5 1/4
(E) none of these

5.

$$1\frac{1}{5} + 2\frac{1}{5} =$$

(A) 3 2/10
(B) 3 1/5
(C) 1 2/5
(D) 1 2/10
(E) none of these

2.

$$6\frac{1}{3} + 2\frac{1}{3} =$$

(F) 4 2/3
(G) 8 2/9
(H) 8 2/3
(J) 8 2/6
(K) none of these

6.

$$5\frac{2}{8} + 6\frac{3}{8} =$$

(F) 1 5/8
(G) 11 5/8
(H) 11 5/16
(J) 11 6/8
(K) none of these

3.

$$2\frac{6}{7}$$
$$+5$$
$$\overline{}$$

(A) 2 1/7
(B) 3 6/7
(C) 5 6/7
(D) 7 6/7
(E) none of these

7.

$$2\frac{3}{10} + 6\frac{4}{10} =$$

(A) 8 1/10
(B) 8 7/20
(C) 12 7/10
(D) 12 7/20
(E) none of these

4.

$$8\frac{1}{7} + 1\frac{2}{7} =$$

(F) 7 1/7
(G) 8 3/7
(H) 9 3/7
(J) 9 3/14
(K) none of these

8.

$$14\frac{1}{2}$$
$$+1$$
$$\overline{}$$

(F) 14 1/2
(G) 15
(H) 15 1/2
(J) 16
(K) none of these

Answers:

A (A)(B)(C)(D)(E) 2 (F)(G)(H)(J)(K) 5 (A)(B)(C)(D)(E) 8 (F)(G)(H)(J)(K)

B (F)(G)(H)(J)(K) 3 (A)(B)(C)(D)(E) 6 (F)(G)(H)(J)(K)

1 (A)(B)(C)(D)(E) 4 (F)(G)(H)(J)(K) 7 (A)(B)(C)(D)(E)

Math Computation: Subtraction—Whole Numbers

Directions: Fill in the circle for the correct answer to each subtraction problem. Choose none of these if the right answer is not given.

Samples

A.

$$8731 - 2181$$

(A) 5440
(B) 6550
(C) 6650
(D) 6912
(E) none of these

B.

$$2700 - 1897$$

(F) 703
(G) 1197
(H) 1803
(J) 1913
(K) none of these

1.

$$9176 - 93$$

(A) 9083
(B) 9123
(C) 9183
(D) 9269
(E) none of these

5.

$$7000 - 2694$$

A) 3406
(B) 4306
(C) 5506
(D) 5694
(E) none of these

2.

$$16,548 - 48 =$$

(F) 16,068
(G) 16,500
(H) 16,508
(J) 16,596
(K) none of these

6.

$$250 - 149$$

(F) 101
(G) 111
(H) 119
(J) 311
(K) none of these

3.

$$2689 - 1345$$

(A) 234
(B) 656
(C) 1344
(D) 4024
(E) none of these

7.

$$5462 - 75 =$$

(A) 4712
(B) 5387
(C) 5413
(D) 5487
(E) none of these

4.

$$3200 - 759 =$$

(F) 2441
(G) 2451
(H) 3559
(J) 3959
(K) none of these

8.

$$2640 - 975$$

(F) 1735
(G) 2335
(H) 2775
(J) 3615
(K) none of these

Answers:

A (A)(B)(C)(D)(E)   **2** (F)(G)(H)(J)(K)   **5** (A)(B)(C)(D)(E)   **8** (F)(G)(H)(J)(K)

B (F)(G)(H)(J)(K)   **3** (A)(B)(C)(D)(E)   **6** (F)(G)(H)(J)(K)

1 (A)(B)(C)(D)(E)   **4** (F)(G)(H)(J)(K)   **7** (A)(B)(C)(D)(E)

Math Computation: Subtraction—Decimals

Directions: Fill in the circle for the correct answer to each subtraction problem. Choose none of these if the right answer is not given.

Samples

A.

$$\begin{array}{r} \$58.79 \\ -\ 15.50 \\ \hline \end{array}$$

(A) $42.20
(B) $43.20
(C) $43.29
(D) $53.29
(E) none of these

B.

$0.52 - 0.36 =$

(F) 6
(G) 0.06
(H) 1.6
(J) 0.6
(K) none of these

1.

$$\begin{array}{r} \$37.95 \\ -\ 29.98 \\ \hline \end{array}$$

(A) $7.97
(B) $12.03
(C) $17.97
(D) $18.87
(E) none of these

5.

$7.7 - 5.9 =$

(A) 2.8
(B) 1.8
(C) 2.2
(D) 1.2
(E) none of these

2.

$$\begin{array}{r} 700.0 \\ -\ \ 0.7 \\ \hline \end{array}$$

(F) 700.0
(G) 700.3
(H) 699.3
(J) 699.08
(K) none of these

6.

$$\begin{array}{r} \$295.00 \\ -\ 67.94 \\ \hline \end{array}$$

(F) $127.46
(G) $228.56
(H) $232.54
(J) $238.56
(K) none of these

3.

$7.8 - 3.4 =$

(A) 0.44
(B) 4.4
(C) 4.8
(D) 44.0
(E) none of these

7.

$14.4 - 5.6 =$

(A) 8.8
(B) 9.8
(C) 11.2
(D) 20.0
(E) none of these

4.

$4.265 - 1.143 =$

(F) 3.122
(G) 31.22
(H) 31.32
(J) 322.2
(K) none of these

8.

$$\begin{array}{r} \$565.94 \\ -\ 565.93 \\ \hline \end{array}$$

(F) $.01
(G) $.10
(H) $1.00
(J) $10.00
(K) none of these

Answers:

A (A)(B)(C)(D)(E) 2 (F)(G)(H)(J)(K) 5 (A)(B)(C)(D)(E) 8 (F)(G)(H)(J)(K)
B (F)(G)(H)(J)(K) 3 (A)(B)(C)(D)(E) 6 (F)(G)(H)(J)(K)
1 (A)(B)(C)(D)(E) 4 (F)(G)(H)(J)(K) 7 (A)(B)(C)(D)(E)

Math Computation: Subtraction—Fractions

Directions: Fill in the circle for the correct answer to each subtraction problem. Choose none of these if the right answer is not given.

Samples

A.

$$\frac{9}{11} - \frac{2}{11} =$$

(A) 2/11
(B) 5/11
(C) 7/11
(D) 9/11
(E) none of these

B.

$$\begin{array}{r} \frac{11}{13} \\ - \frac{5}{13} \\ \hline \end{array}$$

(F) 7/13
(G) 16/13
(H) 4/13
(J) 6/13
(K) none of these

1.

$$\frac{3}{5} - \frac{2}{5} =$$

(A) 1/10
(B) 1/5
(C) 5/5
(D) 5/10
(E) none of these

5.

$$\begin{array}{r} \frac{6}{7} \\ - \frac{2}{7} \\ \hline \end{array}$$

(A) 4/7
(B) 8/7
(C) 4/14
(D) 12/14
(E) none of these

2.

$$\frac{5}{8} - \frac{4}{8} =$$

(F) 1/8
(G) 1/16
(H) 9/8
(J) 9/16
(K) none of these

6.

$$\begin{array}{r} \frac{7}{8} \\ - \frac{4}{8} \\ \hline \end{array}$$

(F) 1/8
(G) 3/8
(H) 11/8
(J) 8
(K) none of these

3.

$$\frac{2}{3} - \frac{1}{3} =$$

(A) 1/3
(B) 1/6
(C) 1
(D) 3
(E) none of these

7.

$$\begin{array}{r} \frac{3}{4} \\ - \frac{1}{2} \\ \hline \end{array}$$

(A) 2/2
(B) 4/6
(C) 1/4
(D) 3/8
(E) none of these

4.

$$\frac{7}{12} - \frac{6}{12} =$$

(F) 1/24
(G) 1/12
(H) 13/12
(J) 13/24
(K) none of these

8.

$$\begin{array}{r} \frac{1}{2} \\ - \frac{3}{8} \\ \hline \end{array}$$

(F) 1/8
(G) 2/8
(H) 1/2
(J) 1/6
(K) none of these

Answers:

A Ⓐ Ⓑ Ⓒ Ⓓ Ⓔ 2 Ⓕ Ⓖ Ⓗ Ⓙ Ⓚ 5 Ⓐ Ⓑ Ⓒ Ⓓ Ⓔ 8 Ⓕ Ⓖ Ⓗ Ⓙ Ⓚ

B Ⓕ Ⓖ Ⓗ Ⓙ Ⓚ 3 Ⓐ Ⓑ Ⓒ Ⓓ Ⓔ 6 Ⓕ Ⓖ Ⓗ Ⓙ Ⓚ

1 Ⓐ Ⓑ Ⓒ Ⓓ Ⓔ 4 Ⓕ Ⓖ Ⓗ Ⓙ Ⓚ 7 Ⓐ Ⓑ Ⓒ Ⓓ Ⓔ

Math Computation: Subtraction—Mixed Numbers

Directions: Fill in the circle for the correct answer to each subtraction problem. Choose none of these if the right answer is not given.

Samples

A.
$$6\frac{1}{2}$$
$$-\,2\frac{1}{2}$$

(A) 4
(B) 4 1/2
(C) 8 1/2
(D) 9
(E) none of these

B.
$$7\frac{7}{8} - 3\frac{4}{8} =$$

(F) 3 3/8
(G) 4 3/8
(H) 4 1/8
(J) 4
(K) none of these

1.
$$5\frac{2}{3}$$
$$-\,1\frac{1}{3}$$

(A) 4
(B) 4 1/6
(C) 4 1/3
(D) 4 3/6
(E) none of these

5.
$$17\frac{8}{11}$$
$$-\,5\frac{3}{11}$$

(A) 12 3/8
(B) 12 5/11
(C) 12 8/11
(D) 12 11/11
(E) none of these

2.
$$5\frac{12}{13}$$
$$-\,4\frac{11}{13}$$

(F) 1
(G) 1 1/13
(H) 1 1/26
(J) 9 1/13
(K) none of these

6.
$$5\frac{4}{9} - 5\frac{2}{9} =$$

(F) 5 2/9
(G) 5 2/18
(H) 6/9
(J) 2/9
(K) none of these

3.
$$6\frac{12}{13} - 5\frac{8}{13} =$$

(A) 11 4/13
(B) 4 4/13
(C) 4 13/4
(D) 1 4/13
(E) none of these

7.
$$8\frac{3}{4}$$
$$-\,6$$

(A) 2
(B) 2 3/4
(C) 14
(D) 14 3/4
(E) none of these

4.
$$6\frac{7}{8} - 5\frac{7}{8} =$$

(F) 1 7/8
(G) 1 1/8
(H) 1 14/8
(J) 1 14/16
(K) none of these

8.
$$7$$
$$-\,5\frac{2}{3}$$

(F) 1 1/3
(G) 2 1/3
(H) 2 2/3
(J) 12 2/3
(K) none of these

Answers: A Ⓐ Ⓑ Ⓒ Ⓓ Ⓔ   2 Ⓕ Ⓖ Ⓗ Ⓙ Ⓚ   5 Ⓐ Ⓑ Ⓒ Ⓓ Ⓔ   8 Ⓕ Ⓖ Ⓗ Ⓙ Ⓚ
B Ⓕ Ⓖ Ⓗ Ⓙ Ⓚ   3 Ⓐ Ⓑ Ⓒ Ⓓ Ⓔ   6 Ⓕ Ⓖ Ⓗ Ⓙ Ⓚ
1 Ⓐ Ⓑ Ⓒ Ⓓ Ⓔ   4 Ⓕ Ⓖ Ⓗ Ⓙ Ⓚ   7 Ⓐ Ⓑ Ⓒ Ⓓ Ⓔ

Math Computation: Multiplication—Whole Numbers

Directions: Fill in the circle for the correct answer to each multiplication problem. Choose none of these if the right answer is not given.

Samples

A.

$$\begin{array}{r} 25 \\ \times\ 4 \\ \hline \end{array}$$

(A) 29
(B) 100
(C) 65
(D) 104
(E) none of these

B.

$50 \times 9 =$

(F) 140
(G) 360
(H) 509
(J) 950
(K) none of these

1.

$$\begin{array}{r} 18 \\ \times\ 24 \\ \hline \end{array}$$

(A) 42
(B) 332
(C) 432
(D) 436
(E) none of these

5.

$73 \times 6 =$

(A) 348
(B) 428
(C) 438
(D) 4218
(E) none of these

2.

$3 \times 6 =$

(F) 4 x 3
(G) 3 x 5
(H) 6 x 4
(J) 2 x 9
(K) none of these

6.

$$\begin{array}{r} 508 \\ \times\ 2 \\ \hline \end{array}$$

(F) 510
(G) 610
(H) 1016
(J) 1106
(K) none of these

3.

$$\begin{array}{r} 490 \\ \times\ 10 \\ \hline \end{array}$$

(A) 490
(B) 500
(C) 4900
(D) 4910
(E) none of these

7.

$$\begin{array}{r} 56 \\ \times\ 55 \\ \hline \end{array}$$

(A) 111
(B) 560
(C) 2530
(D) 3080
(E) none of these

4.

$124 \times 20 =$

(F) 144
(G) 248
(H) 2480
(J) 4080
(K) none of these

8.

$$\begin{array}{r} 236 \\ \times\ 54 \\ \hline \end{array}$$

(F) 944
(G) 1180
(H) 11,744
(J) 13,034
(K) none of these

Answers:

A Ⓐ Ⓑ Ⓒ Ⓓ Ⓔ   2 Ⓕ Ⓖ Ⓗ Ⓙ Ⓚ   5 Ⓐ Ⓑ Ⓒ Ⓓ Ⓔ   8 Ⓕ Ⓖ Ⓗ Ⓙ Ⓚ

B Ⓕ Ⓖ Ⓗ Ⓙ Ⓚ   3 Ⓐ Ⓑ Ⓒ Ⓓ Ⓔ   6 Ⓕ Ⓖ Ⓗ Ⓙ Ⓚ

1 Ⓐ Ⓑ Ⓒ Ⓓ Ⓔ   4 Ⓕ Ⓖ Ⓗ Ⓙ Ⓚ   7 Ⓐ Ⓑ Ⓒ Ⓓ Ⓔ

Math Computation: Multiplication—Decimals

Directions: Fill in the circle for the correct answer to each multiplication problem. Choose none of these if the right answer is not given.

Samples

A.

$7 \times 5.1 =$

(A) 3.57
(B) 35.0
(C) 35.7
(D) 5.8
(E) none of these

B.

$$\begin{array}{r} \$25.50 \\ \times\ 3 \\ \hline \end{array}$$

(F) $7.65
(G) $25.53
(H) $65.50
(J) $76.50
(K) none of these

1.

$$\begin{array}{r} 0.9 \\ \times\ 0.3 \\ \hline \end{array}$$

(A) .0027
(B) 0.27
(C) 2.7
(D) 27
(E) none of these

5.

$$\begin{array}{r} \$54.36 \\ \times\ 4 \\ \hline \end{array}$$

(A) $54.40
(B) $206.24
(C) $217.44
(D) $218.44
(E) none of these

2.

$.94 \times .32 =$

(F) .0470
(G) .2008
(H) .2908
(J) .3008
(K) none of these

6.

$$\begin{array}{r} \$49.99 \\ \times\ 2 \\ \hline \end{array}$$

(F) $50.01
(G) $88.88
(H) $99.98
(J) $100.00
(K) none of these

3.

$6.92 \times 4 =$

(A) 6.96
(B) 10.92
(C) 26.78
(D) 27.68
(E) none of these

7.

$$\begin{array}{r} \$99.06 \\ \times\ 5 \\ \hline \end{array}$$

(A) $99.11
(B) $440.30
(C) $458.00
(D) $495.30
(E) none of these

4.

$$\begin{array}{r} 14.2 \\ \times\ 2 \\ \hline \end{array}$$

(F) .284
(G) 2.84
(H) 28.4
(J) 284
(K) none of these

8.

$$\begin{array}{r} .005 \\ \times\ .05 \\ \hline \end{array}$$

(F) .00025
(G) .0025
(H) .025
(J) .25
(K) none of these

Answers:

A Ⓐ Ⓑ Ⓒ Ⓓ Ⓔ   2 Ⓕ Ⓖ Ⓗ Ⓙ Ⓚ   5 Ⓐ Ⓑ Ⓒ Ⓓ Ⓔ   8 Ⓕ Ⓖ Ⓗ Ⓙ Ⓚ

B Ⓕ Ⓖ Ⓗ Ⓙ Ⓚ   3 Ⓐ Ⓑ Ⓒ Ⓓ Ⓔ   6 Ⓕ Ⓖ Ⓗ Ⓙ Ⓚ

1 Ⓐ Ⓑ Ⓒ Ⓓ Ⓔ   4 Ⓕ Ⓖ Ⓗ Ⓙ Ⓚ   7 Ⓐ Ⓑ Ⓒ Ⓓ Ⓔ

Math Computation: Multiplication—Fractions

Directions: Fill in the circle for the correct answer to each multiplication problem. Choose none of these if the right answer is not given.

Samples

A.

$$\frac{3}{4} \times \frac{1}{4} =$$

(A) 3/4
(B) 3/8
(C) 3/16
(D) 1
(E) none of these

B.

$$\frac{4}{5} \times \frac{5}{8} =$$

(F) 1/2
(G) 9/13
(H) 20/13
(J) 25/32
(K) none of these

1.

$$\frac{1}{3} \times \frac{3}{5} =$$

(A) 9/5
(B) 1/5
(C) 3/8
(D) 4/8
(E) none of these

5.

$$\frac{1}{8} \times \frac{4}{5} =$$

(A) 5/32
(B) 4/13
(C) 5/13
(D) 1/10
(E) none of these

2.

$$\frac{1}{12} \times \frac{3}{4} =$$

(F) 4/36
(G) 3/16
(H) 1/16
(J) 1
(K) none of these

6.

$$\frac{1}{10} \times \frac{1}{2} =$$

(F) 2/20
(G) 1/12
(H) 2/12
(J) 1/8
(K) none of these

3.

$$\frac{3}{10} \times \frac{5}{10} =$$

(A) 8/100
(B) 3/20
(C) 8/20
(D) 8/10
(E) none of these

7.

$$\frac{3}{7} \times \frac{5}{7} =$$

(A) 8/49
(B) 15/49
(C) 21/35
(D) 8/14
(E) none of these

4.

$$\frac{7}{8} \times 1 =$$

(F) 1 7/8
(G) 7/8
(H) 8/7
(J) 8/9
(K) one of these

8.

$$\frac{3}{5} \times \frac{3}{5} =$$

(F) 3/5
(G) 6/10
(H) 15/15
(J) 9/25
(K) none of these

Answers:

A Ⓐ Ⓑ Ⓒ Ⓓ Ⓔ   2 Ⓕ Ⓖ Ⓗ Ⓙ Ⓚ   5 Ⓐ Ⓑ Ⓒ Ⓓ Ⓔ   8 Ⓕ Ⓖ Ⓗ Ⓙ Ⓚ

B Ⓕ Ⓖ Ⓗ Ⓙ Ⓚ   3 Ⓐ Ⓑ Ⓒ Ⓓ Ⓔ   6 Ⓕ Ⓖ Ⓗ Ⓙ Ⓚ

1 Ⓐ Ⓑ Ⓒ Ⓓ Ⓔ   4 Ⓕ Ⓖ Ⓗ Ⓙ Ⓚ   7 Ⓐ Ⓑ Ⓒ Ⓓ Ⓔ

Math Computation: Division—Whole Numbers

Directions: Fill in the circle for the correct answer to each division problem. Choose none of these if the right answer is not given.

Samples

A.

$300 \div 5 =$

- (A) 5
- (B) 6
- (C) 50
- (D) 60
- (E) none of these

B.

$8\overline{)63}$

- (F) 8 R1
- (G) 8
- (H) 7 R7
- (J) 6 R15
- (K) none of these

1.

$4\overline{)64}$

- (A) 11
- (B) 12
- (C) 14
- (D) 15
- (E) none of these

5.

$744 \div 62 =$

- (A) 10 R24
- (B) 11
- (C) 11 R12
- (D) 12
- (E) none of these

2.

$637 \div 7 =$

- (F) 9 R7
- (G) 81
- (H) 91
- (J) 811
- (K) none of these

6.

$38\overline{)766}$

- (F) 20 R6
- (G) 21 R6
- (H) 26
- (J) 206
- (K) none of these

3.

$82\overline{)1722}$

- (A) 20 R22
- (B) 21
- (C) 22 R8
- (D) 201
- (E) none of these

7.

$9 \div 2 =$

- (A) 3 R3
- (B) 4
- (C) 4 R1
- (D) 40 R1
- (E) none of these

4.

$590 \div 10 =$

- (F) 5 R9
- (G) 59
- (H) 60
- (J) 509
- (K) none of these

8.

$4\overline{)158}$

- (F) 38 R6
- (G) 39
- (H) 39 R2
- (J) 44 R2
- (K) none of these

Answers:

A (A)(B)(C)(D)(E) 2 (F)(G)(H)(J)(K) 5 (A)(B)(C)(D)(E) 8 (F)(G)(H)(J)(K)

B (F)(G)(H)(J)(K) 3 (A)(B)(C)(D)(E) 6 (F)(G)(H)(J)(K)

1 (A)(B)(C)(D)(E) 4 (F)(G)(H)(J)(K) 7 (A)(B)(C)(D)(E)

Math Concepts/Applications: Numeration

Directions: Read each item and find the correct answer. Fill in the answer circle for your choice.

Samples

A What is another way to write 3 thousands 9 tens 4 ones?

(A) 394

(B) 3094

(C) 3904

(D) 3940

B. To estimate the sum of 8372 and 7931 to the nearest thousand, you should add . . .

(F) 7000 and 7000

(G) 8000 and 7000

(H) 8000 and 8000

(J) 8000 and 9000

1. In which number does the 8 stand for 8 hundreds?

(A) 1584

(B) 4518

(C) 5814

(D) 8541

5. Which is the numeral for six thousand eighty-seven?

(A) 687

(B) 6087

(C) 60,087

(D) 687,000

2. Which number is greater than 6979?

(F) 6798

(G) 6978

(H) 6879

(J) 6987

6. What is the value of the 5 in 654,732?

(F) 500

(G) 5000

(H) 50,000

(J) 500,000

3. 984 rounded to the nearest ten is . . .

(A) 900

(B) 980

(C) 990

(D) 1000

7. 568,291 rounded to the nearest thousand is?

(A) 560,000

(B) 568,200

(C) 568,000

(D) 570,000

4. Which is the expanded form of 7230?

(F) 700 + 20 + 3

(G) 700 + 200 + 30

(H) 7000 + 20 + 3

(J) 7000 + 200 + 30

8. Which is the standard form for 6 hundreds 7 ones?

(F) 67

(G) 607

(H) 670

(J) 6007

GO→

Answers:

A (A) (B) (C) (D)   2 (F) (G) (H) (J)   5 (A) (B) (C) (D)   8 (F) (G) (H) (J)

B (F) (G) (H) (J)   3 (A) (B) (C) (D)   6 (F) (G) (H) (J)

1 (A) (B) (C) (D)   4 (F) (G) (H) (J)   7 (A) (B) (C) (D)

Math Concepts/Applications: Numeration *(cont.)*

9. What is the twelfth letter of the alphabet?

   (A) F

   (B) L

   (C) G

   (D) N

---

10. Which number would be thirty if rounded to the nearest 10?

   (F) 22

   (G) 24

   (H) 26

   (J) 39

---

11. What number is missing from this number pattern?

   61, 57, 53, _____ , 45, 41

   (A) 51

   (B) 52

   (C) 47

   (D) 49

---

12. Which answer shows counting by fives?

   (F) 5, 9, 13, 17

   (G) 20, 25, 30, 35

   (H) 6, 12, 18, 24

   (J) 1, 3, 5, 7

---

13. What is the Roman numeral for 19?

   (A) XIX

   (B) XXI

   (C) XVIIII

   (D) VVVIIII

---

14. This function table shows input numbers and output numbers. The rule used to change the numbers from input to output is shown above the table. Which number is missing from the table?

Rule: Add 3 and then multiply by 2.

Input	Output
2	10
6	?
10	26

   (F) 12

   (H) 18

   (G) 16

   (J) 20

---

15. What number is the arrow pointing to?

15   26

   (A) 17

   (B) 19

   (C) 21

   (D) 25

---

16. Which two pictures have the same portion of the square shaded?

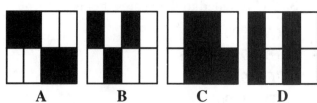

    A   B   C   D

   (F) A and B

   (G) B and C

   (H) C and D

   (J) A and D

STOP

Answers:

   9 Ⓐ Ⓑ Ⓒ Ⓓ   **12** Ⓕ Ⓖ Ⓗ Ⓙ   **15** Ⓐ Ⓑ Ⓒ Ⓓ

   10 Ⓕ Ⓖ Ⓗ Ⓙ   **13** Ⓐ Ⓑ Ⓒ Ⓓ   **16** Ⓕ Ⓖ Ⓗ Ⓙ

   11 Ⓐ Ⓑ Ⓒ Ⓓ   **14** Ⓕ Ⓖ Ⓗ Ⓙ

Math Concepts/Applications: Number Sentences

Directions: Read each question and find the correct answer. Fill in the answer circle for your choice.

Samples

A. What number is needed to make this number sentence true?

$$55 - \boxed{} = 19$$

(A) 30
(B) 34
(C) 36
(D) 74

B. Which sign will make this number sentence true?

$$24 \boxed{} 6 = 2 \times 2$$

(F) +
(G) –
(H) x
(J) ÷

---

1. Which sign will correctly complete this number sentence?

$$9 \boxed{} 7 = 16$$

(A) +
(B) –
(C) x
(D)

4. Which sign will make this number sentence true?

$$30 \boxed{} 3 = 90$$

(F) +
(G) –
(H) x
(J) ÷

---

2. What number is missing from this number sentence?

$$\boxed{} \times 8 = 48$$

(F) 5
(G) 6
(H) 7
(J) 56

5. What number goes in the box to make this sentence true?

$$\boxed{} \div 8 = 7$$

(A) 49
(B) 56
(C) 63
(D) 64

---

3. Which sign will make this number sentence true?

$$9 \boxed{} 4 = 2 + 3$$

(A) +
(B) –
(C) x
(D) ÷

6. What number will make this number sentence true?

$$6 + 24 + \boxed{} = 45$$

(F) 5
(G) 10
(H) 15
(J) 20

Answers: A Ⓐ Ⓑ Ⓒ Ⓓ   1 Ⓐ Ⓑ Ⓒ Ⓓ   3 Ⓐ Ⓑ Ⓒ Ⓓ   5 Ⓐ Ⓑ Ⓒ Ⓓ
         B Ⓕ Ⓖ Ⓗ Ⓙ   2 Ⓕ Ⓖ Ⓗ Ⓙ   4 Ⓕ Ⓖ Ⓗ Ⓙ   6 Ⓕ Ⓖ Ⓗ Ⓙ

Math Concepts/Applications: Number Theory

Directions: Read each question and find the correct answer. Fill in the answer circle for your choice.

Samples

A. The same number will make both number sentences correct. What is the number?

24 ÷ 6 = _____   _____ x 6 = 24

(A) 2
(B) 3
(C) 4
(D) 5

B. Which fraction has the same value as 0.3?

(F) 3/10
(G) 1/3
(H) 2/3
(J) 3/3

---

1. What number makes the number sentence true?

15 x _____ = 0

(A) 0
(B) 1
(C) 10
(D) 15

4. Which fraction means the same as 5/10?

(F) 1/2
(G) 1/3
(H) 1/5
(J) 10/1

---

2. Which answer choice shows two even numbers?

(F) 15, 24
(G) 4, 18
(H) 22, 33
(J) 9, 25

5. Which number sentence is in the same family as 2 + _____ = 10?

(A) 10 + 2 = _____
(B) 10 + _____ = 2
(C) 2 – 10 = _____
(D) 10 - _____ = 2

---

3. Which number is <u>not</u> evenly divisible by 12?

(A) 24
(B) 36
(C) 40
(D) 48

6. What number makes this number sentence true?

11 x _____ = 11

(F) 0
(G) 1
(H) 10
(J) 11

Answers:

A (A) (B) (C) (D)   1 (A) (B) (C) (D)   3 (A) (B) (C) (D)   5 (A) (B) (C) (D)

B (F) (G) (H) (J)   2 (F) (G) (H) (J)   4 (F) (G) (H) (J)   6 (F) (G) (H) (J)

Math Concepts/Applications: Geometry

Directions: Read each question and find the correct answer. Fill in the answer circle for your choice.

Samples

A. What is the name of this figure?

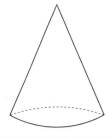

(A) cube

(B) cone

(C) pyramid

(D) cylinder

B. These are the dimensions of Mrs. Brown's new rug. What is the perimeter of the rug?

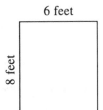

(F) 12 ft.

(G) 16 ft.

(H) 28 ft.

(J) 48 ft.

---

1. Find the figure in which the dotted line is not a line of symmetry.

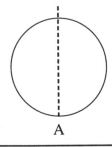   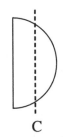   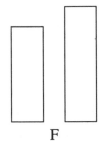   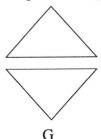

    A   B   C   D

---

2. Which answer choice shows a pair of congruent figures?

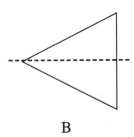   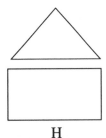   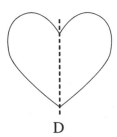   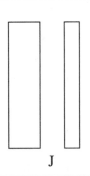

    F   G   H   J

---

3. Which pair of lines are parallel?

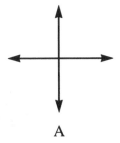   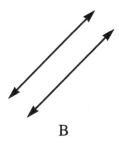      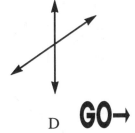

    A   B   C   D **GO→**

Answers: **A** Ⓐ Ⓑ Ⓒ Ⓓ   **1** Ⓐ Ⓑ Ⓒ Ⓓ   **2** Ⓕ Ⓖ Ⓗ Ⓙ   **3** Ⓐ Ⓑ Ⓒ Ⓓ
              B Ⓕ Ⓖ Ⓗ Ⓙ

Math Concepts/Applications: Geometry *(cont.)*

4. These are the dimensions of Mr. Green's garden. What is the area of the garden?

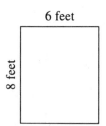

6 feet

8 feet

(F) 12 sq. ft.

(G) 16 sq. ft.

(H) 28 sq. ft.

(J) 48 sq. ft.

5. This shape is called a . . .

(A) square.

(B) triangle.

(C) rectangle.

(D) circle.

---

6. Which one of these shapes does not have any curved surfaces?

 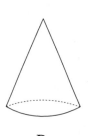 

F   G   H   J

---

7. Which one of these shapes is a cylinder?

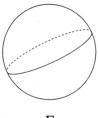  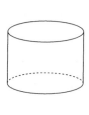 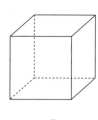

A   B   C   D

---

8. Similar figures have the same shape but they are of different sizes. Which pair of figures below is similar?

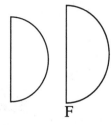 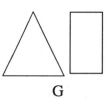 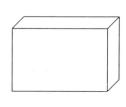 

F   G   H   J

Answers: **4** Ⓕ Ⓖ Ⓗ Ⓙ   **6** Ⓕ Ⓖ Ⓗ Ⓙ   **8** Ⓕ Ⓖ Ⓗ Ⓙ

5 Ⓐ Ⓑ Ⓒ Ⓓ   **7** Ⓐ Ⓑ Ⓒ Ⓓ

Math Concepts/Applications: Measurement—Time and Money

Directions: Read each question and find the correct answer. Fill in the answer circle for your choice.

Samples

A. What time is shown on this clock?

(A) 12:0

(B) 10:00

(C) 12:50

(D) 10:12

B. What is the total value of these coins?

(F) 9¢

(G) 44¢

(H) 45¢

(J) $1.00

---

1. Which clock shows that the time is 4:30?

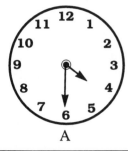   

    A   B   C   D

---

2. Which group of coins has the total value of 46¢?

    F   G   H   J

---

3. Find the group of coins with the least value.

(A) 10 dimes, 50 pennies

(B) 4 quarters, 4 dimes, 1 nickel

(C) 1 dollar, 3 dimes, 2 nickels

(D) 3 dimes, 8 nickels, 5 pennies

4. What time is shown on this clock?

(F) 8:09

(G) 8:45

(H) 9:08

(J) 9:40 **GO→**

Answers:

A Ⓐ Ⓑ Ⓒ Ⓓ   1 Ⓐ Ⓑ Ⓒ Ⓓ   3 Ⓐ Ⓑ Ⓒ Ⓓ

B Ⓕ Ⓖ Ⓗ Ⓙ   2 Ⓕ Ⓖ Ⓗ Ⓙ   4 Ⓕ Ⓖ Ⓗ Ⓙ

Math Concepts/Applications: Measurement— Time and Money *(cont.)*

5. Which answer choice is another way of writing 85¢?

(A) $.85

(B) ¢.85

(C) .85¢

(D) $8.2

7. What time is shown on this clock?

(A) 3:04

(B) 3:25

(C) 4:03

(D) 4:15

6. Which one of these has a greater value than seventy-eight cents?

(F) 7 dimes

(G) 75 pennies

(H) 16 nickels

(J) 3 quarters

8. What time will it be half an hour after the time shown on this clock?

(F) 10:15

(G) 11:00

(H) 11:15

(J) 11:45

9. Which clock shows the time is 6:45?

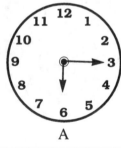         

A   B   C   D

10. Which group of coins has the value of 72¢?

F   G   H   J   **GO→**

Answers:

5 (A) (B) (C) (D)   7 (A) (B) (C) (D)   9 (A) (B) (C) (D)

6 (F) (G) (H) (J)   8 (F) (G) (H) (J)   10 (F) (G) (H) (J)

Math Concepts/Applications: Measurement— Time and Money *(cont.)*

July						
Sun.	Mon.	Tues.	Wed.	Thurs.	Fri.	Sat.
	1	2	3	4	5	6
7	8	9	10	11	12	13
14	15	16	17	18	19	20
21	22	23	24	25	26	27
28	29	30	31			

11. The month on this calendar page begins on which day of the week?

   (A) Sunday
   (B) Monday
   (C) Friday
   (D) Tuesday

12. On which day of the week does the Fourth of July fall?

   (F) Sunday
   (G) Wednesday
   (H) Thursday
   (J) Saturday

13. The third Saturday of this month falls on which date?

   (A) 6
   (B) 13
   (C) 20
   (D) 27

14. How many days does July have?

   (F) 28
   (G) 29
   (H) 30
   (J) 31

Answers: **11** Ⓐ Ⓑ Ⓒ Ⓓ   **13** Ⓐ Ⓑ Ⓒ Ⓓ
                12 Ⓕ Ⓖ Ⓗ Ⓙ   **14** Ⓕ Ⓖ Ⓗ Ⓙ

Math Concepts/Applications: Measurement—Length

Directions: Read each item and find the correct answer. Fill in the answer circle for your choice.

Sample

A. How many inches long is the pencil?

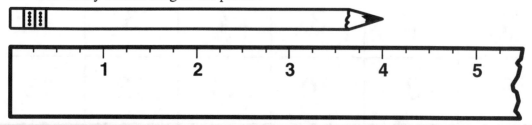

(A) 4.5
(B) 4
(C) .4
(D) 3.4

---

1. About how many centimeters long is the key?

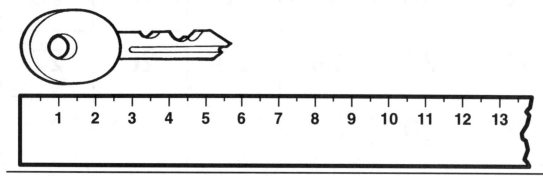

(A) 6.7
(B) 6.2
(C) 6
(D) 5.2

---

2. How many centimeters long is the stick?

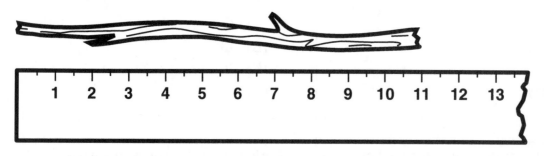

(F) 10.1
(G) 11
(H) 11.5
(J) 10.5

---

3. The length of a dollar bill is about . . .	**4.** 1 foot =
(A) 1 inch.	(F) 6 inches
(B) 6 inches.	(G) 9 inches
(C) 1 foot.	(H) 12 inches
(D) 6 feet.	(J) 15 inches

Answers: A Ⓐ Ⓑ Ⓒ Ⓓ   1 Ⓐ Ⓑ Ⓒ Ⓓ   3 Ⓐ Ⓑ Ⓒ Ⓓ
                              2 Ⓕ Ⓖ Ⓗ Ⓙ   4 Ⓕ Ⓖ Ⓗ Ⓙ

Math Concepts/Applications: Measurement—Weight and Capacity

Directions: Read each question and find the correct answer. Fill in the answer circle for your choice.

Samples

A. How much does this rock weigh?

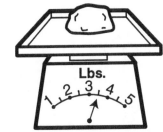

(A) 3 lbs.

(B) 3 1/2 lbs.

(C) 4 lbs.

(D) 5 lbs.

B. How many cups are there in a quart?

(F) 2

(G) 3

(H) 4

(J) 5

---

1. How much do these oranges weigh?

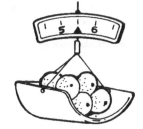

(A) 4 1/2 lbs.

(B) 5 lbs.

(C) 5 1/2 lbs.

(D) 6 lbs.

4. How many quarts are in a gallon?

(F) 4

(G) 6

(H) 8

(J) 12

---

2. Gerry just weighed himself on the scale. How much does he weigh?

(F) 85 lbs.

(G) 87 lbs.

(H) 88 lbs.

(J) 90 lbs.

5. How many pints are in 4 quarts?

(A) 4

(B) 8

(C) 10

(D) 12

---

3. How many ounces are in a pound?

(A) 10

(B) 12

(C) 14

(D) 16

6. 1 ton = _____?

(F) 000 pounds

(G) 1200 pounds

(H) 1600 pounds

(J) 2000 pounds

Answers:

A (A) (B) (C) (D) 1 (A) (B) (C) (D) 3 (A) (B) (C) (D) 5 (A) (B) (C) (D)

B (F) (G) (H) (J) 2 (F) (G) (H) (J) 4 (F) (G) (H) (J) 6 (F) (G) (H) (J)

Math Concepts/Applications: Measurement—Temperature

Directions: Read the question and use the thermometer to find the correct answer. Fill in the answer circle for your choice.

Sample

A. What temperature does this thermometer show?

(A) 73°

(B) 74°

(C) 75°

(D) 76°

1. What temperature does this thermometer show?

(A) 32°

(B) 33.3°

(C) 32.4°

(D) 32.2°

2. What temperature does this thermometer show?

(F) -6.3°

(G) -6.6°

(H) -7.2°

(J) -7.4°

Answers: A Ⓐ Ⓑ Ⓒ Ⓓ   1 Ⓐ Ⓑ Ⓒ Ⓓ   2 Ⓕ Ⓖ Ⓗ Ⓙ

Math Concepts/Applications: Probability and Statistics

Directions: Read each problem. Look for the best answer. Fill in the answer circle for your choice.

Sample

A. How many glasses of lemonade were sold on Saturday at Ron's lemonade stand?

(A)	5 glasses
(B)	6 glasses
(C)	50 glasses
(D)	55 glasses

This graph shows how many personal computers were sold by a computer store during the first six months of the year. Use the graph to answer questions 1 and 2.

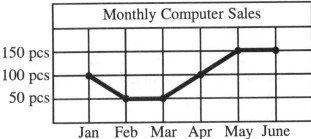

1. How many personal computers were sold in March?

(A) 50
(B) 100
(C) 150
(D) 200

2. In which two months were the most personal computers sold?

(F) January and February
(G) February and March
(H) April and May
(J) May and June

3. Suppose that you spun this spinner 100 times. Which number would the arrow land on the most often?

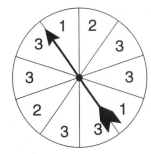

(A) Number 1
(B) Number 2
(C) Number 3
(D) You cannot tell.

4. At College Park Elementary School, 6 out of 10 students buy lunch every day. There are 300 students in the school. What is the probability that a student does not buy lunch every day?

(F) 6 out of 10
(G) 6 out of 300
(H) 4 out of 10
(J) 10 out of 300

Answers: A Ⓐ Ⓑ Ⓒ Ⓓ   1 Ⓐ Ⓑ Ⓒ Ⓓ   3 Ⓐ Ⓑ Ⓒ Ⓓ

2 Ⓕ Ⓖ Ⓗ Ⓙ   4 Ⓕ Ⓖ Ⓗ Ⓙ

Math Concepts/Applications: Estimation

Directions: Read each problem. Look for the best answer. Fill in the answer circle for your choice.

Samples

A. At the ballpark, programs cost $3.95 and T-shirts are $14.95 each. About how much would it cost to buy a T-shirt and a program?

(A) $17.00
(B) $18.00
(C) $19.00
(D) $20.00

B. What is the best estimate of the <u>area</u> of this square?

6.2 meters

(F) 62 square meters
(G) 36 square meters
(H) 24 square meters
(J) 6 square meters

1. Each row in one section of a stadium holds 103 people. There are 98 rows in the section. What is the best way to estimate the number of people that can sit in that section of the stadium?

(A) 105 x 98
(B) 110 x 90
(C) 100 x 90
(D) 100 x 100

2. Which one of these is the best estimate of 29 plus 21 plus 42?

(F) 80
(G) 90
(H) 100
(J) 110

3. Students and their parents baked a total of 730 cupcakes for a big school bake sale. If they can pack 8 cupcakes in a box, about how many boxes will they have for the sale?

(A) 70
(B) 80
(C) 90
(D) 100

4. Paul had $20.00 to spend when he went to the mall. He bought a book for $6.95 and spent $4.89 on a hamburger and shake for lunch. About how much money did he still have when he left the mall?

(F) $10.00
(G) $9.00
(H) $8.00
(J) $7.00

5. There are 2.54 centimeters in an inch. About how many centimeters are there in 1 foot?

(A) 10
(B) 20
(C) 30
(D) 60

6. A professional football player weighed 307 pounds. His friend weighed 198. About how much heavier was the football player than his friend?

(F) 300 pounds
(G) 150 pounds
(H) 115 pounds
(J) 100 pounds

Answers:

A (A) (B) (C) (D)   1 (A) (B) (C) (D)   3 (A) (B) (C) (D)   5 (A) (B) (C) (D)

B (F) (G) (H) (J)   2 (F) (G) (H) (J)   4 (F) (G) (H) (J)   6 (F) (G) (H) (J)

Math Concepts/Applications: Strategies

Directions: Read each problem. Look for the correct answer. Fill in the answer circle for your choice.

Samples

A. Gabby bought a game. She needs to know the price of the game, but she cannot find her receipt. She remembers paying for the game with a twenty dollar bill. What other information does she need in order to figure out how much the game cost?
(A) how many pieces are in the game
(B) how much change she received
(C) how much allowance she gets
(D) how much money she gave the clerk

B. Side AB is 12 units. What else do you need to know to find the area of this rectangle?

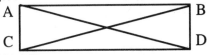

(F) Side AD
(G) Side CD
(H) Side BD
(J) Side BC

1. A man is driving his car at an average speed of 65 miles per hour. He drives for 4 hours. Knowing this, which one of these could you find?
(A) the number of stops he made
(B) the distance he traveled
(C) the direction in which he traveled
(D) the number of other people in the car

2. There are 38 weeks in a school year. Students attend school 6 hours a day, 5 days a week. Using this information, which one of these could you figure out?
(F) what students do on weekends
(G) hours students spend at recess each day
(H) what students do after school
(J) hours students spend in school each year

3. A certain tree adds 1/2 inch to the circumference of its trunk every year. It is 3 feet around now. How could you find out what the circumference of its trunk would in 10 years?
(A) 3 feet + (1/2 inch + 10 years)
(B) 1/2 inch + (3 feet x 10 years)
(C) 1/2 inch x 3 feet x 10 years
(D) 3 feet + (1/2 inch x 10 years)

4. There were 5008 books in the school library. New books were added, making a total of 5695 books. How could you figure out how many new books were added.
(F) 5008 + 5695 = _____
(G) 5008 + _____ = 5695
(H) 5008 – _____ = 5695
(J) _____ + 5695 = 5008

5. Three fifth grade classes are going on a field trip in two buses. There are two classes of 30 students and one class of 20 students. If the teachers want an even number on each bus, what should they do?
(A) (30 + 30 + 20) ÷ 2
(B) (30 + 20) ÷ 2
(C) (30 + 20) x 2
(D) (30 + 30 + 20) x 2

6. Anderson Elementary School has 354 students. The 214 students of Winton Elementary School will join them while their school is being repaired. How many students will there be altogether?
(F) 354 ÷ 214
(G) 354 x 214
(H) 354 – 214
(J) 354 + 214

Answers:
A Ⓐ Ⓑ Ⓒ Ⓓ   1 Ⓐ Ⓑ Ⓒ Ⓓ   3 Ⓐ Ⓑ Ⓒ Ⓓ   5 Ⓐ Ⓑ Ⓒ Ⓓ
B Ⓕ Ⓖ Ⓗ Ⓙ   2 Ⓕ Ⓖ Ⓗ Ⓙ   4 Ⓕ Ⓖ Ⓗ Ⓙ   6 Ⓕ Ⓖ Ⓗ Ⓙ

Math Concepts/Applications: Problem Solving and Data Analysis

Directions: Read each problem. Look for the correct answer. Fill in the answer circle for your choice.

Samples

A. Lupe receives $3.00 an hour when she baby-sits. On Wednesday she worked for 3 hours. On Friday she worked for 5 hours, and on Saturday she worked for 7 hours. How much money did Lupe earn altogether?

  (A) $15.00
  (B) $24.00
  (C) $36.00
  (D) $45.00

B. Mrs. Roberts had a party to which she invited 15 guests. She served a cake which cost $16.00 and punch which cost $14.00. How much did Mrs. Roberts spend on each guest?

  (F) $2.00   (H) $16.00
  (G) $14.00   (J) $30.00

The graph below shows how many concert tickets a radio station gave away during a recent week-long contest. Use the graph to answer questions 1 through 3.

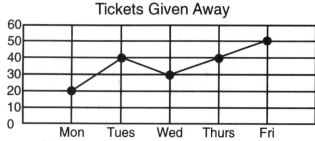

Tickets Given Away

1. On which day were 20 tickets given away?

  (A) Monday   (C) Wednesday
  (B) Tuesday   (D) Thursday

2. On which day were the most tickets given away?

  (F) Monday   (H) Thursday
  (G) Wednesday   (J) Friday

3. How many tickets were given away on Thursday and Friday altogether?

  (A) 40   (C) 90
  (B) 50   (D) 95

Read the paragraph below. Use the information in the paragraph to answer questions 4 through 6.

Bev has 2 horses. She feeds them and gives them water every morning. Every afternoon Bev brushes the horses and gives them each a quart of oats. Feeding and watering the horses takes about 15 minutes a day. Then Bev rides both horses for a total of 60 minutes. She sets a timer to make sure that each horse gets an equal amount of time.

4. How many minutes does Bev spend feeding and watering the horses every week?

  (F) 15   (G) 60
  (H) 105   (J) 160

5. What numbers can be used to figure out how many minutes a day Bev rides each horse?

  (A) 15 and 2   (C) 60 and 15
  (B) 15 and 60   (D) 60 and 2

6. Which number sentence can be used to figure out how many minutes a day Bev spends with her horses?

  (F) 15 x 60 =   (H) 15 x 60 x 2 =
  (G) 15 + 60 =   (J) 15 + 60 + 2 =

Answers:

A Ⓐ Ⓑ Ⓒ Ⓓ   1 Ⓐ Ⓑ Ⓒ Ⓓ   3 Ⓐ Ⓑ Ⓒ Ⓓ   5 Ⓐ Ⓑ Ⓒ Ⓓ

B Ⓕ Ⓖ Ⓗ Ⓙ   2 Ⓕ Ⓖ Ⓗ Ⓙ   4 Ⓕ Ⓖ Ⓗ Ⓙ   6 Ⓕ Ⓖ Ⓗ Ⓙ

Math Concepts/Applications: Reasonable Answers

Directions: Read each problem. Look for the best answer. Fill in the answer circle for your choice.

Samples

A. At noon 198 students eat lunch in the school cafeteria. As many as 10 students can sit at each table. About how many tables are there in the cafeteria?

(A) 10

(B) 19

(C) 20

(D) 21

B. A school bus can hold 60 students. A group of 90 students is going on a field trip. How many buses will they need?

(F) 1

(G) 1 1/2

(H) 2

(J) 2 1/2

---

1. A half-gallon is four times larger than a pint, and a pint is twice as large as a cup. How would you find out how many cups there are in a half-gallon?

(A) 4 x 4 x 4

(B) 4 + 4 + 2

(C) 4 x 2

(D) 4 x 4

2. About how tall is a regular door?

(F) 12 inches

(G) 36 inches

(H) 7 feet

(J) 15 feet

3. One dozen eggs fit into a regular egg carton. How many cartons would you need to store 40 eggs?

(A) 2

(B) 3

(C) 4

(D) 5

---

4. Suppose you are using a calculator to multiply 10 x 100. How many zeroes would be in the answer?

(F) 1

(G) 2

(H) 3

(J) 4

Answers:
A Ⓐ Ⓑ Ⓒ Ⓓ 1 Ⓐ Ⓑ Ⓒ Ⓓ 3 Ⓐ Ⓑ Ⓒ Ⓓ

B Ⓕ Ⓖ Ⓗ Ⓙ 2 Ⓕ Ⓖ Ⓗ Ⓙ 4 Ⓕ Ⓖ Ⓗ Ⓙ

Teacher Scripts

NOTE: The boxed information for each skill on the following pages references the Student Practice Pages (SPP).

Word Analysis: Consonant Sounds/Beginning | SPP 31 |

- Open your book to page _____. (Check to make sure everyone has found the right place.)

- On this page you will match consonant sounds with the beginning sounds of words. Look at the directions at the top of the page and read them to yourself as I read them aloud. (Read directions to students.)

- Look at sample A. What is the word with the underlined letter? (call) What sound does the underlined letter stand for? /k/ Yes, the underlined letter in call stands for the /k/ sound. Which of the three words below it has the same sound? (take) Yes, the answer is take. The word take has the same /k/ sound as the word call. Fill in the circle for answer choice A in item A at the bottom of the page.

- (Take time to explain the answer choice rows at the bottom of the page. Point out that these are numbered to correspond to the item numbers. Tell the students that the answer choices and answer circles are alternately labeled A, B, C and F, G, H. They must match both the item numbers and the answer choice letters for each item. Copy the answer section from the bottom of the page and demonstrate as you go along.)

- Now look at sample B, right next to sample A. What is the word with the underlined letters? (trip) Find the word that has the same sound as the underlined letters in the word trip. Then find the answers for sample B at the bottom of the page. Fill in the circle for the answer you chose.

- Which answer did you choose? (extra) The word <u>extra</u> has the same sound as the beginning sound in the word <u>trip</u>. Which answer choice letter goes with <u>extra</u>? (G) Find item B at the bottom of the page and mark answer choice <u>G</u>. (Check to make sure everyone understands how to do this.)

- Now you are going to finish the page. For each question, read the word with the underlined letter or letters. Then look at the answer choices and find the word that has the same sound. Remember, the consonant sound you are looking for may be at the beginning, in the middle, or at the end of a word.

Teacher Scripts

Word Analysis: Consonant Sounds—Middle and Ending

- Open your book to page _____. (Check to make sure that everyone has found the right place.)

- On this page you will match consonant sounds with the middle or ending sounds of words. Look at the directions at the top of the page and read them to yourself as I read them aloud. (Read the directions to your students.)

- Look at sample A. What is the word with the underlined letter? (face) What sound does the underlined letter stand for? /s/ Yes, the underlined letter in face stands for the /s/ sound. Which of the three words below it has the same sound? (soup) Yes, the answer is soup. The word soup has the same /s/ sound as the word face. Fill in the circle for answer choice A in item A at the bottom of the page.

- (Take time to explain the answer choice rows at the bottom of the page. Point out that these are numbered to correspond to the item numbers. Tell the students that the answer choices and answer circles are alternately labeled A, B, C and F, G, H. They must match both the item numbers and the answer choice letters for each item. Copy the answer section from the bottom of the page and demonstrate as you go along.)

- Now look at sample B which is next to sample A. What is the word with the underlined letters? (sent) Find the word that has the same sound as the underlined letters in the word sent. Then find the answer circles for sample B at the bottom of the page. Fill in the circle for the answer of your choice.

- Which answer did you choose? (pants) The word pants has the same sound as the sound in the word sent. Which answer choice letter goes with pants? (G) Find item B at the bottom of the page and fill in answer choice G. (Check to make sure that everyone understands how to do this.)

- Now you are going to finish the page. For each question, read the word with the underlined letter or letters. Then look at the answer choices and find the word that has the same sound. Remember, the consonant sound you are looking for may be at the beginning, in the middle, or at the end of the answer word.

Teacher Scripts

Word Analysis: Consonant Sounds—Initial and Final

- Open your book to page _____. (Check to make sure that everyone has found the right place.)

- On this page you will match words with the same beginning or ending sounds. Look at the directions at the top of the page and read them to yourself as I read them aloud. (Read the directions to your students.)

- Look at sample A. Look at the words in this section. Who can read them aloud for us? Now listen carefully. Which word begins with the same sounds as stare? (stop) Which letter is next to the word stop? (B) Fill in answer circle B in sample A at the bottom of the page. (Check to make sure that everyone understands how to do this.)

- Look again at the words in sample A. Which words begin with the same letter as stop? (share and skid) Say these three words with stare. (stop, share, skid) Can you hear why only stop is correct? Only stop has the same beginning sounds as stare. Say these two words together: stare, stop. Do not be confused by words that begin with the same letter as the word I say. Match the sounds, not the letters.

- Now look at sample B. Who can read the words in this section aloud for us? Listen carefully. Which word has the same ending sound as four? (more) What letter is next to the word more? (H) Find the row for sample B at the bottom of the page and fill in circle H. (Review the directions for finding the item numbers and answer choice letters at the bottom of the page.)

- Now we will do the rest of the page. Make sure that you listen carefully to my directions for matching beginning or ending sounds. Sometimes you will need to match a single sound. Sometimes you will need to match more than one sound or a combination of sounds. If you are matching more than one sound, some of the answer choices might have one of the same sounds. But only one answer choice will have all of the same beginning or ending sounds.

- Listen carefully to the word I say. Then read the answer choices and decide which word begins or ends with the same sound or sounds as the word I say. Fill in the answer circle for that word.

- Item 1. Fill in the circle for the word that has the same beginning sound as tenth . . . the same *beginning* sound as tenth.

- Item 2. Fill in the circle for the word that has the same beginning sound as someone . . . the same *beginning* sound as someone.

- Item 3. Fill in the circle for the word that has the same beginning sound as run . . . the same *beginning* sound as run.

- Item 4. Fill in the circle for the word that has the same beginning sound as glad . . . the same *beginning* sound as glad.

- Item 5. Fill in the circle for the word that has the same beginning sound as swallow . . . the same *beginning* sound as swallow.

- Find item 6 near the top of the second column. Fill in the circle for the word that has the same ending sound as four . . . the same *ending* sound as four.

- Item 7. Fill in the circle for the word that has the same ending sound as fort . . . the same *ending* sound as fort.

- Item 8. Fill in the circle for the word that has the same ending sound as cake . . . the same *ending* sound as cake.

- Item 9. Fill in the circle for the word that has the same ending sound as sang . . . the same *ending* sound as sang.

- Item 10. Fill in the circle for the word that has the same ending sound as made . . . the same *ending* sound as made.

Teacher Scripts

Word Analysis: Consonant Sounds—Initial and Final   SPP 34

- Open your book to page _____. (Check to make sure that everyone has found the right place.)

- On this page you will match words that begin or end with the same sounds. Look at the directions at the top of the page and read them to yourself as I read them aloud. (Read the directions to your students.)

- Look at the words in sample A. Who can read them aloud for us? Now listen carefully. Which word begins with the same sounds as the word trip? (truck) Which letter is under the word truck? (B) Fill in answer circle B in sample A at the bottom of the page.

- Now look at sample B. Who can read the words in sample B out loud for us? Which letters are underlined in each word? (lt, nd, th) The letters that are underlined in each word stand for the sounds at the end of the words. The letters are underlined to help you match the ending sounds. Now listen carefully. Which of the words in sample B ends with the same sound as the word fault . . . fault? (tilt) What letter is under the word tilt? (F) Fill in answer circle F in sample B at the bottom of the page. (Check to see that the students have found the answer circles for the samples and filled in the correct ones.)

- Now we will do the rest of the page. Listen carefully to the word I say. Then read the answer choices and decide which word begins or ends with the same sound or sounds as the word I said. The underlined letters in the words will help you. Fill in the circle for your answer choice.

- Item 1. Fill in the answer circle for the word that *begins* with the same sound as the word swan . . . swan.

- Item 2. Fill in the answer circle for the word that *begins* with the same sound as the word bread . . . bread.

- Item 3. Fill in the answer circle for the word that *begins* with the same sound as the word dread . . . dread.

- Item 4. Fill in the answer circle for the word that *begins* with the same sound as the word sleep . . . sleep.

- Item 5. Fill in the answer circle for the word that *ends* with the same sound as the word sand . . . sand.

- Item 6. Fill in the answer circle for the word that *ends* with the same sound as the word lamp . . . lamp.

- Item 7. Fill in the answer circle for the word that *ends* with the same sound as the word cracked . . . cracked.

- Item 8. Fill in the answer circle for the word that *ends* with the same sound as the word dash . . . dash.

Teacher Scripts

Word Analysis: Consonant Sounds/Vowel Sounds

- Open your book to page _____. (Check to make sure that everyone has found the right place.)

- On this page you will match words that begin or end with the same sounds. Look at the directions at the top of the page and read them to yourself as I read them aloud. (Read the directions to your students.)

- Look at sample A. There are three answer choices in sample A. Who can read them out loud for us? Which letters are underlined? (th, tr, st) The letters that are underlined in each word stand for the sound at the beginning of the word. The letters are underlined to help you match the sounds. Now listen carefully. Which of the words in sample A begins with the same sound as the word treat . . . treat? (truck) What letter is under the word truck? (B) Fill in answer circle B in sample A at the bottom of the page.

- Now look at sample B. The word at the beginning of the row has an underlined part. Find the word that has the same vowel sound as the underlined part. Which word did you choose? (roam) Yes, roam has the same vowel sound as cone. What letter is under roam? (D) Fill in answer circle D in sample B at the bottom of the page. (Check to see that the students have found the answer circles for the samples and filled in the correct ones.)

- Now we will do the rest of the page. Listen carefully to the word I say. Then read the answer choices and decide which word begins or ends with the same sound or sounds as the word I said. The underlined letters in the words will help you. Fill in the circle for your answer choice.

- Item 1. Find the word that has the same *beginning* sound as help . . . help. Fill in the circle for your answer.

- Item 2. Find the word that has the same *beginning* sound as clap . . . clap. Fill in the circle for your answer.

- Item 3. Find the word that has the same *ending* sound as wand . . . wand. Fill in the circle for your answer.

- Item 4. Find the word that has the same *ending* sound as toward . . . toward. Fill in the circle for your answer.

- Look at items 5 through 8. The first word in each row has a part underlined. As we did in sample B, fill in the answer circle for the other word in the row that has the same vowel sound.

- Work by yourself to finish the page.

Teacher Scripts

Word Analysis: Consonant Sounds

- Open your book to page _____. (Check to make sure that everyone has found the right place.)

- On this page you will find words that do not have the same consonant sounds as other words. Look at the directions at the top of the page and read them to yourself as I read them aloud. (Read the directions to your students.)

- Look at sample A. Read the first word. What part of the word jelly is underlined? (the letter j) Now say each answer choice word to yourself and listen for the same sound as the j in jelly. Which word does not have the same sound as the j in jelly? (gas) What letter is under the word gas? (C) Now look at the answer rows at the bottom of the page. Find the four answer circles that follow the capital letter A. These four circles are for sample A. Fill in the answer circle that has a C in it. (Check to see that the students have done this correctly.)

- Now look at sample B. Read the first word. Then say the four answer choices to yourself and listen for the same sound as the underlined part of the first word. Find the word that does not have the same sound. Which word does not have the same sound as the th in breathe? (through) What letter is under the word through? (G) Now find the answer circles for sample B at the bottom of the page. Fill in the circle with a G in it because the word through does not have the same sound as the underlined part of breathe. (Check to see that the students have done this correctly.)

- Now you will work by yourself to do the rest of the page. Remember, you are to look for the word that does not have the same sound as the underlined part of the first word. Match the sounds, not the letters. Then fill in the answer circle for your choice at the bottom of the page.

Word Analysis: Vowel Sounds

- Open your book to page _____. (Check to make sure that everyone has found the right place.)

- On this page you will match vowel sounds. Look at the directions at the top of the page and read them to yourself as I read them aloud. (Read the directions to your students.)

- Look at sample A. What is the word with the underlined letter? (skip) What sound does the underlined letter stand for? /i/ Yes, the underlined letter in skip stands for the short /i/ vowel sound. Which one of the three words below skip has the same vowel sound? (fill) The word fill has the same vowel sound as the word skip. Now find the answer circles for sample A at the bottom of the page. Fill in the circle with a C in it because the word fill has the same sound as the underlined part of skip. (Check to see that the students have done this correctly.)

- Now look at sample B. What is the word with the underlined letters? (food) Which answer has the same vowel sound as food? Fill in answer circle H for sample B at the bottom of the page because the word moon has the same vowel sound as the word food. (Check to see that the students have done this correctly.)

- Now you will work by yourself to finish the page. Find a match for the vowel sound of each word. Remember the same vowel sound may be spelled in different ways. Match the sounds, not the letters. Then fill in the circle for your answer choice at the bottom of the page.

Teacher Scripts

Word Analysis: Vowel Sounds   SPP 38

- Open your book to page _____. (Check to make sure that everyone has found the right place.)

- On this page you will match words with the same vowel sounds. Look at the directions at the top of the page and read them to yourself as I read them aloud. (Read the directions to your students.)

- Look at sample A. One word in the box, hat, has a part that is underlined. Say the word and listen to the sound of the underlined part. What vowel sound do you hear in hat? (short /a/) Now say each answer choice and listen for the vowel sound in each word. Which word has the same short /a/ vowel sound as hat? Find the answer choices for sample A at the bottom of the page and fill in circle D.

- Now look at sample B. Say the word with the underlined part. Now say each answer choice. Which word has the same vowel sound as the underlined part of rice? (kind, answer choice G) Fill in circle G for sample B at the bottom of the page.

- Now you will work by yourself to finish the page. Find a match for the vowel sound of each word. Remember the same vowel sound may be spelled in different ways. Match the sounds, not the letters. Then fill in the answer circle for your choice at the bottom of the page.

Word Analysis: Vowel Sounds   SPP 39

- Open your book to page _____. (Check to make sure that everyone has found the right place.)

- On this page you will match words with the same vowel sounds. Look at the directions at the top of the page and read them to yourself as I read them aloud. (Read the directions to your students.)

- Look at sample A. Read the first word. What vowel sound do you hear in the word mole? (long /o/) Now read the four other words in the row. Say each answer choice to yourself and listen to the vowel sound in each word. Which word has a vowel sound like the vowel sound in mole? (road, answer choice C) Fill in circle C for sample A at the bottom of the page.

- Now look at sample B. Read the first word. What vowel sound do you hear in the word clock? (short /o/) Now read the four other words in the row. Say each answer choice to yourself and listen to the vowel sound in each word. Which word has a vowel sound like the vowel sound in clock? (drop, answer choice G) Fill in circle G for sample B at the bottom of the page.

- Now you will work by yourself to finish the page. Find a match for the vowel sound of each word. Remember the same vowel sound may be spelled in different ways. Match the sounds, not the letters. Then fill in the answer circle for your choice at the bottom of the page.

Teacher Scripts

Word Analysis: Compound Words SPP 40

- Open your book to page _____. (Check to make sure that everyone has found the right place.)
- On this page you will match words together to make compound words. Look at the directions at the top of the page and read them to yourself as I read them aloud. (Read the directions to your students.)
- Look at sample A. Read the underlined word. Now read the four answer choices. One of these words can be added to the underlined word to make a new word. Which word can be added to side to make a new word? (walk) Yes, if the word walk is added to side, it makes a compound word: sidewalk. Fill in circle D for sample A at the bottom of the page.
- Now you will work by yourself to finish the page. Read each underlined word and find the answer choice that can be added to it to form a compound word. Then fill in the answer circle for your choice at the bottom of the page.

Word Analysis: Compound Words SPP 41

- Open your book to page _____. (Check to make sure that everyone has found the right place.)
- On this page you will find compound words. Compound words are words that are made up of two or more smaller words. Look at the directions at the top of the page and read them to yourself as I read them aloud. (Read the directions to your students.)
- Look at sample A. Read the sentence and look at the underlined word part. Now read the four answer choices. What are they? (case, end, mark, and keeper) Fill in circle A for sample A at the bottom of the page because the word *bookcase* is the compound word that fits best in the sentence. The other words also make compound words when they are attached to book (bookend, bookmark, bookkeeper), but these words do not make as much sense in the sentence.
- Now you will work by yourself to finish the page. Read each sentence and look at the underlined word part. Then choose the answer that can be added to the word part to form a compound word. Fill in the answer circle for your choice at the bottom of the page.

Word Analysis: Root Words and Affixes SPP 42

- Open your book to page _____. (Check to make sure that everyone has found the right place.)
- On this page you will find the root words and affixes of words. Affixes can be either prefixes or suffixes. Look at the directions at the top of the page and read them to yourself as I read them aloud. (Read the directions to your students.)
- Look at sample A. The first word, international, is underlined. What is the root word of international? (nation) Now look for the word nation among the answer choices. What letter is under the word nation? (C) Find the answer circles for sample A at the bottom of the page. Fill in answer circle C for sample A because nation is the root word of international.
- Look at sample B. Read the underlined word. You are to find the prefix of submarine. What is the root word of submarine? (marine) What prefix was added at the beginning of the word submarine? (sub) Now look at the four answer choices. Which answer choice is the correct one? (choice F, sub) Find the answer circles for sample B and fill in circle F.
- Look at sample C. Read the underlined word. You are to find the suffix of wonderful. What is the root word of wonderful? (wonder) What suffix was added at the end of the word wonderful? (ful) Now look at the four answer choices. Which answer choice is the correct one? (choice D, ful) Find the answer circles for sample C and fill in circle D.
- Work by yourself to finish the page. Read the directions and the items. Fill in the answer circles for your choices at the bottom of the page.

Teacher Scripts

Word Analysis: Syllabication SPP 43

- Open your book to page _____. (Check to make sure that everyone has found the right place.)

- On this page you will divide words into syllables. Look at the directions at the top of the page and read them to yourself as I read them aloud. (Read the directions to your students.)

- Look at sample A. What is the word in this sample? (himself) Yes, the word is himself. Listen to the parts of the word: him-self. Fill in the circle for answer choice A in sample A because this answer shows the correct way to divide the word into syllables.

- Now look at sample B. What is the word in this sample? (because) Which answer choice shows the correct way to divide the word because into syllables? (G) Find the answer circles for sample B at the bottom of the page and fill in circle G.

- Work by yourself to finish the page. In each item find the answer that has been correctly divided into syllables. Fill in the answer circle for your choice at the bottom of the page.

Vocabulary: Synonyms SPP 44

- Open your book to page _____. (Check to make sure that everyone has found the right place.)

- On this page you will find words that have the same or almost the same meanings. Look at the directions at the top of the page and read them to yourself as I read them aloud. (Read the directions to your students.)

- Look at sample A. Read the phrase. Which word is underlined? (slight) Now read the four words under the phrase. Each word makes sense in the phrase. You can have a huge change, an important change, a small change, or a slow change, so you have to think about the meaning of the word slight to find the right answer. Which answer choice has the same or almost the same meaning as slight? (small) What letter is in front of the word small? (C) Find the answer circles for sample A at the bottom of the page and fill in circle C.

- Now look at sample B. Read the phrase to yourself and think about the meaning of the underlined word. Then read the four words under the phrase. Which word in the phrase is underlined? (distant) Which word has the same or almost the same meaning as distant? (faraway) Which letter is in front of the word faraway? (G) Find the answer circles for sample B at the bottom of the page and fill in circle G.

- Work by yourself to finish the page. In each item find the word that has the same or almost the same meaning as the underlined word in the phrase. Fill in the answer circle for your choice at the bottom of the page.

Teacher Scripts

Vocabulary: Antonyms

SPP 45

- Open your book to page _____. (Check to make sure that everyone has found the right place.)
- On this page you will find words that have opposite meanings. Look at the directions at the top of the page and read them to yourself as I read them aloud. (Read the directions to your students.)
- Look at sample A. Read the phrase. Which word is underlined? (valuable) Now read the four words under the phrase. Each word makes sense in the phrase. Statues can be ancient, worthless, beautiful, or modern, so you have to think about the meaning of the word valuable to find the right answer. Which answer choice word means the opposite of valuable? (worthless) What letter is in front of the word worthless? (B) Find the answer circles for sample A at the bottom of the page and fill in circle B.
- Now look at sample B. Read the phrase to yourself and think about the meaning of the underlined word. Then read the four words under the phrase. Which word in the phrase is underlined? (obedient) Which answer choice word means the opposite of obedient? (naughty) Which letter is in front of the word naughty? (H) Find the answer circles for sample B at the bottom of the page and fill in circle H.
- Work by yourself to finish the page. In each item find the word that has the opposite meaning as the underlined word in the phrase. Fill in the answer circle for your choice at the bottom of the page.

Vocabulary: Word Meanings

SPP 46

- Open your book to page _____. (Check to make sure that everyone has found the right place.)
- On this page you will answer questions about word meanings. Look at the directions at the top of the page and read them to yourself as I read them aloud. (Read the directions to your students.)
- Look at sample A. Listen as I read the sentence. Then read the answer choices to yourself as I read them out loud. This is the sentence: An ancient ruin is one that is very—A. old . . . B. new . . . C. ugly . . . D. small. Which word completes the sentence correctly? (old) Yes, old is the correct answer because ancient means very old. Find the answer circles for sample A at the bottom of the page and fill in circle A for old.
- Now look at sample B. Listen as I read the sentence. Then read the answer choices to yourself as I read them out loud. This is the sentence: A cooperative person is—F. generous . . . G. helpful . . . H. naughty . . . J. polite. Which word completes the sentence correctly? (helpful) Find the answer circles for sample B at the bottom of the page and fill in circle G for helpful.
- Now we will finish the page. Listen carefully as I read each sentence. Then follow along in your booklet as I read the answer choices. Choose the best answer for each item.
- Item 1. Something that feels fluffy is—A. hard . . . B. soft . . . C. rough . . . D. slippery.
- Item 2. If you are flexible, you can—F. jump . . . G. run . . . H. bend . . . J. sleep.
- Item 3. To guard something is to—A. lose it . . . B. break it . . . C. release it . . . D. protect it.
- Item 4. To inquire is to—F. ask . . . G. answer . . . H. reply . . . J. fail.
- Item 5. A journey is—A. a visit . . . B. a trip . . . C. a diary . . . D. an adventure.
- Item 6. A pastime can be—F. a career . . . G. a clock . . . H. a hobby . . . J. an experience.
- Item 7. A thief is a—A. robber . . . B. tool . . . C. police officer . . . D. store.
- Item 8. To pause is to—F. proceed . . . G. stop . . . H. pass . . . J. finish.
- Item 9. To yell is to—A. complain . . . B. whisper . . . C. shout . . . D. rip.
- Item 10. To recall is to—F. phone . . . G. forget . . . H. discuss . . . J. remember.

Teacher Scripts

Vocabulary: Derivations SPP 47

- Open your book to page _____. (Check to make sure that everyone has found the right place.)
- On this page you will find words that have come to us from other languages. Look at the directions at the top of the page and read them to yourself as I read them aloud. (Read the directions to your students.)
- Look at sample A. Read the question and think about what you are supposed to do. (discuss) Now, which answer probably comes from the Latin word granum meaning a seed? Which word sounds like the Latin word and means a kind of seed? (grain) What letter is in front of the word grain? (B) Find the answer circles for sample A at the bottom of the page and fill in circle B.
- Now look at sample B. Which answer probably comes from the German word schnarren meaning to growl? Which word sounds like the German word and means a growling kind of noise? (snore) What letter is in front of the word snore? (H) Find the answer circles for sample B at the bottom of the page and fill in circle H.
- Work by yourself to finish the page. In each item find the word that probably comes from the word given in the question. Think about both the sound and the meaning. Fill in the answer circle for your choice at the bottom of the page.

Vocabulary: Multiple Meanings SPP 48

- Open your book to page _____. (Check to make sure that everyone has found the right place.)
- On this page you will find words that have two meanings. Look at the directions at the top of the page and read them to yourself as I read them aloud. (Read the directions to your students.)
- Look at sample A. There are two underlined word meanings in this sample. Both meanings are for the same word. Read the first meaning. Read the second meaning. Now read each of the answer choice words and check them against both meanings. Which word can mean a kind of bird and went in head first? (dove) Which letter is in front of the word dove? (D) Find the answer circles for sample A at the bottom of the page and fill in circle D.
- Now look at sample B. Read the two underlined meanings. Now read each of the answer choice words and check them against both meanings. Which word can mean a source of water and a metal coil? (spring) Which letter is in front of the word spring? (G) Find the answer circles for sample B at the bottom of the page and fill in circle G.
- Work by yourself to finish the page. In each item find the word that fits both of the underlined meanings. Fill in the answer circle for your choice at the bottom of the page.

Vocabulary: Multiple Meanings SPP 49

- Open your book to page _____. (Check to make sure that everyone has found the right place.)
- On this page you will find words that have more than one meaning. Look at the directions at the top of the page and read them to yourself as I read them aloud. (Read the directions to your students.)
- Look at sample A. Read the two sentences for sample A to yourself. (pause) Now look at the four answer choices below the sentences. Think carefully. Which one of the four answer choices will fit in both sentences? (pause) The correct answer is D, note. (He left a note to tell his mother where he was going. The musician hit a wrong note. If necessary, explain the two meanings of note.) Find the answer circles for sample A at the bottom of the page and fill in circle D.
- Look at sample B. Read the sentences and find the word that fits best in both sentences. (pause) Which answer choice is correct? (G) Yes, pass fits in both sentences. Find the answer circles for sample B at the bottom of the page and fill in circle G.
- Work by yourself to finish the page. In each item find the word that fits best in both sentences. Fill in the answer circle for your choice at the bottom of the page.

Teacher Scripts

Vocabulary: Affix Meanings

SPP 50

- Open your book to page _____. (Check to make sure that everyone has found the right place.)

- On this page you will identify the meanings of prefixes and suffixes in words. Look at the directions at the top of the page and read them to yourself as I read them aloud. (Read the directions to your students.)

- Look at sample A. There are two words with the prefix in underlined. A prefix is one or more letters added before a word to form a different word. Read the two words. Now think about the meanings of the words inactive and indirect. What does the prefix mean in both words? (not) Inactive means not active and indirect means not direct. Look at the four answer choices. Which answer choice gives the meaning of the prefix in? (answer choice B, not) Find the answer circles for sample A at the bottom of the page and fill in circle B.

- Look at sample B. There are two words with the suffix less underlined. A suffix is one or more letters added after a word to form a different word. Read the first word. What does speechless mean? (with no ability to speak) What does worthless mean? (with little or no worth) Now look at the four answer choices. Which answer choice best tells the meaning of the suffix less as used in the words speechless and worthless? (answer choice G, without) Find the answer circles for sample B at the bottom of the page and fill in circle G.

- Work by yourself to finish the page. In each item find the answer that best tells the meaning of the prefix or suffix that is underlined in the two words. Fill in the answer circle for your choice at the bottom of the page.

Vocabulary: Words in Context

SPP 51, 52

- Open your book to page _____. (Check to make sure that everyone has found the right place.)

- On this page you will find the words that fit best in the sentences that you read. Look at the directions at the top of the page and read them to yourself as I read them aloud. (Read the directions to your students.)

- Look at sample A. Read the sentence. A word is underlined. If you do not know the word, the sentence will help you figure out its meaning. Read the sentence. Which word is underlined? (gems) Now look at the four words under the sentence. Which word has the same or almost the same meaning as the underlined word and makes sense with the other words in the sentence? (jewels) Yes, jewels means the same thing as the word gems in this sentence. What letter is next to the word jewels? (B) Find the answer circles for sample A at the bottom of the page and fill in circle B.

- Now look at sample B. This is a sentence with a missing word. Read the sentence. Now read the sentence with each of the answer choices in place of the blank. Which word makes the most sense in the sentence? (gloomy) What is the complete sentence? (After two weeks of gloomy weather, we were glad when the sun broke through the clouds.) Why are the other answer choices not as good? (They do not make sense with the other words in the sentence.) Look at the answer choices again. What letter is next to gloomy? (G) Find the answer circles for sample B at the bottom of the page and fill in circle G.

- Now you can work by yourself to finish the exercise. Do questions 1 through 4 in the same way that we did sample A. When you come to the word **Go** after question 4, turn to the next page. Then do questions 5 through 8 the same way that we did sample B. For questions 9 through 12, read the directions carefully. Find the words that will make the most sense in the paragraph. Fill in the answer circles for your choices at the bottom of the pages. Work until you come to the word **Stop.**

Teacher Scripts

Reading Comprehension: Listening

- Turn to page _____ in your test booklet. (Check to make sure that everyone has found the right place.)

- On this page you will listen to stories and answer questions about them. Look at the directions at the top of the page and read them to yourself as I read them aloud. (Read the directions to your students.)

- Find sample A. Listen to the story, the question, and the answer choices I am about to read. Here is the story:

    "Mom," said Donald, "may I go to the park and play baseball with some of the guys?"

    "Yes," said his mother, "but be home for lunch because Grandma is coming."

- Here is the question for sample A. Donald asked to play baseball in the—A. park . . . B. field . . . C. street . . . D. yard. What is the answer? (park) Find the answer circles for sample A at the bottom of the page and fill in circle A for park.

- Now look at sample B. Here is the question for sample B. Donald's Grandma is coming for—F. breakfast . . . G. lunch . . . H. dinner . . . J. tea. What is the answer? (lunch) Find the answer circles for sample B at the bottom of the page and fill in circle G for lunch.

- Now we will finish the page together. Listen carefully as I read the stories and the answer choices. Fill in the circles for your answers as you did in the samples.

- Find items 1 and 2. Listen to this story.

    North American black bears are sometimes called "the clowns of the woods" because of their funny tricks. They may dance, stand on their heads, and stretch out their paws to beg for food. Black bears can run fast and are skillful tree climbers. Although they do not usually fight, they will defend their cubs.

- Item 1. Because North American black bears do tricks, they are sometimes called—

    A. beggars . . . B. dancers . . . C. tree climbers . . . D. clowns.

- Item 2. Black bears will fight to defend their—F. cubs . . . G. food . . . H. trees . . . J. tricks.

- Find items 3 through 5. Listen to the story.

    The astronauts had landed on the moon. The surface looked silvery gray under their feet as they bounded along. When they looked up, they could see the earth. It looked very blue against the blackness of space. It was so beautiful that they could hardly stop looking long enough to do the scientific experiments that were the reason for their mission.

    The astronauts gathered samples of rocks. They measured their own reactions: blood pressure, pulse, and body temperature. They set up some test instruments that would keep working after they left. Then they were ready to return to earth.

- Item 3. The astronauts were on the moon to—A. look around . . . B. climb . . . C. do experiments . . . D. land.

- Item 4. From the moon the earth looked—F. silver . . . G. gray . . . H. blue . . . J. black.

Teacher Scripts

Reading Comprehension: Listening *(cont.)*

- Item 5. They left some instruments that would keep working to measure—A. blood pressure . . . B. pulse . . . C. rocks . . . D. The story does not say.

- Find items 6 and 7. Listen to the story.

  The Children's Library is offering after-school activities called "Fun with Magnets, Electricity, and Simple Machines." Students in grades three through six are invited to take part. Anyone who is interested can sign up at the Children's Library on Main Street.

- Item 6. What kind of activities are being offered at the Children's Library? F. music . . . G. acting . . . H. art . . . J. science

- Item 7. If you want to take part, you must—A. pay a fee . . . B. sign up . . . C. bring a parent . . . D. make a poster.

- Find the box with items 8 through 10. Listen to the story.

  Marci cleaned her room and sorted out her toys. She found a box of stuffed animals that she had not played with in a long time. She looked at them all lovingly and remembered how much fun she had had with each one. She took one brown bear, gave him a hug, and set him up on a shelf. "Mother," Marci said, "do you think I could give the old stuffed animals in this box to the children's hospital? I don't play with them anymore, and they might make someone happy."

- Item 8. What is the best word to describe Marci? F. mean . . . G. impatient . . . H. generous . . . J. lazy

- Item 9. Marci probably put the brown bear up on a shelf because he was—A. too old . . . B. too dirty . . . C. her sister's . . . D. her favorite.

- Item 10. What other toys were in Marci's room? F. dolls . . . G. games . . . H. blocks . . . J. The story does not say.

Teacher Scripts

Reading Comprehension: Stories

Explanatory Notes

1. The sample for "Reading Comprehension: Stories" consists of one page. A short story is followed by five questions. The skills tested are indicated by the numbers listed in the "Table of Contents." In the sample, these skills are

   3 (Main Ideas)   17 (Character)
   2 (Details)   1 (Word Meanings)
   7 (Drawing Conclusions)

   The sample will give students an idea of the story format.

2. The Student Practice Pages for "Reading Comprehension: Stories" consist of four sections, each of which is comprised of five pages. Each section contains two stories. Part of a continued story appears on each page and is followed by five questions. Within each section, all of the reading comprehension skills are tested once. Skill 1, Word Meaning is tested five times.

   In this way, each two-story section tests a full range of comprehension skills. If you include all four stories in your practice test, you will assess each skill four times. Word meanings will be assessed twenty times.

   The comprehension skills are listed by number in the "Table of Contents" and below for your convenience.

1. **Word Meanings**	12. **Relationships**
2. **Details**	13. **Author's Purpose**
3. **Main Idea**	14. **Figurative Language**
4. **Sequence**	15. **Interpreting Events**
5. **Cause and Effect**	16. **Plot**
6. **Inferring the Main Idea**	17. **Characters**
7. **Drawing Conclusions**	18. **Mood**
8. **Predicting Outcomes**	19. **Setting**
9. **Identifying Feelings**	20. **Making Comparisons**
10. **Reality and Fantasy**	21. **Analogies**
11. **Fact and Opinion**	

Note: The comprehension skill numbers are noted on the appropriate answer key pages at the back of this book.

Teacher Scripts

Reading Comprehension: Stories—Sample (Skills 3, 2, 4, 11, 1)   SPP 54

- Turn to page _____ in your test booklet. (Check to make sure that everyone has found the right place.)

- On this page you will answer questions about a story you read. Find the directions at the top of the page and read them to yourself as I read them aloud. (Read the directions to your students.)

- Read the story in the first column to yourself. Look at the five questions in the second column. Each question has four answer choices. Check back in the story to decide on your answers. Fill in the circles by your answer choices at the bottom of the page.

- Which answer did you choose for item number 1? (C, how Jeff's plans affect his family) Yes, this story is mainly about how Jeff's plans affect his family. Which answer did you choose for the item number 2? (G, a detective) When Jeff wanted to be a detective, he used a notebook and pencil. Which answer did you choose for item number 3? (C, he knows Jeff will want him to take part in the project) Jeff's brother knows this because he has had experience with Jeff's other career plans. Which answer did you choose for item number 4? (G, making new plans) This is the best description of Jeff. Which answer did you choose for item number 5? (A, mixed up in) Involved means to be mixed up in something.

- Now you are ready to read more stories and answer questions about them.

Reading Comprehension: Stories—Sections 1–4 (All Skills)   SPP 55–74

- Turn to page _____ in your test booklet. (Check to make sure that everyone has found the right place.)

- On the following pages you will answer questions about the stories you will read. Find the directions at the top of the page and read them to yourself as I read them aloud.

- Read the story in the first column to yourself. Look at the five questions in the second column. Each question has four answer choices. Check back in the story to decide on your answers. Fill in the circles by your answer choices at the bottom of the page.

- When you come to the arrow at the bottom, turn to the next page to read more of the stories. Keep going until you come to the stop sign.

Teacher Scripts

Critical Reading: Interpreting Figurative Language

SPP 75

- Turn to page _____ in your test booklet. (Check to make sure that everyone has found the right place.)

- On this page you will identify the meanings of phrases in sentences. Find the directions at the top of the page and read them to yourself as I read them aloud.

- Look at sample A. Read the sentence. Find the underlined phrase "ate like a pig." Think about what the phrase "ate like a pig" really means in the sentence. What do you really mean when you say "He ate like a pig"? (C, ate far too much) Find the answer choices for sample A at the bottom of the page and fill in answer circle C because "ate far too much" means the same thing as the phrase "ate like a pig."

- Now look at sample B. Read the sentence to yourself. What is the underlined phrase? (roared fiercely) Think about the real meaning of the phrase. Imagine the wind roaring fiercely. Now read the answer choices. Which answer choice has the same or almost the same meaning as the phrase "roared fiercely" as it is used in the sentence? (F, blew loudly) Find the answer choices for sample B at the bottom of the page and fill circle F.

- Work by yourself to finish the page. In each item, look for the answer choice that tells the meaning of the phrase as it is used in the sentence. Fill in your answer choice at the bottom of the page.

Critical Reading: Recognizing Story Structures

SPP 76

- Turn to page _____ in your test booklet. (Check to make sure that everyone has found the right place.)

- On this page you will answer questions about passages you will read. Find the directions at the top of the page and read them to yourself as I read them aloud.

- Look at sample A. Read the passage and then read the question and the answer choices. Look back at the passage to check. Where might you read a passage like this one? (B, newspaper article) Information like this, about a current event, would most likely be found in a newspaper article. Find the answer choices for sample A at the bottom of the page and fill in circle B for newspaper article.

- Work by yourself to finish the page. In each item, read the passage and the question. Then choose the answer that you think is correct. Fill in your answer choice at the bottom of the page.

Teacher Scripts

Spelling

Note:

- The formats for testing spelling skills differ widely among the tests, even from grade level to grade level. As often as possible, these testing formats are identified for you on the title line at the beginning of each script and practice page.

- You may want to give your students the benefit of trying all of these formats, or you may wish to use the *Spelling List* (page 192) to create more practice pages of your own in the appropriate format(s). The *Spelling List* contains many words that are tested as well as those used as distracters in the various spelling items.

Spelling Skills (CAT/CTBS)

> **SPP 77**

- Turn to page _____ in your test booklet. Find the number _____ at the top of the page and put your finger on it. (Check to make sure that everyone has found the right number.)

- On this page you will find the correct spellings of words that complete sentences. Look at the directions at the top of the page. Read them to yourself as I read them aloud. (Read the directions to your students.)

- Look at sample A. There is a sentence with a blank. The blank shows that a word is missing. Read the sentence. Now look at the four words under the sentence. One word shows the right way to spell the missing word. Which answer choice shows the correct spelling of the word that belongs in the sentence? (choice B) Yes, c-a-l-e-n-d-a-r is the correct spelling of the word calendar. Find the answer circles for sample A at the bottom of the page and fill in circle B.

- Now look at sample B. Read the sentence. Look at the four answer choices and find the correct spelling of the missing word. Which answer choice shows the correct spelling of the word that belongs in the sentence? (choice J) Yes, a-s-s-i-g-n-m-e-n-t is the correct spelling of the word assignment. Find the answer circles for sample B at the bottom of the page and fill in circle J.

- Work by yourself. Finish the rest of the page in the same way that we did the samples. Fill in your answer choices at the bottom of the page.

Spelling Skills (CAT/CTBS)

> **SPP 78**

- Turn to page _____ in your test booklet. Find the number _____ at the top of the page and put your finger on it. (Check to make sure that everyone has found the right number.)

- On this page you will see how well you can spell words. Look at the directions at the top of the page. Read them to yourself as I read them aloud. (Read the directions to your students.)

- Look at sample A. Read the four phrases. Find the underlined word that is spelled incorrectly. Which answer has an incorrectly spelled word? (choice C) The correct spelling of explain is e-x-p-l-a-i-n. Find the answer circles for sample A at the bottom of the page and fill in circle C.

- Look at sample B. Read the four phrases. Find the underlined word that is spelled incorrectly. Which answer has an incorrectly spelled word? (choice F) The correct spelling of hurricane is h-u-r-r-i-c-a-n-e. Find the answer circles for sample B at the bottom of the page and fill in circle F.

- Work by yourself. Finish the rest of the page in the same way that we did the samples. Fill in your answer choices at the bottom of the page.

Teacher Scripts

Spelling

Spelling Skills (ITBS)

SPP 79

- Turn to page _____ in your test booklet. Find the number _____ at the top of the page and put your finger on it. (Check to make sure that everyone has found the right number.)

- On this page you will look for words with spelling mistakes. Look at the directions at the top of the page. Read them to yourself as I read them aloud. (Read the directions to your students.)

- Look at sample A. Look at the first word. Does it have a spelling mistake? (no) Look at the second word. Is it spelled correctly? (no) What is the word? (answer) How should answer be spelled? Yes, the word answer is spelled a-n-s-w-e-r, not a-n-s-e-r. Find the answer circles for sample A at the bottom of the page and fill in circle 2 because the second word has a spelling mistake.

- Look at sample B. Read the last answer choice. (no mistake) You should choose this answer only if all of the words in an item are spelled correctly. Now read the words in sample B and look for a word with a spelling mistake. Did you find a word with a mistake? (no) Which answer should you choose? (choice 5, no mistake) Find the answer circles for sample B at the bottom of the page and fill in circle 5.

- Work by yourself. Finish the rest of the page in the same way that we did the samples. Fill in your answer choices at the bottom of the page.

Spelling Skills (SAT)

SPP 80

- Turn to page _____ in your test booklet. Find the number _____ at the top of the page and put your finger on it. (Check to make sure that everyone has found the right number.)

- On this page you will look for words with spelling mistakes. Look at the directions at the top of the page. Read them to yourself as I read them aloud. (Read the directions to your students.)

- Look at sample A. Read the four words. Which word is spelled incorrectly? What is the correct answer? (B) Yes, B is the right answer because the word difference is spelled incorrectly. Who can tell me how it should be spelled? Find the answer circles for sample A at the bottom of the page and fill in circle B.

- Now look at sample B. Read the four words. Which word is spelled incorrectly? What is the correct answer? (J) Yes, J is the right answer because the word knowledge is spelled incorrectly. Who can tell me how it should be spelled? Find the answer circles for sample B at the bottom of the page and fill in circle J.

- Work by yourself. Finish the rest of the page in the same way that we did the samples. Fill in your answer choices at the bottom of the page.

Teacher Scripts

Spelling

Spelling Skills (SAT)

SPP 81

- Turn to page _____ in your test booklet. Find the number _____ at the top of the page and put your finger on it. (Check to make sure that everyone has found the right number.)

- On this page you will be looking for the word that is spelled incorrectly for the way it is used in a phrase. Look at the directions at the top of the page. Read them to yourself as I read them aloud. (Read the directions to your students.)

- Look at sample A. Which underlined word is spelled incorrectly for the way it is used in the phrase? Which answer did you choose? (A) Yes, A is the correct answer because the word whole is spelled incorrectly. How should the word be spelled in this phrase? (h-o-l-e) Find the answer circles for sample A at the bottom of the page and fill in circle A.

- Now look at sample B. Which underlined word is spelled incorrectly for the way it is used in the phrase? Which answer did you choose? (F) Yes, F is the correct answer because the word new is spelled incorrectly. How should the word be spelled in this phrase? (k-n-e-w) Find the answer circles for sample B at the bottom of the page and fill in circle F.

- Now work by yourself. Finish the rest of the page in the same way that we did the samples. Fill in your answer choices at the bottom of the page.

Spelling Skills (MAT)

SPP 82

- Turn to page_____ in your test booklet. Find the number_____at the top of the page and put your finger on it. (Check to see if everyone has found the number.)

- On this page you will look for words that have spelling mistakes. Look at the directions at the top of the page. Read them to yourself as I read them aloud. (Read the directions to your students.)

- Look at sample A. Read the sentence with the underlined words to yourself. Find the underlined word that has a spelling error. If there is no error, choose the last answer, no mistake. Which word has a spelling error? (the second one) Answer B, c-h-a-l-e-n-g-e, has a spelling error and should be spelled c-h-a-l-l-e-n-g-e. Find the answer circles for sample A at the bottom of the page and fill in circle B.

- Now do sample B. Find the underlined word that has a spelling error. If there is no error, choose the last answer, no mistake. Which answer choice is correct? (H) Yes, all of the words are spelled correctly. Find the answer circles for sample B at the bottom of the page and fill in circle H.

- Work by yourself to finish the page. In each item, read the sentence and look at the underlined words. Choose the word that has a spelling error. If there is no error, choose the last answer, no mistake. Fill in your answer choices at the bottom of the page.

Teacher Scripts

Spelling

Spelling Skills (MAT)

- Turn to page _____ in your test booklet. Find the number _____ at the top of the page and put your finger on it. (Check to make sure that everyone has found the right number.)

- On this page you will be looking for the correct spellings of the words that you hear. Look at the directions at the top of the page. Read them to yourself as I read them aloud. (Read the directions to your students.)

- Look at sample A. There are four words in this section. I am going to say a word, then read a sentence using the word, and then say the word one more time. Listen and look at the answer choices. Happy . . . Those children are happy . . . happy. Which answer choice shows the right spelling of the word happy? (choice B) Choice B, h-a-p-p-y, is the correct spelling of happy. Find the answer circles for sample A at the bottom of the page and fill in circle B.

- Now look at sample B. Listen and find the correct spelling of the word I say. Basket . . . Put the peaches in the basket . . . basket. Which answer choice shows the correct spelling of basket? (choice G) Find the answer circles for sample B at the bottom of the page and fill in circle G.

- Now we will do the rest of the page. I will read the word for each question, a sentence using the word, and then say the word once more. Listen and choose the answer for the correct spelling of the word.

- Item 1. Find the correct spelling for farmer . . . The farmer plowed his field . . . farmer.

- Item 2. lamb . . . Mary had a little lamb . . . lamb.

- Item 3. meet . . . She will meet her friends after school . . . meet.

- Item 4. except . . . Everyone went to the party except me . . . except.

- Item 5. chapter . . . Read the second chapter . . . chapter.

- Item 6. bought . . . He bought a present for his mother . . . bought.

- Item 7. night . . . We went to the movies last night . . . night.

- Item 8. worst . . . It was the worst storm we ever had . . . worst.

- Item 9. safety . . . Today we had a safety lesson . . . safety.

- Item 10. puppies . . . David's dog has six puppies . . . puppies.

Teacher Scripts

Language Mechanics: Capitalization (CAT/CTBS)

- Turn to page _____ in your test booklet. Find the number _____ at the top of the page and put your finger on it. (Check to make sure that everyone has found the right number.)

- On this page you will find mistakes in capitalization. Look at the directions at the top of the page. Read them to yourself as I read them aloud. (Read the directions to your students.)

- Look at sample A. This sentence has been divided into four parts. Read the first part of the sentence. Is there a word in this part that needs a capital letter? (no) Read the second part. Do you see a word in this part of the sentence that should begin with a capital letter? (yes) Which word is it? (new) Why should new begin with a capital letter? (New is part of the name of a city, and the names of cities always begin with capital letters.) What letter is under the second part of the sentence? (B) Find the answer circles for sample A at the bottom of the page and fill in circle B.

- Now look at sample B. Read the word that comes after the sentence. What is it? (*none*) The word *none* has a letter under it. You should fill in the answer circle for the word *none* only if no other capital letter is needed in the sentence. Now look at the sentence in sample B. Read each part to yourself and look for a word that should begin with a capital letter. Is there a word in any of the four parts of the sentence that needs a capital letter? (no) What should you do? (fill in the answer circle for none) Find the answer circles for sample B at the bottom of the page and fill in circle K.

- Do the rest of the page by yourself. Do items 1 through 8 in the same way that we did the samples. Fill in your answer choices at the bottom of the page.

Language Mechanics: Capitalization (ITBS)

- Turn to page _____ in your test booklet. Find the number _____ at the top of the page and put your finger on it. (Check to make sure that everyone has found the right number.)

- On this page you will look for capitalization mistakes. Look at the directions at the top of the page. Read them to yourself as I read them aloud. (Read the directions to your students.)

- Look at sample A. Each item in this lesson contains one or two sentences written on three lines. Now read line 4. (*no mistakes*) You should choose this answer only if an item does not have a capitalization mistake. Now read line 1 of sample A. Is there a capitalization mistake in this line? (no) Read line 2. Do you see a mistake in capitalization? (Yes, the word he should begin with a capital letter.) Why? (The first word of a sentence always begins with a capital letter.) Find the answer circles for sample A at the bottom of the page and fill in circle 2 because there is a capitalization mistake in line 2.

- Now look at sample B. Read the item to yourself line by line and look for a capitalization mistake. Did you find a mistake? (no) What should you do if an item does not have a mistake in capitalization? (fill in answer circle 4, *no mistakes*) Find the answer circles for sample B at the bottom of the page and fill in circle 4 because there are no capitalization mistakes.

- Do the rest of the page by yourself. Do items 1 through 10 in the same way that we did the samples. Fill in your answer choices at the bottom of the page.

Teacher Scripts

Language Mechanics: Capitalization (SAT) SPP 86

- Turn to page _____ in your test booklet. Find the number _____ at the top of the page and put your finger on it. (Check to make sure that everyone has found the right number.)

- On this page you will look for correctly capitalized words. Look at the directions at the top of the page. Read them to yourself as I read them aloud. (Read the directions to your students.)

- Look at sample A. Read the sentence. Which group of words is capitalized correctly? (B) Yes, B is the correct answer because the words in the name of a holiday always begin with capital letters. Find the answer circles for sample A at the bottom of the page and fill in circle B.

- Now look at sample B. Read the sentence. Which group of words is capitalized correctly? (J) Yes, J is the correct answer because the first word and important words in a title always begin with capital letters. Find the answer circles for sample B at the bottom of the page and fill in circle J.

- Do the rest of the page by yourself. Do items 1 through 8 in the same way that we did the samples. Fill in your answer choices at the bottom of the page.

Language Mechanics: Punctuation (CAT/CTBS) SPP 87

- Turn to page _____ in your test booklet. Find the number _____ at the top of the page and put your finger on it. (Check to make sure that everyone has found the right number.)

- On this page you will be looking for places in sentences where punctuation marks are needed. Look at the directions at the top of the page. Read them to yourself as I read them aloud. (Read the directions to your students.)

- Look at sample A. Read the sentence. Now look at the row of four punctuation marks underneath the sentence. What are they? (period, colon, comma, quotation mark) Look at the sentence and check to see if it needs one of these punctuation marks. Does the sentence need a punctuation mark? (yes) Does it need a period, a colon, a comma, or a quotation mark? (a comma) Where is the comma needed? (after the word knives) Why? (Commas are used to separate words in a series.) What letter is in front of the comma? (C) Find the answer circles for sample A at the bottom of the page and fill in circle C.

- Now look at sample B. Read the word at the end of the row of punctuation marks. What is the word? (*none*) The word *none* has a letter in front of it. You should fill in the answer circle for the word *none* only if no other punctuation mark is needed in a sentence. Now read the sentence in sample B to yourself. Then check to see if the sentence needs one of the punctuation marks given in the row of answer choices. Does the sentence need quotation marks, a comma, a period, or an exclamation mark? (no) That's right. The sentence has the correct punctuation. Not one of the punctuation marks under the sentence is needed. What letter is in front of the word none? (K) Find the answer circles for sample B at the bottom of the page and fill in circle K.

- Do the rest of the page by yourself. Do items 1 through 8 in the same way that we did the samples. Fill in your answer choices at the bottom of the page.

Teacher Scripts

Language Mechanics: Punctuation (CAT/CTBS) | SPP 88

- Turn to page _____ in your test booklet. Find the number _____ at the top of the page and put your finger on it. (Check to make sure that everyone has found the right number.)

- On this page you will be looking for the correct punctuation for parts of sentences. Look at the directions at the top of the page. Read them to yourself as I read them aloud. (Read the directions to your students.)

- Look at sample A. Read the sentence. Now look at the underlined part. It is the end of a quotation. What punctuation do you see? (quotation mark) Is this punctuation correct? (yes) The underlined part is also at the end of a sentence. What punctuation is needed at the end of a sentence? (an end mark) Read the sentence in sample A again. Does the underlined part have an end mark? (no) What end mark is needed? (a period) So the underlined part of the sentence should end with a period and quotation marks. Examine the answer choices and find the one that shows the correct punctuation for the underlined part of the sentence. Which one did you choose? (choice B) Find the answer circles for sample A at the bottom of the page and fill in circle B because it shows a period and quotation mark correctly used at the end of a sentence.

- Now look at sample B. Read the last answer choice. What is it? (*correct as it is*) You should fill in the answer circle for correct as it is only if the underlined part of the sentence already has the correct punctuation. Read the sentence in sample B to yourself. Does the underlined part of the sentence have the correct punctuation? (yes) What should you do? (fill in the answer circle for *correct as it is*) Find the answer circles for sample B at the bottom of the page and fill in circle K.

- Do the rest of the page by yourself. Do items 1 through 6 in the same way that we did the samples. Fill in your answer choices at the bottom of the page.

Language Mechanics: Punctuation (ITBS) | SPP 89

- Turn to page _____ in your test booklet. Find the number _____ at the top of the page and put your finger on it. (Check to make sure that everyone has found the right number.)

- On this page you will look for punctuation mistakes. Look at the directions at the top of the page. Read them to yourself as I read them aloud. (Read the directions to your students.)

- The items on this page contain one or two sentences written on three lines. Look at sample A. Which answer should you choose if an item does not have a punctuation mistake? (answer 4, *no mistakes*) Read line 1 of sample A. Is there a punctuation mistake in this line? (no) Read line 2. Do you see a mistake? (no) Read line 3. Does line 3 have a mistake in punctuation? (no) What should you do now? (fill in answer circle 4, *no mistakes*) Find the answer circles for sample A at the bottom of the page and fill in circle 4.

- Now look at sample B. Read the item to yourself line by line and stop if you find a line with a punctuation mistake. Did you find a mistake? (yes, in line 1) What is the mistake? (Quotation marks are needed in front of the word "Let's.") Yes, quotation marks are used around the exact words someone says. There are quotation marks at the end of Randy's words in line 3, but quotation marks are missing at the beginning of Randy's words in line 1. Find the answer circles for sample B at the bottom of the page and fill in circle 1 because there is a punctuation mistake in line 1.

- Do the rest of the page by yourself. Do items 1 through 10 in the same way that we did the samples. Fill in your answer choices at the bottom of the page.

Teacher Scripts

Language Mechanics: Punctuation (SAT)

- Turn to page _____ in your test booklet. Find the number _____ at the top of the page and put your finger on it. (Check to make sure that everyone has found the right number.)

- On this page you will be looking for correct punctuation. Look at the directions at the top of the page. Read them to yourself as I read them aloud. (Read the directions to your students.)

- Look at sample A. Read the sentence. Which word has the correct punctuation? Which answer did you choose? (B) Yes, B is the correct answer because this sentence is a question. A question should always be followed by a question mark. Find the answer circles for sample A at the bottom of the page and fill in circle B.

- Now look at sample B. Read the sentence. Which words have the correct punctuation? Which answer did you choose? (J) Yes, J is the correct answer because the name of a city should always be separated from the name of a state with a comma. Find the answer circles for sample B at the bottom of the page and fill in circle J.

- Do the rest of the page by yourself. Do items 1 through 8 in the same way that we did the samples. Fill in your answer choices at the bottom of the page.

Language Mechanics: Capitalization and Punctuation

- Turn to page _____ in your test booklet. Find the number _____ at the top of the page and put your finger on it. (Check to make sure that everyone has found the right number.)

- On this page you will look for sentences that have the correct capitalization and punctuation. Look at the directions at the top of the page. Read them to yourself as I read them aloud. (Read the directions to your students.)

- Read the sentences in sample A. Which one is correctly written with no capitalization or punctuation errors? (the third one, choice C) Yes, the third sentence is written correctly. There are no capitalization or punctuation mistakes. Find the answer circles for sample A at the bottom of the page and fill in circle C.

- Now look at sample B. This is a different type of item. Read the sentence with the underlined part. Then look at the answer choices. Find the answer choice that shows the correct capitalization and punctuation for the underlined part. If the part is correct, choose *correct as it is*. Which answer did you choose? (J) Yes, the underlined part is correct. Find the answer circles for sample B at the bottom of the page and fill in circle J.

- Do the rest of the page by yourself. For items 1 through 3, choose the sentence that has correct capitalization and punctuation. For items 4 through 6, choose the answer choice that shows the correct capitalization and punctuation for the underlined part. Choose *correct as it is* only if the underlined part has no errors. Fill in your answer choices at the bottom of the page.

Teacher Scripts

Language Expression: Usage

- Turn to page _____ in your test booklet. Find the number _____ at the top of the page and put your finger on it. (Check to make sure that everyone has found the right number.)

- On this page you will choose the best words to complete sentences or the pronouns to replace nouns in sentences. Look at the directions at the top of the page. Read them to yourself as I read them aloud. (Read the directions to your students.)

- Look at sample A. Find the sentence with a blank. The blank shows that one or more words are missing. Read the sentence. Now look at the words under the sentence. Which word best fits in the sentence? (choice D, taller) What is the complete sentence? (Bob's sister is taller than his mother.) Find the answer circles for sample A at the bottom of the page and fill in circle D.

- Now look at sample B. Read the sentence with the underlined part. Examine the answer choices. Which pronoun can replace the underlined words? (choice G, We) What is the complete sentence with the pronoun? (We went to the movies.) Find the answer circles for sample B at the bottom of the page and fill in circle G.

- Do the rest of the page by yourself. Do items 1 through 8 in the same way that we did the samples. Fill in your answer choices at the bottom of the page.

Language Expression: Usage

- Turn to page _____ in your test booklet. Find the number _____ at the top of the page and put your finger on it. (Check to make sure that everyone has found the right number.)

- On this page you will look for words that are used incorrectly. Look at the directions at the top of the page. Read them to yourself as I read them aloud. (Read the directions to your students.)

- In sample A there are sentences written on three lines. What does it say on line 4? (*no mistakes*) You should choose this answer only when an item does not have a usage mistake. Now, let's read the item line by line and listen for a usage mistake. Read line 1. Is there a mistake in the use of a word? (Yes, the word "he" is not needed in the sentence.) That's right. A pronoun should be used instead of a noun, not in addition to a noun. Find the answer circles for sample A at the bottom of the page and fill in circle 1 because there is a usage mistake in line 1.

- Now look at sample B. Read the item to yourself line by line and listen for a line that does not sound right. Did you find a mistake in the use of a word? (no) Find the answer circles for sample B at the bottom of the page and fill in circle 4 for *no mistakes*.

- Do the rest of the page by yourself. Read items 1 through 10 line-by-line and look for a usage mistake in each one in the same way that we did the samples. Fill in your answer choices at the bottom of the page.

Teacher Scripts

Language Expression: Grammar and Syntax **SPP 94, 95**

- Turn to page _____ in your test booklet. Find the number _____ at the top of the page and put your finger on it. (Check to make sure that everyone has found the right number.)

- On this page you will answer many different questions about sentences and the words in them. Look at the directions at the top of the page. Read them to yourself as I read them aloud. (Read the directions to your students.)

- Look at sample A. Read the first line of words to yourself as I read it aloud. The kitten is crying for some milk. Now look at item A. You have to decide whether the group of words makes a complete sentence, and if it is a sentence, you must decide what kind it is. Do the words in the box make a complete sentence? (yes) What kind of sentence do the words make? (a statement) Which answer choice should you fill in? (choice C, a statement) Find the answer circles for sample A at the bottom of the page and fill in circle C.

- Now look at sample B. This question is also about the group of words in the box. Read item B and its answer choices. To find the subject of a sentence, you might ask yourself, "Whom is the sentence about? Who is crying for some milk?" What is the subject of the sentence? (the kitten) Which answer circle should you choose? (E) Find the answer circles for sample B at the bottom of the page and fill in circle E.

- Do the rest of the page yourself. When you come to the arrow and the word GO at the bottom of the page, turn the page and go on until you get to the word STOP. Do items 1 through 14 in the same way that we did the samples. Fill in your answer choices at the bottom of the page.

Language Expression: Sentences **SPP 96**

- Turn to page _____ in your test booklet. Find the number _____ at the top of the page and put your finger on it. (Check to make sure that everyone has found the right number.)

- On this page you will find the subjects and predicates of sentences. Look at the directions at the top of the page. Read them to yourself as I read them aloud. (Read the directions to your students.)

- Look at sample A. Read the sentence. Four parts of the sentence are underlined. Which underlined part is the simple subject of the sentence? (boys) Yes, the sentence is about boys. What letter is under the word boys? (B) Find the answer circles for sample A at the bottom of the page and fill in circle B.

- Look at sample B. Read the sentence. Four parts of the sentence are underlined. Which underlined part is the simple predicate of the sentence? (lands) Yes, lands is the simple predicate, or verb, of the sentence; it tells what the subject, plane, does. What letter is under the word lands? (H) Find the answer circles for sample B at the bottom of the page and fill in circle H.

- Now look at sample C. There are four answer choices. You are to find the complete sentence— the one that is not a fragment or a run-on. Read the first answer. Is it a complete sentence? (no) Why not? (It is a fragment.) Read the rest of the answers. Which answer is a complete sentence? (choice B) Find the answer circles for sample C at the bottom of the page and fill in circle B.

- Do the rest of the page by yourself. Read the directions for each group of items and do items 1 through 10 in the same way that we did the samples. Fill in your answer choices at the bottom of the page.

Teacher Scripts

Language Expression: Sentences

SPP 97

- Turn to page _____ in your test booklet. Find the number _____ at the top of the page and put your finger on it. (Check to make sure that everyone has found the right number.)

- On this page you will identify the subjects and predicates of the sentences. Look at the directions at the top of the page. Read them to yourself as I read them aloud. (Read the directions to your students.)

- Look at sample A. Read the sentences. Which one has the complete subject underlined? (B) Yes, sentence B has the complete subject underlined. Find the answer circles for sample A at the bottom of the page and fill in circle B.

- Look at sample B. Read the sentences. Which one has the complete predicate underlined? (J) Yes, sentence J has the complete predicate underlined. Find the answer circles for sample B at the bottom of the page and fill in circle J.

- Do the rest of the page by yourself. Read the directions for each group of items and do items 1 through 6 in the same way that we did the samples. Fill in your answer choices at the bottom of the page.

Language Expression: Sentence Combining

SPP 98

- Turn to page _____ in your test booklet. Find the number _____ at the top of the page and put your finger on it. (Check to make sure that everyone has found the right number.)

- On this page you will be looking for sentences that are the best combination of two or three sentences. Look at the directions at the top of the page. Read them to yourself as I read them aloud. (Read the directions to your students.)

- Look at sample A. Read the two underlined sentences. These two sentences can be combined into one sentence. The new sentence should have the same meaning as the underlined sentences, and it should not repeat the two sentences word for word. Now read the four answer choices. Read carefully and look for the sentence that is the best combination of the two underlined sentences. Which sentence is the best combination of the sentences? (choice B, Examples of our work and our art are on the bulletin board.) Find the answer circles for sample A at the bottom of the page and fill in circle B.

- Do the rest of the page by yourself. Do items 1 through 3 in the same way that we did the samples. Fill in your answer choices at the bottom of the page.

Teacher Scripts

Language Expression: Paragraphs and Topic Sentences

- Turn to page _____ in your test booklet. Find the number _____ at the top of the page and put your finger on it. (Check to make sure that everyone has found the right number.)

- On this page you will be looking for topic sentences. You will also be looking for the best sentences to develop topic sentences. Look at the directions at the top of the page. Read them to yourself as I read them aloud. (Read the directions to your students.)

- Look at sample A. There is a blank at the beginning of the paragraph. It shows that the topic sentence is missing. Read the paragraph and then read the four answer choices. Look for the topic sentence—the sentence that tells the main idea of the paragraph. You may want to reread the paragraph after you read each answer choice to help you decide if the sentence tells the main idea of the paragraph. (pause) Which answer choice gives the topic sentence of the paragraph? (C) Yes, the paragraph tells about what Leonardo da Vinci did in addition to being an artist and a sculptor. Find the answer circles for sample A at the bottom of the page and fill in circle C.

- In sample B you will see the topic sentence of a paragraph. Let's read it. Remember, the topic sentence tells the main idea of a paragraph. You are to find the group of sentences that best explain or develop the idea expressed by the topic sentence. You may want to read the topic sentence just before you read each answer choice to help you decide if the sentences explain the idea expressed in the topic sentence. Which answer choice is the best group of sentences? (G) Yes, these sentences tell about the first man-made satellite. Find the answer circles for sample B at the bottom of the page and fill in circle G.

- Work by yourself to finish the rest of the page. Read the directions carefully and then do the items the same way that we did the samples. Fill in your answer choices at the bottom of the page.

Language Expression: Paragraphs and Sentence Sequence

- Turn to page _____ in your test booklet. Find the number _____ at the top of the page and put your finger on it. (Check to make sure that everyone has found the right number.)

- On this page you will be putting the sentences of paragraphs in the correct order. Look at the directions at the top of the page. Read them to yourself as I read them aloud. (Read the directions to your students.)

- Look at sample A. There are four sentences. Each sentence has a number in front of it. Let's read sentence 1, sentence 2, sentence 3, and sentence 4. The four sentences belong to the same paragraph but the sentences are not in the correct order. Think about the order in which the events in the paragraph happened and look for key words that will help you figure out the correct order for the sentences. Now read the sentences to yourself. Which sentence should come first in the paragraph? (sentence 1) Which sentence should come second? (sentence 3) Which sentence should come next? (sentence 2) Which sentence should come last? (sentence 4) The correct order is sentence 1, sentence 3, sentence 2, and sentence 4. To check this, read the paragraph with the sentences in the correct order. Now look at the answer choices under the sentences. They show the numbers 1, 2, 3, and 4 in different orders. The numbers stand for the numbers of the sentences. Which answer choice shows the numbers in the correct order for the sentences in the paragraph? (choice B) Find the answer circles for sample A at the bottom of the page and fill in circle B.

- Work by yourself to finish the rest of the page. Do these items the same way that we did the sample. Fill in your answer choices at the bottom of the page.

Teacher Scripts

Language Expression: Writing

Note:

- The Grade 3 TAAS test includes three student-generated writing samples: descriptive, informative, and narrative. The Grade 5 TAAS test includes five student-generated writing samples: the three listed above, plus classificatory and persuasive. Each one includes a page of instructions and guidelines to help the students get organized. The teacher reads these aloud while the students read along. Any pre-writing instructions that you are accustomed to giving your students would be appropriate. Students are encouraged to use scratch paper to brainstorm and make notes. The prompts for descriptive, narrative, and persuasive writing are pictures.

- The tests include instructions and time for pre-writing and writing a first draft. Writing samples are scored with a rubric. If you use the writing process, both you and your students will be familiar with this procedure.

- The scoring emphasis is on content. The only time for concern about errors in mechanics is when there are so many of them that it is hard to read the piece.

Language Expression: Descriptive Writing (TAAS)   `SPP 101`

- Turn to page _____ in your test booklet. Find the number _____ at the top of the page and put your finger on it. (Check to make sure that everyone has found the right number.)

- In this lesson you will write about a picture. Before you begin writing, you will use scratch paper to brainstorm and organize your ideas.

- Use the best English you can, but do not worry about mistakes. The most important thing is to write clearly about the picture and tell about all of the things you see. Use the notes that you made on scratch paper to stay organized.

Language Expression: Informative Writing (TAAS)   `SPP 102`

- Turn to page _____ in your test booklet. Find the number _____ at the top of the page and put your finger on it. (Check to make sure that everyone has found the right number.)

- In this lesson you will write about how to do something. Before you begin writing, you will use scratch paper to list all of the steps you should take and then organize them in order from the first to the last.

- Use the best English you can, but do not worry about mistakes. The most important thing is to describe every step in the correct order. Use the notes that you made on the scratch paper to stay organized.

Teacher Scripts

See Writing Note About the TAAS Tests on Previous Page

Language Expression: Narrative Writing (TAAS)   **SPP 103**

- Turn to page _____ in your test booklet. Find the number _____ at the top of the page and put your finger on it. (Check to make sure that everyone has found the right number.)

- In this lesson you will write a story that you have made up by yourself. The picture and directions will help you get started. Before you begin writing, you will use scratch paper to brainstorm and organize your ideas. Use your imagination to think up great ideas.

- Use the best English you can, but do not worry about mistakes. The most important thing is to write clearly so that the person reading your story can imagine what is happening from the beginning to the end. Use the notes that you made on the scratch paper to remember your ideas and stay organized.

Language Expression: Classificatory Writing (TAAS)   **SPP 104**

- Turn to page _____ in your test booklet. Find the number _____ at the top of the page and put your finger on it. (Check to make sure that everyone has found the right number.)

- In this lesson you will write about being able to predict the future. Before you begin writing, use scratch paper to list all of the good and bad things that you can think of about having this ability.

- Use the best English you can, but do not worry about mistakes. The most important thing is to write clearly so that your readers will understand what you are trying to say. Use the notes you made on the scratch paper to stay organized.

Language Expression: Persuasive Writing (TAAS)   **SPP 105**

- Turn to page _____ in your test booklet. Find the number _____ at the top of the page and put your finger on it. (Check to make sure that everyone has found the right number.)

- In this lesson you will try to convince your readers to agree with you. Before you begin writing, decide on your position and then use your scratch paper to list reasons to support your position.

- Use the best English you can, but do not worry about mistakes. The most important thing is to write clearly and explain why you think your readers should agree with you. Use the notes you made on the scratch paper to stay organized.

Teacher Scripts

Work-Study Skills: Library Skills (Reference Sources) SPP 106

- Turn to page _____ in your test booklet. Find the number _____ at the top of the page and put your finger on it. (Check to make sure that everyone has found the right number.)

- On this page you will be looking for the best sources for different types of information. You will also be finding information on a library catalog card. Look at the directions at the top of the page. Read them to yourself as I read them aloud. (Read the directions to your students.)

- Look at sample A. Read the question. Are there key words in the question that will help you find the answer? (locations . . . countries in Asia) Now read the four answer choices. Which source should you use to find the location of the countries in Asia? (globe) A globe shows a map of the earth so you could use a globe to find the location of the countries in Asia. What letter is in front of the word globe? (A) Find the answer circles for sample A at the bottom of the page and fill in circle A.

- Now look at sample B. Read the question carefully to yourself. Are there key words in the question that will help you find the answer? (titles . . . books by A. A. Milne) Now read the answer choices and find the source that could help you locate the titles of all of the books by A. A. Milne that are in the library. Which answer choice is the best source to find the information asked for in the question? (choice H, author cards of the card catalog) Since you want to find the titles of all of the books by just one author, it is best to look at the author cards. There will be a card for each title of a book written by that author. Find the answer circles for sample B at the bottom of the page and fill in circle H.

- Do the rest of the page by yourself. Do items 1 through 4 in the same way that we did the samples. Then read the directions above the library card catalog and do items 5 and 6. Fill in your answer choices at the bottom of the page.

Work-Study Skills: Parts of a Book SPP 107

- Turn to page _____ in your test booklet. Find the number _____ at the top of the page and put your finger on it. (Check to make sure that everyone has found the right number.)

- On this page you will use a table of contents and title page of a book to find information. Look at the directions at the top of the page. Read them to yourself as I read them aloud. (Read the directions to your students.)

- Look at sample A. Look at the table of contents on the left side of the page. Read the information in the table of contents and then read the question. What key words will help you answer the question? (information . . . in Chapter 2) What is the title of Chapter 2? (Who Were the Forty-Niners?) Now read the four answer choices. Which answer choice would be found in Chapter 2? (choice C) Find the answer circles for sample A at the bottom of the page and fill in circle C.

- Now you will do the rest of the page by yourself. Use the title page from a book to answer questions 1 through 4. Fill in your answer choices at the bottom of the page.

Teacher Scripts

Work-Study Skills: Table of Contents

SPP 108

- Turn to page _____ in your test booklet. Find the number _____ at the top of the page and put your finger on it. (Check to make sure that everyone has found the right number.)

- On this page you will use a table of contents to answer questions. Look at the directions at the top of the page. Read them to yourself as I read them aloud. (Read the directions to your students.)

- Look at the table of contents on the left side of the page. Read the information above the table of contents and in the table of contents itself.

- Read the question in sample A. What key words will help you answer the question? (foods . . . France at Christmas) Now look at the answers. They are chapter numbers. Check the answer choices. In which chapter would you find out about foods served in France at Christmas? (chapter 1, "Christmas Feasts in France") So which answer choice is correct? (1) Find the answer circles for sample A at the bottom of the page and fill in circle 1.

- Now look at sample B. Read the question and the answers. Which answer gives you information you might find in chapter 5? (answer choice 3) Find the answer circles for sample B at the bottom of the page and fill in circle 3.

- Finish the rest of the page by yourself. Use the table of contents on the left side of the page to do items 1 through 4. Read the information above and in the table of contents itself before you read the questions. Fill in your answer choices at the bottom of the page.

Work-Study Skills: Index

SPP 109

- Turn to page _____ in your test booklet. Find the number _____ at the top of the page and put your finger on it. (Check to make sure that everyone has found the right number.)

- On this page you will use an index from a book to answer questions. Look at the directions at the top of the page. Read them to yourself as I read them aloud. (Read the directions to your students.)

- Look at the index on the left side of the page. Read the information above and in the index itself.

- Read the question in sample A. What key word will help you answer the question? (comets) Now look at the answers. They are page numbers. Check the answer choices. On which page would you find information about comets? (45) So which answer is correct? (3) Find the answer circles for sample A at the bottom of the page and fill in circle 3.

- Now look at sample B. Read the question and the answers. Which answer gives you the page number for information about telescopes? (answer choice 4, 160) Find the answer circles for sample B at the bottom of the page and fill in circle 4.

- Do the rest of the page by yourself. Use the index on the left side of the page to do items 1 through 4. Read the information above and in the index itself before you read the questions. Fill in your answer choices at the bottom of the page.

Teacher Scripts

Work-Study Skills: Alphabetizing

- Turn to page _____ in your test booklet. Find the number _____ at the top of the page and put your finger on it. (Check to make sure that everyone has found the right number.)

- On this page you will be putting words in alphabetical order. Look at the directions at the top of the page. Read them to yourself as I read them aloud. (Read the directions to your students.)

- Look at the four words in sample A. If you put the words in alphabetical order, which one would come first? (answer B, bench) Yes, bench would come first in alphabetical order. Find the answer circles for sample A at the bottom of the page and fill in answer circle B.

- Now look at the four words in sample B. Which of these words would come last in alphabetical order? Remember, if words start with the same letter, look at the second or even the third letter to put them in alphabetical order. Which word would be last? (answer H, zero) Find the answer circles for sample B at the bottom of the page and fill in circle H.

- Do the rest of the page by yourself. Read the directions for each section and then do the items in the same way that we did the samples. Fill in your answer choices at the bottom of the page.

Work-Study Skills: Dictionary Skills

- Turn to page _____ in your test booklet. Find the number _____ at the top of the page and put your finger on it. (Check to make sure that everyone has found the right number.)

- On this page you will use entries from a dictionary to find information. Look at the directions at the top of the page. Read them to yourself as I read them aloud. (Read the directions to your students.)

- Look at sample A. There is a dictionary entry for the word camper. Read the dictionary entry. Then read the question for sample A and find the answer in the entry. Which answer did you choose? (B, noun) Right. Camper is a noun. Find the answer circles for sample A at the bottom of the page and fill in answer circle B.

- Now use the dictionary entry to answer questions 1 through 5. Fill in your answer choices at the bottom of the page.

Work-Study Skills: Outlines and Schedules

- Turn to page _____ in your test booklet. Find the number _____ at the top of the page and put your finger on it. (Check to make sure that everyone has found the right number.)

- On this page you will answer questions about ways to organize information. Look at the directions at the top of the page. Read them to yourself as I read them aloud. (Read the directions to your students.)

- Look at the schedule at the top of the left side of the page. You will use this schedule to answer the question in sample A. What are the key words in the question? (1:00, doing) Look at the schedule. What is the answer to the question? (answer C, warming up) Find the answer circles for sample A at the bottom of the page and fill in answer circle C.

- Now study the outline below the schedule. Use it to answer questions 1 through 3. Fill in your answer choices at the bottom of the page.

Teacher Scripts

Work-Study Skills: Maps

- Turn to page _____ in your test booklet. Find the number _____ at the top of the page and put your finger on it. (Check to make sure that everyone has found the right number.)
- On this page you will use the information on maps to answer questions. Look at the directions at the top of the page. Read them to yourself as I read them aloud. (Read the directions to your students.)
- Look at the map below the directions on the left side of the page. Read the explanation above the map. Now take a little time to examine the map and see where things are located.
- Read the question in sample A and look for the key words. Key words are the words in the question that will help you find the answer. What are the key words in sample A? (farthest . . . Natural History Museum) Look at the map. Find the Natural History Museum. Now check each answer for sample A and find the place that is farthest away from the Natural History Museum. Which place is it? (the restaurant) What is the number of the correct answer? (4) Find the answer circles for sample A at the bottom of the page and fill in circle 4.
- Now look at sample B. Read the question to yourself and look for the key words. What are the key words in the question? (southeast corner, Wilson Blvd. and 3rd Street, north across the street) Look at the map and find the answer. What place is located directly north, across the street from the southeast corner of Wilson Blvd. and 3rd Street? (High Park) Which answer is correct? (answer 1, in the park) Find the answer circles for sample B at the bottom of the page and fill in circle 1.
- Now you will do the rest of the page. Use the map on the left side of the page to do items 1 through 4. Read the explanation and study the map before you answer the questions. Fill in your answer choices at the bottom of the page.

Work-Study Skills: Graphs and Tables

- Turn to page _____ in your test booklet. Find the number _____ at the top of the page and put your finger on it. (Check to make sure that everyone has found the right number.)
- On this page you will use information on graphs and tables to answer questions. Look at the directions at the top of the page. Read them to yourself as I read them aloud. (Read the directions to your students.)
- Look at the graph below the directions on the left side of the page. Read the title of the graph. Look at the bottom of the graph. What does each picture on the graph stand for? (4 students) How many students would half of a picture stand for? (2) Now look at sample A. Read the question. The question has a key number and key words that will help you. What are they? (18, from which area) Now read the answers. Then look at the graph and figure out how many students came from each area listed as an answer. There were 18 students from which area? (Atlantic States) What is the number of the correct answer? (3) Find the answer circles for sample A at the bottom of the page and fill in circle 3.
- Now look at sample B. Read the question. What are the key words? (how many more, Atlantic States, Southwestern States) Now figure out the answer. How many more students came from the Atlantic States than from Southwestern States? (2) Which answer should you fill in? (answer 1) Find the answer circles for sample B at the bottom of the page and fill in circle 1.
- Do the rest of the page by yourself. Use the table on the left side of the page to do items 1 and 2. Use the graph on the right side of the page to do items 3 and 4. Be sure to read the title of the table and the explanation above the graph before you answer the questions. Fill in your answer choices at the bottom of the page.

Teacher Scripts

Math Computation: Addition—Whole Numbers

SPP 115

- Turn to page _____ in your test booklet. Find the number _____ at the top of the page and put your finger on it. (Check to make sure that everyone has found the right number.)

- On this page you will be looking for the answers to addition problems. Look at the directions at the top of the page. Read them to yourself as I read them aloud. (Read the directions to your students.)

- Look at sample A. What are you being asked to do? (add 77 and 13) Look at the five answer choices. What are they? (80, 84, 89, 90, and *none of these*) You should fill in the answer circle for *none of these* only if the right answer is not given as one of the answer choices. Now do the problem. Use scratch paper if you need to. Add carefully. What is the answer to 77 plus 13? (90) What letter is next to the answer 90? (D) Find the answer circles for sample A at the bottom of the page and fill in circle D.

- Now look at sample B. What are you being asked to do? (add 448 and 374) You might want to rewrite the problem in a vertical form on scratch paper to make it easier to add. Remember to line the problem up so that one number is directly under the other. Add the problem carefully. What is the answer to 448 plus 374? (822) Is 822 one of the answer choices? (no) Since the right answer to the problem is not given as an answer choice, you should fill in the circle for *none of these*. What letter is next to *none of these*? (K) Find the answer circles for sample B at the bottom of the page and fill in circle K.

- Do the rest of the page by yourself. Do items 1 through 8 in the same way that we did the samples. If you need to, rewrite and work the problems on scratch paper. Fill in your answer choices at the bottom of the page.

Math Computation: Addition—Decimals

SPP 116

- Turn to page _____ in your test booklet. Find the number _____ at the top of the page and put your finger on it. (Check to make sure that everyone has found the right number.)

- On this page you will be looking for the answers to decimal addition problems. Look at the directions at the top of the page. Read them to yourself as I read them aloud. (Read the directions to your students.)

- Look at sample A. What are you being asked to do? (add $7.62 and $8.98) Look at the five answer choices. What are they? ($15.60, $16.50, $16.60, $16.61, and *none of these*) You should fill in the answer circle for *none of these* only if the right answer is not given as one of the answer choices. Now add the problem. Use scratch paper if you need to. Add carefully. What is the answer to $7.62 plus $8.98? ($16.60) What letter is next to the answer $16.60? (C) Find the answer circles for sample A at the bottom of the page and fill in circle C.

- Now look at sample B. What are you being asked to do? (add 3.5 and 9.7) You might want to rewrite the problem in a vertical form on scratch paper to make it easier to add. Remember to line the problem up so that the decimal points are under one another. Carefully add the problem. What is the answer to 3.5 plus 9.7? (13.2) Is 13.2 one of the answer choices? (no) Since the right answer to the problem is not given as an answer choice, you should fill in the circle for none of these. What letter is next to *none of these*? (K) Find the answer circles for sample B at the bottom of the page and fill in circle K.

- Do the rest of the page by yourself. Do items 1 through 8 in the same way that we did the samples. If you need to, rewrite and add the problems on scratch paper. Fill in your answer choices at the bottom of the page.

Teacher Scripts

Math Computation: Addition—Fractions

- Turn to page _____ in your test booklet. Find the number _____ at the top of the page and put your finger on it. (Check to make sure that everyone has found the right number.)

- On this page you will find the answers to fraction addition problems. Look at the directions at the top of the page. Read them to yourself as I read them aloud. (Read the directions to your students.)

- Look at sample A. What are you being asked to do? (add 1/3 and 1/3) Look at the five answer choices. What are they? (2/3, 2/6, 1/6, 1, and *none of these*) You should fill in the answer circle for *none of these* only if the right answer is not given as one of the answer choices. Now carefully add the problem. Use scratch paper if you need to. What is the answer to 1/3 plus 1/3? (2/3) What letter is next to the answer 2/3? (A) Find the answer circles for sample A at the bottom of the page and fill in circle A.

- Now look at sample B. What are you being asked to do? (add 3/8 and 2/8) You might want to rewrite the problem in a vertical form on scratch paper to make it easier to add. Now carefully add the problem. What is the answer to 3/8 plus 2/8? (5/8) Is 5/8 one of the answer choices? (yes) What letter is next to 5/8? (G) Find the answer circles for sample B at the bottom of the page and fill in circle G.

- Do the rest of the page by yourself. Do items 1 through 8 in the same way that we did the samples. If you need to, rewrite and work the problems on scratch paper. Fill in your answer choices at the bottom of the page.

Math Computation: Addition—Mixed Numbers

- Turn to page _____ in your test booklet. Find the number _____ at the top of the page and put your finger on it. (Check to make sure that everyone has found the right number.)

- On this page you will find the answers to mixed number addition problems. Look at the directions at the top of the page. Read them to yourself as I read them aloud. (Read the directions to your students.)

- Look at sample A. What are you being asked to do? (add 2 2/4 and 1 1/4) Look at the five answer choices. What are they? (3 3/4, 3 2/4, 3 3/8, 3 3/16, and *none of these*) You should fill in the answer circle for *none of these* only if the right answer is not given as one of the answer choices. Now carefully add the problem. Use scratch paper if you need to. What is the answer to 2 2/4 plus 1 1/4? (3 3/4) What letter is next to the answer 3 3/4? (A) Find the answer circles for sample A at the bottom of the page and fill in circle A.

- Now look at sample B. What are you being asked to do? (add 5 2/5 and 10 2/5) You might want to rewrite the problem in a vertical form on scratch paper to make it easier to add. Now carefully add the problem. What is the answer to 5 2/5 plus 10 2/5? (15 4/5) What letter is next to the answer 15 4/5? (G) Find the answer circles for sample B at the bottom of the page and fill in answer circle G.

- Do the rest of the page by yourself. Do items 1 through 8 in the same way that we did the samples. If you need to, rewrite and add the problems on scratch paper. Fill in your answer choices at the bottom of the page.

Teacher Scripts

Math Computation: Subtraction—Whole Numbers

SPP 119

- Turn to page _____ in your test booklet. Find the number _____ at the top of the page and put your finger on it. (Check to make sure that everyone has found the right number.)

- On this page you will be looking for the answers to subtraction problems. Look at the directions at the top of the page. Read them to yourself as I read them aloud. (Read the directions to your students.)

- Look at sample A. What are you being asked to do? (subtract 2181 from 8731) Look at the five answer choices. What are they? (5440, 6550, 6650, 6912, and *none of these*) You should fill in the answer circle for *none of these* only if the right answer is not given as one of the answer choices. Now carefully subtract the problem. Use scratch paper if you need to. What is the answer to 8731 minus 2181? (6550) What letter is next to the answer 6550? (B) Find the answer circles for sample A at the bottom of the page and fill in circle B.

- Now look at sample B. What are you being asked to do? (subtract 1897 from 2700) Now do the problem. Use scratch paper if you need to. Remember to line the problem up so that one number is directly under another. Subtract carefully. What is the answer to 2700 minus 1897? (803) Is 803 one of the answer choices? (no) Since the right answer to the problem is not given as an answer choice, you should fill in the circle for *none of these*. What letter is next to *none of these*? (K) Find the answer circles for sample B at the bottom of the page and fill in circle K.

- Do the rest of the page by yourself. Do items 1 through 8 in the same way that we did the samples. If you need to, rewrite and subtract the problems on scratch paper. Fill in your answer choices at the bottom of the page.

Math Computation: Subtraction—Decimals

SPP 120

- Turn to page _____ in your test booklet. Find the number _____ at the top of the page and put your finger on it. (Check to make sure that everyone has found the right number.)

- On this page you will be finding the answers to decimal subtraction problems. Look at the directions at the top of the page. Read them to yourself as I read them aloud. (Read the directions to your students.)

- Look at sample A. What are you being asked to do? (subtract $15.50 from $58.79) Look at the five answer choices. What are they? ($42.20, $43.20, $43.29, $53.29, and *none of these*) You should fill in the answer circle for *none of these* only if the right answer is not given as one of the answer choices. Now carefully subtract the problem. Use scratch paper if you need to. What is the answer to $58.79 minus $15.50? ($43.29) What letter is next to the answer $43.29? (C) Find the answer circles for sample A at the bottom of the page and fill in circle C.

- Now look at sample B. What are you being asked to do? (subtract 0.36 from 0.52) You might want to rewrite the problem in a vertical form on scratch paper to make it easier to subtract. Now carefully do the problem. What is the answer to 0.52 minus 0.36? (0.16) What letter is next to the answer 0.16? (H) Find the answer circles for sample B at the bottom of the page and fill in circle H.

- Do the rest of the page by yourself. Do items 1 through 8 in the same way that we did the samples. If you need to, rewrite and subtract the problems on scratch paper. Fill in your answer choices at the bottom of the page.

Teacher Scripts

Math Computation: Subtraction—Fractions

SPP 121

- Turn to page _____ in your test booklet. Find the number _____ at the top of the page and put your finger on it. (Check to make sure that everyone has found the right number.)

- On this page you will be finding the answers to subtraction problems with fractions. Look at the directions at the top of the page. Read them to yourself as I read them aloud. (Read the directions to your students.)

- Look at sample A. What are you being asked to do? (subtract 2/11 from 9/11) Look at the five answer choices. What are they? (2/11, 5/11, 7/11, 9/11, and *none of these*) You should fill in the answer circle for *none of these* only if the right answer is not given as one of the answer choices. Now carefully do the problem. Use scratch paper if you need to. What is the answer to 9/11 minus 2/11? (7/11) What letter is next to 7/11? (C) Find the answer circles for sample A at the bottom of the page and fill in circle C.

- Now look at sample B. What are you being asked to do? (subtract 5/13 from 11/13) Now carefully subtract the problem. Use scratch paper if you need to. What is the answer to 11/13 minus 5/13? (6/13) What letter is next to the answer 6/13? (J) Find the answer circles for sample B at the bottom of the page and fill in circle J.

- Do the rest of the page by yourself. Do items 1 through 8 in the same way that we did the samples. If you need to, rewrite and subtract the problems on scratch paper. Fill in your answer choices at the bottom of the page.

Math Computation: Subtraction—Mixed Numbers

SPP 122

- Turn to page _____ in your test booklet. Find the number _____ at the top of the page and put your finger on it. (Check to make sure that everyone has found the right number.)

- On this page you will be finding the answers to subtraction problems with mixed numbers. Look at the directions at the top of the page. Read them to yourself as I read them aloud. (Read the directions to your students.)

- Look at sample A. What are you being asked to do? (subtract 2 1/2 from 6 1/2) Look at the five answer choices. What are they? (4, 4 1/2, 8 1/2, 9, and *none of these*) You should fill in the answer circle for *none of these* only if the right answer is not given as one of the answer choices. Now carefully subtract the problem. Use scratch paper if you need to. What is the answer to 6 1/2 minus 2 1/2? (4) What letter is next to the answer 4? (A) Find the answer circle for sample A at the bottom of the page and fill in circle A.

- Now look at sample B. What are you being asked to do? (subtract 3 4/8 from 7 7/8) You might want to rewrite the problem on scratch paper, in a vertical form, to make it easier to subtract. Now carefully subtract the problem. What is the answer to 7 7/8 minus 3 4/8? (4 3/8) What letter is next to 4 3/8? (G) Find the answer circles for sample B at the bottom of the page and fill in circle G.

- Do the rest of the page by yourself. Do items 1 through 8 in the same way that we did the samples. If you need to, rewrite and subtract the problems on scratch paper. Fill in your answer choices at the bottom of the page.

Teacher Scripts

Math Computation: Multiplication—Whole Numbers **SPP 123**

- Turn to page _____ in your test booklet. Find the number _____ at the top of the page and put your finger on it. (Check to make sure that everyone has found the right number.)

- On this page you will find the answers to multiplication problems. Look at the directions at the top of the page. Read them to yourself as I read them aloud. (Read the directions to your students.)

- Look at sample A. What are you being asked to do? (multiply 25 by 4) Look at the five answer choices. What are they? (29, 100, 65, 104, and *none of these*) You should fill in the answer circle for *none of these* only if the right answer is not given as one of the answer choices. Now carefully multiply the problem. Use scratch paper if you need to. What is the answer to 25 times 4? (100) What letter is next to the answer 100? (B) Find the answer circles for sample A at the bottom of the page and fill in circle B.

- Now look at sample B. What are you being asked to do? (multiply 50 by 9) Now carefully multiply the problem. Use scratch paper if you need to. What is the answer to 50 times 9? (450) Is 450 one of the answer choices? (no) Since the right answer to the problem is not given as an answer choice, you should fill in the circle for *none of these*. What letter is next to *none of these*? (K) Find the answer circles for sample B at the bottom of the page and fill in circle K.

- Do the rest of the page by yourself. Do items 1 through 8 in the same way that we did the samples. If you need to, rewrite and multiply the problems on scratch paper. Fill in your answer choices at the bottom of the page.

Math Computation: Multiplication—Decimals **SPP 124**

- Turn to page _____ in your test booklet. Find the number _____ at the top of the page and put your finger on it. (Check to make sure that everyone has found the right number.)

- On this page you will be finding the answers to multiplication problems with decimals in them. Look at the directions at the top of the page. Read them to yourself as I read them aloud. (Read the directions to your students.)

- Look at sample A. What are you being asked to do? (multiply 7 by 5.1) Look at the five answer choices. What are they? (3.57, 35.0, 35.7, 5.8, and *none of these*) You should fill in the answer circle for *none of these* only if the right answer is not given as one of the answer choices. Now carefully multiply the problem. Use scratch paper if you need to. You might want to rewrite the problem in a vertical form to make it easier to multiply. What is the answer to 7 times 5.1? (35.7) What letter is next to the answer 35.7? (C) Find the answer circles for sample A at the bottom of the page and fill in answer circle C.

- Now look at sample B. What are you being asked to do? (multiply $25.50 by 3) Now multiply the problem. Use scratch paper if you need to. What is the answer to $25.50 times 3? ($76.50) What letter is next to the answer $76.50? (J) Find the answer circles for sample B at the bottom of the page and fill in circle J.

- Do the rest of the page by yourself. Do items 1 through 8 in the same way that we did the samples. If you need to, rewrite and multiply the problems on scratch paper. Fill in your answer choices at the bottom of the page.

Teacher Scripts

Math Computation: Multiplication—Fractions

SPP 125

- Turn to page _____ in your test booklet. Find the number _____ at the top of the page and put your finger on it. (Check to make sure that everyone has found the right number.)

- On this page you will find the answers to fraction multiplication problems. Look at the directions at the top of the page. Read them to yourself as I read them aloud. (Read the directions to your students.)

- Look at sample A. What are you being asked to do? (multiply 3/4 by 1/4) Look at the five answer choices. What are they? (3/4, 3/8, 3/16, 1, and *none of these*) You should fill in the answer circle for *none of these* only if the right answer is not given as one of the answer choices. Now carefully multiply the problem. Use scratch paper if you need to. What is the answer to 3/4 times 1/4? (3/16) What letter is next to the answer 3/16? (C) Find the answer circles for sample A at the bottom of the page and fill in circle C.

- Now look at sample B. What are you being asked to do? (multiply 4/5 by 5/8) Carefully multiply the problem. Use scratch paper if you need to. What is the answer to 4/5 times 5/8? (1/2) What letter is next to the answer 1/2? (F) Find the answer circles for sample B at the bottom of the page and fill in circle F.

- Do the rest of the page by yourself. Do items 1 through 8 in the same way that we did the samples. If you need to, rewrite and multiply the problems on scratch paper. Fill in your answer choices at the bottom of the page.

Math Computation: Division—Whole Numbers

SPP 126

- Turn to page _____ in your test booklet. Find the number _____ at the top of the page and put your finger on it. (Check to make sure that everyone has found the right number.)

- On this page you will find the answers to division problems. Look at the directions at the top of the page. Read them to yourself as I read them aloud. (Read the directions to your students.)

- Look at sample A. What are you being asked to do? (divide 300 by 5) Look at the five answer choices. What are they? (5, 6, 50, 60, and *none of these*) You should fill in the answer circle for *none of these* only if the right answer is not given as one of the answer choices. Now carefully divide the problem. Use scratch paper if you need to. What is the answer to 300 divided by 5? (60) What letter is next to the answer 60? (D) Find the answer circles for sample A at the bottom of the page and fill in circle D.

- Now look at sample B. What are you being asked to do? (divide 63 by 8) Divide the problem. Use scratch paper if you need to. What is the answer to 63 divided by 8? (7 R7) What letter is next to the answer 7 R7? (H) Find the answer circles for sample B at the bottom of the page and fill in circle H.

- Do the rest of the page by yourself. Do items 1 through 8 in the same way that we did the samples. If you need to, rewrite and divide the problems on scratch paper. Fill in your answer choices at the bottom of the page.

Teacher Scripts

Math Concepts/Applications: Numeration $\boxed{\textbf{SPP 127, 128}}$

- Turn to page _____ in your test booklet. Find the number _____ at the top of the page and put your finger on it. (Check to make sure that everyone has found the right number.)
- On this page you will find the answers to problems about numbers. Look at the directions at the top of the page. Read them to yourself as I read them aloud. (Read the directions to your students.)
- Look at sample A. Read the question. The question contains key words and numbers. Key words and numbers are important words and numbers in a problem that will help you to find the answer. Read the question in sample A to yourself again and look for the key words and numbers. What are they? (3 thousand, 9 tens, 4 ones) Look at the four answer choices. Which one has the same value as 3 thousands 9 tens 4 ones? (choice B, 3094) Find the answer circles for sample A at the bottom of the page and fill in circle B.
- Now look at sample B. Read the problem. Find the key words and numbers. Remember, key words and numbers are the important words and numbers in a problem that will help you to find the answer. What are the key words and numbers in this problem? (estimate, sum of 8372 and 7931, nearest thousand) What should you do to find the answer? (round 8372 and 7931 to the nearest thousand) Round the numbers now. Use scratch paper if you need to. What is 8372 rounded to the nearest thousand? (8000) What is 7931 rounded to the nearest thousand? (8000) Examine the answer choices. Which one shows the numbers that you should add to estimate the sum of 8372 and 7931? (choice H, 8000 and 8000) Find the answer circles for sample B at the bottom of the page and fill in circle H.
- Do the rest of the page by yourself. When you see the arrow and the word GO at the bottom of the page, go on to the next page. Do all of the items in the same way that we did the samples. Use scratch paper if you need to. Fill in your answer choices at the bottom of the page. Stop when you reach the word STOP.

Math Concepts/Applications: Number Sentences $\boxed{\textbf{SPP 129}}$

- Turn to page _____ in your test booklet. Find the number _____ at the top of the page and put your finger on it. (Check to make sure that everyone has found the right number.)
- On this page you will be looking for the numbers and operation signs that make the number sentences true. Look at the directions at the top of the page. Read them to yourself as I read them aloud. (Read the directions to your students.)
- Look at sample A. Read the question and the number sentence. Find the number that goes in the box to make the number sentence true. One way to find the number is to try each answer choice in the box to see if it works. Use your scratch paper if you need to. Try answer choice A, 30, in the number sentence. Does 55 minus 30 equal 19? (no) Now try answer choice B, 34. Does 55 minus 34 equal 19? (no) Try answer choice C, 36. Does 55 minus 36 equal 19? (yes) Find the answer circles for sample A at the bottom of the page and fill in circle C.
- Now look at sample B. Read the problem. Find the number that goes in the box to make the number sentence true. One way to find the answer is to do the computing on the right side of the equal sign first. What is 2 x 2? (4) So, 24 box 6 must equal 4. What operation sign will make this sentence true? (the division sign) Look at the answer choices. Which one shows the division sign? (J) Find the answer circles for sample B at the bottom of the page and fill in answer circle J.
- Do the rest of the page by yourself. Do items 1 through 6 in the same way that we did the samples. Use scratch paper if you need to. Fill in your answer choices at the bottom of the page.

Teacher Scripts

Math Concepts/Applications: Number Theory

SPP 130

- Turn to page _____ in your test booklet. Find the number _____ at the top of the page and put your finger on it. (Check to make sure that everyone has found the right number.)

- On this page you will be looking for the correct numbers and completing number sentences. Look at the directions at the top of the page. Read them to yourself as I read them aloud. (Read the directions to your students.)

- Look at sample A. Read the question and the number sentences. What are you being asked to find? (the number that makes both sentences true) Now look at the first number sentence. What is 24 divided by 6? (4) Look at the second number sentence. Does 4 also make the second number sentence true? (yes) So 4 is the correct answer. Look at the four answer choices. What letter is in front of the answer 4? (C) Find the answer circles for sample A at the bottom of the page and fill in circle C.

- Now look at sample B. Read the question. What are the key words and numbers in the question? (fraction, same value as 0.3) Now look at the answer choices. Which one has the same value as the decimal three tenths? (choice A, 3/10) Yes, the fraction 3/10 has the same value as the decimal 0.3 (three tenths). Find the answer circles for sample B at the bottom of the page and fill in circle F.

- Do the rest of the page by yourself. Do items 1 through 6 in the same way that we did the samples. Look for the key words and numbers. Use scratch paper if you need to. Fill in your answer choices at the bottom of the page.

Math Concepts/Applications: Geometry

SPP 131, 132

- Turn to page _____ in your test booklet. Find the number _____ at the top of the page and put your finger on it. (Check to make sure that everyone has found the right number.)

- On this page you will be looking for the answers to questions about shapes. Look at the directions at the top of the page. Read them to yourself as I read them aloud. (Read the directions to your students.)

- Look at sample A. Read the question. Examine the figure carefully. Then read the four answer choices and decide which one gives the name of the figure. What is the name of the figure? (cone) So which answer choice is correct? (B) Find the answer circles for sample A at the bottom of the page and fill in circle B.

- Now look at sample B. Read the question and examine the picture. What are the key words and numbers in the question and picture? (perimeter, 6 ft., 8 ft.) If you remember that the perimeter of a figure is the distance around it, you will be able to figure out the answer to this question. How many sides does the rug have? (4) How many numbers should you add together to find the perimeter of this rug? (4) How do you know the numbers for the two sides that are not labeled? (They are the same as the ones that are across from them.) So what four numbers should you add? (6, 8, 6, 8) What is the perimeter of the rug? (28 ft.) What letter is in front of that answer choice? (H) Find the answer circles for sample B at the bottom of the page and fill in circle H.

- Now work by yourself. When you come to the arrow and the word GO at the bottom of the page, turn to the next page. Do all of the items in the same way that we did the samples. Stop when you reach the word STOP. Fill in your answer choices at the bottom of the page.

Teacher Scripts

Math Concepts/Applications: Measurement—Time and Money | SPP 133 – 135 |

- Turn to page _____ in your test booklet. Find the number _____ at the top of the page and put your finger on it. (Check to make sure that everyone has found the right number.)
- On this page you will be looking for the answers to questions about time and money. Look at the directions at the top of the page. Read them to yourself as I read them aloud. (Read the directions to your students.)
- Look at sample A. Read the question. Examine the clock carefully. Then read the four answer choices and decide which one gives the time shown on the clock. What is the time? (10:00) So which answer choice is correct? (B) Find the answer circles for sample A at the bottom of the page and fill in circle B.
- Now look at sample B. Read the question. What are the key words and numbers in the question? (value, coins) What coins do you see? (3 dimes, 2 nickels, 4 pennies) What is the value of a dime? (10 cents) What is the value of a nickel? (5 cents) What is the value of a penny? (1 cent) Now figure out the value of all of the coins together. What is it? (44 cents) What letter is in front of the answer choice 44¢? (G) Find the answer circles for sample B at the bottom of the page and fill in answer circle G.
- Now work by yourself. When you come to the arrow and the word GO at the bottom of the page, turn to the next page. Do all of the items in the same way that we did the samples. Stop when you reach the word STOP. Fill in your answer choices at the bottom of the page.

Math Concepts/Applications: Measurement—Length | SPP 136 |

- Turn to page _____ in your test booklet. Find the number _____ at the top of the page and put your finger on it. (Check to make sure that everyone has found the right number.)
- On this page you will be finding the answers to questions about length measurement. Look at the directions at the top of the page. Read them to yourself as I read them aloud. (Read the directions to your students.)
- Look at sample A. Read the question. Examine the picture of the pencil and the inch ruler. Then read the four answer choices and decide which one gives the correct length of the pencil. What is the length of the pencil? (4 inches) So which answer choice is correct? (B) Find the answer circles for sample A at the bottom of the page and fill in circle B.
- Now work by yourself to finish the rest of this page. Do items 1 and 2 in the same way that we did the sample. Then answer the questions in items 3 and 4. Fill in your answer choices at the bottom of the page.

Math Concepts/Applications: Measurement—Weight and Capacity | SPP 137 |

- Turn to page _____ in your test booklet. Find the number _____ at the top of the page and put your finger on it. (Check to make sure that everyone has found the right number.)
- On this page you will be finding the answers to questions about weight and capacity. Look at the directions at the top of the page. Read them to yourself as I read them aloud. (Read the directions to your students.)
- Look at sample A. Read the question and look carefully at the picture of a scale. Then read the four answer choices and decide which one gives the correct weight of the rock. What is the weight of the rock? (3 1/2 pounds) So which answer choice is correct? (B) Find the answer circles for sample A at the bottom of the page and fill in circle B.
- Look at sample B. How many cups are there in a quart? (choice H, 4) Yes, there are 4 cups in a quart. Find the answer circles for sample B at the bottom of the page and fill circle H.
- Now work by yourself to finish the page. Do items 1 through 6 in the same way that we did the samples. Fill in your answer choices at the bottom of the page.

Teacher Scripts

Math Concepts/Applications: Measurement—Temperature

- Turn to page _____ in your test booklet. Find the number _____ at the top of the page and put your finger on it. (Check to make sure that everyone has found the right number.)
- On this page you will be reading thermometers to answer the questions. Look at the directions at the top of the page. Read them to yourself as I read them aloud. (Read the directions to your students.)
- Look at sample A. Read the question and look at the thermometer. What is the correct answer? (76°) Look at the four answer choices. Which one is correct? (D) Find the answer circles for sample A at the bottom of the page and fill in circle D.
- Do the rest of the page by yourself. Fill in your answer choices at the bottom of the page.

Math Concepts/Applications: Measurement—Probability and Statistics

- Turn to page _____ in your test booklet. Find the number _____ at the top of the page and put your finger on it. (Check to make sure that everyone has found the right number.)
- On this page you will be using charts and graphs to answer the questions. Look at the directions at the top of the page. Read them to yourself as I read them aloud. (Read the directions to your students.)
- Look at sample A. Read the question and look at the graph. What is the correct answer? (55 glasses) Look at the four answer choices. Which one is correct? (D) Find the answer circles for sample A at the bottom of the page and fill in circle D.
- Do the rest of the page by yourself. Fill in your answer choices at the bottom of the page.

Math Concepts/Applications: Estimation

- Turn to page _____ in your test booklet. Find the number _____ at the top of the page and put your finger on it. (Check to make sure that everyone has found the right number.)
- On this page you will be estimating the answers to the questions. Look at the directions at the top of the page. Read them to yourself as I read them aloud. (Read the directions to your students.)
- Look at sample A. Read the question. What are the key words in this problem? (about how much) One way to find the answer to this problem is to round each amount to the nearest dollar. Use scratch paper if you need to. What is $3.95 rounded to the nearest dollar? ($4.00) What is $14.95 rounded to the nearest dollar? ($15.00) What is the sum of $4.00 and $15.00? ($19.00) Is $19.00 one of the answer choices? (yes, choice C) Find the answer circles for sample A at the bottom of the page and fill in circle C.
- Now look at sample B. Read the question. What are the key words in this question? (estimate, area, square) How do you find the area of a square? (multiply the length of one side by the length of another) What is something that you know about a square? (all four sides are equal) Does that knowledge give you the information you need to figure out this problem? (yes) Remember, you are being asked to estimate, so what should you do next? (round 6.2 to the nearest meter) Now do the problem. Use scratch paper if you need to. What is the approximate area of the square? (36 square meters, choice G) Find the answer circles for sample B at the bottom of the page and fill in circle G.
- Do the rest of the page by yourself. Do items 1 through 6 in the same way that we did the samples. Use scratch paper if you need to. Fill in your answer choices at the bottom of the page.

Teacher Scripts

Math Concepts/Applications: Strategies SPP 141

- Turn to page _____ in your test booklet. Find the number _____ at the top of the page and put your finger on it. (Check to make sure that everyone has found the right number.)

- On this page you will be figuring out how to solve the problems. Look at the directions at the top of the page. Read them to yourself as I read them aloud. (Read the directions to your students.)

- Look at sample A. Read the question and the answer choices. Which answer is correct? (B) Yes, B is the correct answer. If you subtract the change that Gabby received from the amount of money that she gave to the clerk, you will know how much the game cost. Find the answer circles for sample A at the bottom of the page and fill in circle B.

- Now look at sample B. Read the question and the answer choices. Which answer is correot? (H) Yes, answer H is correct because the area of a rectangle is found by multiplying the length of one side by the height of another. Find the answer circles for sample B at the bottom of the page and fill in circle H.

- Do the rest of the page by yourself. Do items 1 through 6 in the same way that we did the samples. Use scratch paper if you need to. Fill in your answer choices at the bottom of the page.

Math Concepts/Applications: Problem Solving and Data Analysis SPP 142

- Turn to page _____ in your test booklet. Find the number _____ at the top of the page and put your finger on it. (Check to make sure that everyone has found the right number.)

- On this page you will be solving problems. Look at the directions at the top of the page. Read them to yourself as I read them aloud. (Read the directions to your students.)

- Look at sample A. Read the question. One way to do this problem is to first add up the hours Lupe worked. How many hours did she work? (15 hours) Then what should you do? (multiply 15 times $3.00) How much money did Lupe earn? (answer D, $45.00) Find the answer circles for sample A at the bottom of the page and fill in circle D.

- Now look at sample B. Read the question. Which answer is correct? (F) Yes, Mrs. Roberts spent $30.00 dollars altogether or $2.00 for each guest. Find the answer circles for sample B at the bottom of the page and fill in circle F.

- Do the rest of the page by yourself. Do items 1 through 6 in the same way that we did the samples. Use scratch paper if you need to. Fill in your answer choices at the bottom of the page.

Math Concepts/Applications: Reasonable Answers SPP 143

- Turn to page _____ in your test booklet. Find the number _____ at the top of the page and put your finger on it. (Check to make sure that everyone has found the right number.)

- On this page you will choose answers that make the most sense. Look at the directions at the top of the page. Read them to yourself as I read them aloud. (Read the directions to your students.)

- Look at sample A. Read the question. One way to do this problem is to first round 198 to the nearest hundred. Then divide by 10. What is the correct answer? (choice C, 20) Find the answer circles for sample A at the bottom of the page and fill in circle C.

- Now look at sample B. Read the question. Which answer is correct? (H) Yes, if there are too many students for one bus, they will need two buses. Find the answer circles for sample B at the bottom of the page and fill in circle H.

- Do the rest of the page by yourself. Use scratch paper if you need to. Fill in your answer choices at the bottom of the page.

Student Practice Pages

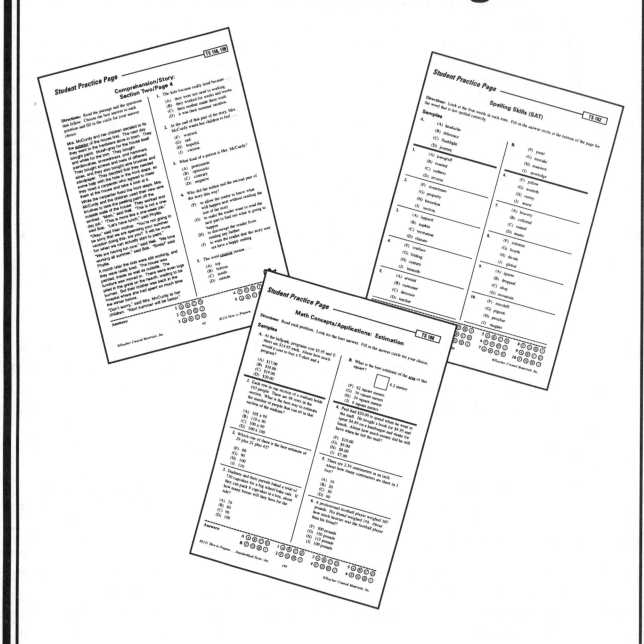

Student's Name _____

Starting Date _____

Teacher Script

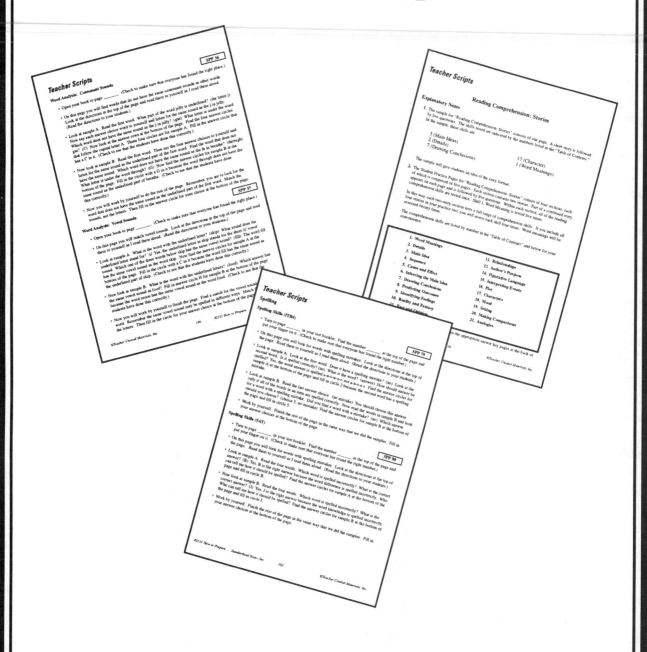

Teacher's Name _____

Starting Date _____

Spelling List

This is a list of selected words that you may wish to add to your spelling program. Many of them appear on the tests as the tested words or as distractors.

ability	apartment	beach
able	appear	beauty
absent	application	before
absolute	approach	bell
absorb	apron	beneath
accelerate	arithmetic	beside
accept	around	blame
account	arrange	blew
ache	arrive	blink
achieve	article	blizzard
acquaint	artistic	blossom
acre	asking	blue
across	asleep	board
address	assignment	boat
admire	assistance	bodies
advantage	attention	books
adventure	auditorium	borrow
against	awake	bottles
aisle	banana	bought
although	bargain	boundary
annual	baseball	brain
answer	basket	branch
anytime	basketful	bravery

Spelling List (cont.)

bread	challenge	company
breeze	chapter	concern
brilliant	cheerful	condition
bristles	chicken	confuse
broken	chrome	continent
bruise	circle	convince
bucket	circus	corner
building	cities	cost
burn	class	country
burrow	clean	courage
business	clear	cousin
button	climate	cover
calendar	close	create
canyon	closet	crowd
captain	clothes	customer
careful	coach	cute
carefully	coastal	debate
carrot	collect	decorate
carry	collection	degree
cause	colleges	delicious
celery	colored	deposit
center	comfort	description
cents	community	destroyed
century	companion	

detect	dust	experiment
develop	duties	explain
development	earn	explanation
dictionary	earth	expressway
difference	eastern	extend
different	eaten	extreme
difficult	echo	fair
dinner	eight	families
disaster	eighth	family
discovered	else	farmer
discussed	empty	fasten
dismiss	energy	favorite
dissolve	entrance	February
distress	equal	figure
disturb	equipment	financial
divide	eraser	finger
doctor	error	finish
dolphin	escape	fish
doubt	estimate	flashlight
dozen	evidence	flea
dried	excellent	flies
drive	except	for
dropped	exist	
during	expedition	

Spelling List (cont.)

forgive	giant	highest
forward	glasses	history
found	global	hole
four	gloves	holiday
fourth	goats	hollow
fragment	graduate	honor
freeze	graph	horse
frequent	grateful	hospital
fresh	great	hour
fried	grew	house
friend	groan	human
friendly	ground	humor
frightened	grown	hundred
frozen	half	hunger
fudge	handful	hurl
gain	handle	hurricane
gallon	happy	hurried
game	harmful	iceberg
garden	harvest	ignore
gasoline	hasn't	I'll
gather	headache	imaginary
gathered	health	imagination
generous	heavy	
ghost	hidden	

Spelling List (cont.)

imagine	kneel	lower
imitate	knew	loyal
imperial	knife	lugging
important	knives	machine
include	knob	made
infant	knocked	magazine
inspect	knowledge	magnet
inspector	knows	maid
instant	lamb	mail
instead	large	male
interest	lately	mansion
interesting	laughter	march
interrupt	lawyer	mast
invisible	learning	match
island	leather	matches
isle	leaving	material
issue	lemon	meadow
jacket	leopard	memory
January	lesson	merriest
jewel	light	mine
journey	listen	miner
juggle	locate	minor
juicy	lonely	
jumped	loose	

Spelling List (cont.)

minute	nearly	outside
mischief	neighbor	oven
mislead	nephew	pail
mistake	nervous	paint
mistrust	new	pair
mittens	nickels	pale
mixture	north	paragraph
moccasin	nose	parallel
monkey	notice	pardon
month	number	passage
monument	obey	passenger
morning	odor	patient
motor	offered	peak
mountain	office	pear
mouse	official	pearl
movement	often	peculiar
mowed	onions	peek
muscles	operate	pencil
music	opinion	people
mystery	opportunity	perfect
napkin	order	permission
narrow	organized	permitted
native	original	
natural	our	

Spelling List (cont.)

personal	promise	reason
phone	property	receive
physically	provide	recently
piece	publish	recognize
pigeon	puppet	recreation
pillow	puppies	refill
plain	purpose	regret
plane	quality	relative
plastic	quart	relax
platform	quarter	rely
pleasure	question	remark
pointed	quiet	remember
powder	raging	remove
prefer	rain	reply
preserve	rained	research
pretty	raise	respect
pride	range	restaurant
prison	rapid	return
prize	raspberries	reverse
probably	rays	reward
problem	reach	rhinoceros
professor	read	right
program	ready	road

Spelling List (cont.)

roasted	search	similar
rode	season	simple
role	secret	singer
roll	section	sister
rose	secure	sizzle
rough	selfish	slender
rows	sense	sliced
rumor	sergeant	smart
sadness	serious	smiling
safety	several	sneeze
said	shadow	snowflakes
sail	shady	soars
salad	share	soften
sale	sheet	solemn
same	shirt	solid
sample	short	some
sandwich	shortly	sometimes
satisfaction	shoulder	sores
Saturday	shovel	sounded
scenery	sight	speed
science	signal	spies
scientific	signed	spill
scold	silence	
screen	silly	

Spelling List (cont.)

spinach	suggestion	thankful
splash	suit	that's
spoke	sum	their
sprinkle	support	themselves
squeeze	sure	there
squirrel	surprise	thin
stairs	surrender	think
stares	suspended	thousand
starve	suspense	threw
statement	swift	throat
station	switch	through
steady	swollen	ticket
stereo	sword	time
store	syllable	tired
story	tail	tomorrow
straight	taking	tournament
strange	tale	town
stranger	taught	track
streak	teach	tractor
strong	teacher	traffic
struggle	temperature	trail
subject	terminal	transmit
sudden	terrific	transparent
sugar	thank	

Spelling List (cont.)

transparent	visitor	where
travel	voice	whether
treasure	waist	which
treatment	wait	whistle
trophy	warm	whole
Tuesday	warmer	wind
tunnel	warmth	window
twice	waste	witch
twist	way	without
uncle	weak	witness
uneasily	wealthy	won
uniform	wear	wonderful
unite	weather	wood
unless	week	worms
unnecessary	weekend	worst
until	weigh	would
use	weight	wrapping
usual	weird	wreck
vanilla	went	write
variable	whale	yellow
vegetables	wheat	yesterday
vehicle	wheel	young

Testing Terms

Assessment

Assessment refers to the systematic and purposeful use of one or more of the various methods of testing student progress and achievement.

Alternative Assessment

Alternative assessment involves innovative ways of keeping track of and evaluating student work and progress. Usually contrasted with traditional, objective, standardized, norm-referenced, and paper-and-pencil testing, it includes methods such as portfolio assessment, observation of assigned tasks, and anecdotal records.

Authentic Assessment

Authentic assessment is the observation and scoring of the performance of a task in real life or, if that is impossible, in a situation that closely matches the standards and challenges of real life.

Criterion-Referenced Assessment

This kind of assessment is compared to and based upon behavioral objectives in which the learner's proficiency in an area of the curriculum is determined by his or her degree of success in completing prescribed tasks and not by comparison to the scores of other learners.

Portfolio Assessment

Portfolio assessment is a longitudinal system of assessment that occurs over a period of time and involves chronologically ordered samples of a student's work that can be compared to identify that student's progress. These samples are stored in an individual container of some kind (a portfolio).

Traditional Assessment

A traditional assessment system involves the periodic collection of data about student achievement by means of objective, standardized, norm-referenced, and paper-and-pencil tests.

Evaluation

Evaluation is the process of judging the information or results obtained from assessment for one purpose or another. (If you assess a student's ability to complete a given task in the fall and then again in the spring, you can evaluate the progress he or she has made by comparing the two assessments.)

Testing Terms *(cont.)*

Information Management

In an information management system, assessment information (test dates, observation checklists, portfolio materials, etc.) regarding student progress is collected, organized, and maintained.

Anecdotal Records

These used to be just lists of teacher observations stated factually and objectively without teacher interpretation or judgment. They were usually kept to document behavior problems. Anecdotal records have, however, taken on a new meaning with new forms of assessment. They have become positive narratives that document the growth and development of students. They are, at least to some extent, subjective since they contain teacher interpretation and judgment. They are often kept in student portfolios and have thus become a part of portfolio assessment.

Checklists

Checklists are convenient forms in a variety of styles. They are designed (or can be designed through the use of task analysis) to help teachers record what they see during observation-based assessment.

Checkpoints

Checkpoints are important assessment points along the way between the beginning and the end of the educational process.

Exit Demonstration (Culminating Activity, Outcome)

Exit demonstration refers to the final culminating activity that proves that a student has mastered an area of the curriculum.

Portfolios

In addition to functioning as a type of assessment, portfolios also function as containers for collecting, organizing, and maintaining student records.

Rubrics

In connection with assessment, a rubric is a scoring guide that differentiates, on an articulated scale, among a group of student samples that respond to the same prompt.

Running Records

A running record is of student miscues (errors) made during the oral reading of a selection.

Testing Terms (cont.)

Standards

Content Standards

These are standards that describe the desired outcomes in various subject areas. (frameworks; curriculum outlines)

Curriculum Standards

The course of study in a given area; an outline of content.

National Standards

A set of standards for the whole country. Currently, a popular movement among one group of educators. Usually understood to include content standards, performance standards, and school delivery standards.

Performance Standards

Standards that define the level and quality of performance that students must exhibit to show mastery of an area of the curriculum.

School Delivery Standards

Standards that indicate whether or not a school has the resources necessary to enable students to meet the performance standards.

Tests

Tests are assessment tools constructed in such a way that achievement can be measured.

Achievement Tests

These are tests designed to assess the amount of information or degree of skill possessed by the test taker, usually objective, standardized, norm-referenced, paper-and-pencil tests.

Cognitive Tests

Cognitive tests are used to assess intellectual functioning.

Norm-Referenced Tests

These tests are based on and judged in comparison with standards determined by testing a selected pool of individuals, forming the standardized sample.

Tests (cont.)

Objective Tests

Tests in which each question is stated in such a way that there is only one correct answer, true/false and multiple-choice tests are examples of objective tests.

Paper-and-Pencil Tests

We refer to tests that are designed to be read either orally by the teacher or silently by the student and answered in writing as paper-and-pencil tests.

Performance Tests

Students are asked to perform tasks while their methods and reasoning processes are observed, monitored, and recorded by means of an instrument (such as a checklist). In most cases, the students' methods and reasoning processes are considered of the same or greater value than the actual results or answers.

Proficiency Tests

Proficiency tests are written to test the objectives that are actually being taught. In order to construct a proficiency test, educators first decide on the things that they really want their students to learn (goals and objectives). Teachers then teach these things and test students to see if they have learned the material.

Psycho-Motor/Perception Tests

These tests used to measure visual-motor skills are usually standardized and norm-referenced.

Standardized Tests

(See *Norm-Referenced Tests, page 204*.)

Writing Sample Tests

Students are asked to demonstrate writing abilities by actually writing in response to given prompts. These writing samples are graded with the use of rubrics.
(See *Rubrics, page 204*.)

Answer Key

Page 31

A	● (B) (C)	A
B	(F) ● (H)	B
1	● (B) (C)	
2	(F) (G) ●	
3	(A) ● (C)	
4	(F) ● (H)	
5	(A) ● (C)	
6	(F) (G) ●	
7	(A) (B) ●	
8	(F) ● (H)	
9	(A) ● (C)	
10	(F) ● (H)	

Page 32

A ● (B) (C)
B (F) ● (H)
1 ● (B) (C)
2 (F) ● (H)
3 (A) (B) ●
4 ● (G) (H)
5 (A) (B) ●
6 (F) ● (H)
7 (A) ● (C)
8 (F) ● (H)
9 (A) ● (C)
10 ● (G) (H)

Page 33

A (A) ● (C) (D)
B (E) (F) (G) ●
1 ● (B) (C) (D)
2 ● (F) (G) (H)
3 (A) (B) (C) ●
4 (E) ● (G) (H)
5 (A) (B) ● (D)
6 (E) (F) ● (H)
7 (A) (B) (C) ●
8 (E) (F) ● (H)
9 ● (B) (C) (D)
10 (E) ● (G) (H)

Page 34

A (A) ● (C)
B ● (G) (H)
1 (A) ● (C)
2 ● (G) (H)
3 (A) ● (C)
4 ● (G) (H)
5 (A) ● (C)
6 ● (G) (H)
7 ● (B) (C)
8 (F) ● (H)

Page 35

A (A) ● (C)
B ● (E) (F) (G)
1 (A) ● (C)
2 (D) (E) ●
3 (A) ● (C)
4 ● (E) (F)
5 (A) ● (C) (D)
6 (E) ● (G) (H)
7 ● (B) (C) (D)
8 (E) ● (G) (H)

Page 36

A (A) (B) ● (D)
B (F) ● (H) (J)
1 (A) (B) ● (D)
2 (F) ● (H) (J)
3 (A) (B) (C) ●
4 ● (G) (H) (J)
5 (A) (B) (C) ●
6 ● (G) (H) (J)
7 (A) ● (C) (D)
8 ● (G) (H) (J)

Answer Key (cont.)

Page 37

A (A) (B) ●	2 (F) ● (H)	5 (A) (B) ●	8 (F) ● (H)
B (F) (G) ●	3 ● (B) (C)	6 ● (G) (H)	9 ● (B) (C)
1 (A) (B) ●	4 (F) (G) ●	7 ● (B) (C)	10 (F) (G) ●

Page 38

A (A) (B) (C) ●	2 (E) (F) ● (H)	5 (A) (B) (C) ●	8 (E) (F) ● (H)
B (E) (F) ● (H)	3 ● (B) (C) (D)	6 ● (F) (G) (H)	9 (A) ● (C) (D)
1 (A) ● (C) (D)	4 (E) (F) ● (H)	7 (A) (B) (C) ●	10 (E) (F) ● (H)

Page 39

A (A) (B) ● (D)	2 (F) ● (H) (J)	5 (A) (B) (C) ●	8 (F) (G) ● (J)
B (F) ● (H) (J)	3 (A) (B) ● (D)	6 (F) ● (H) (J)	
1 (A) (B) ● (D)	4 ● (G) (H) (J)	7 ● (B) (C) (D)	

Page 40

A (A) (B) (C) ●	3 (A) (B) ● (D)	6 (F) ● (H) (J)	9 (A) ● (C) (D)
1 ● (B) (C) (D)	4 (F) (G) (H) ●	7 (A) (B) ● (D)	
2 (F) ● (H) (J)	5 ● (B) (C) (D)	8 ● (G) (H) (J)	

Page 41

A ● (B) (C) (D)	3 (A) (B) (C) ●	6 (E) (F) ● (H)
1 (A) ● (C) (D)	4 ● (F) (G) (H)	7 (A) (B) ● (D)
2 ● (F) (G) (H)	5 (A) (B) (C) ●	8 (E) (F) (G) ●

Page 42

A (A) (B) ● (D)	1 (A) (B) ● (D)	4 ● (G) (H) (J)
B ● (G) (H) (J)	2 (F) ● (H) (J)	5 (A) (B) (C) ●
C (A) (B) (C) ●	3 (A) (B) (C) ●	6 (F) ● (H) (J)

Answer Key (cont.)

Page 43

A — A	3 — A	7 — A	11 — A
B — G	4 — F	8 — H	12 — H
1 — B	5 — B	9 — C	
2 — H	6 — H	10 — H	

Page 44

A — C	2 — F	5 — B	8 — H
B — G	3 — B	6 — J	9 — C
1 — C	4 — F	7 — B	10 — F

Page 45

A — B	2 — G	5 — A	8 — F
B — H	3 — D	6 — J	9 — B
1 — C	4 — H	7 — A	10 — G

Page 46

A — A	2 — H	5 — B	8 — G
B — G	3 — D	6 — H	9 — C
1 — B	4 — F	7 — A	10 — J

Page 47

A — B	1 — D	3 — D	5 — A
B — H	2 — H	4 — G	6 — F

Page 48

A — D	1 — C	3 — B	5 — A
B — G	2 — F	4 — H	6 — J

Answer Key (cont.)

Page 49

A (A) (B) (C) ●   1 ● (B) (C) (D)   3 (A) ● (C) (D)   5 (A) (B) ● (D)

B (F) ● (H) (J)   2 (F) (G) (H) ●   4 (F) (G) ● (J)   6 ● (G) (H) (J)

Page 50

A (A) ● (C) (D)   2 (F) (G) ● (J)   5 (A) (B) ● (D)   8 (F) ● (H) (J)

B (F) ● (H) (J)   3 (A) (B) (C) ●   6 (F) (G) (H) ●

1 ● (B) (C) (D)   4 (F) (G) ● (J)   7 ● (B) (C) (D)

Page 51

A (A) ● (C) (D)   1 (A) (B) ● (D)   3 (A) ● (C) (D)

B (F) ● (H) (J)   2 ● (G) (H) (J)   4 (F) (G) ● (J)

Page 52

5 (A) (B) ● (D)   7 (A) (B) (C) ●   9 (A) (B) ● (D)   11 (A) ● (C) (D)

6 (F) ● (H) (J)   8 (F) ● (H) (J)   10 ● (G) (H) (J)   12 (F) (G) (H) ●

Page 53

A ● (B) (C) (D)   2 ● (G) (H) (J)   5 (A) (B) (C) ●   8 (F) (G) ● (J)

B (F) ● (H) (J)   3 (A) (B) ● (D)   6 (F) (G) (H) ●   9 (A) (B) (C) ●

1 (A) (B) (C) ●   4 (F) (G) ● (J)   7 (A) ● (C) (D)   10 (F) (G) (H) ●

Page 54

1 (A) (B) ● (D) #3   4 (F) ● (H) (J) #11

2 (F) ● (H) (J) #2   5 ● (B) (C) (D) #1

3 (A) (B) ● (D) #4

Answer Key *(cont.)*

Page 55

1 Ⓐ Ⓑ ● Ⓓ #3
2 ● Ⓖ Ⓗ Ⓙ #2
3 Ⓐ ● Ⓒ Ⓓ #4

4 Ⓕ Ⓖ Ⓗ ● #11
5 Ⓐ Ⓑ ● Ⓓ #1

Page 56

1 Ⓐ Ⓑ ● Ⓓ #6
2 ● Ⓖ Ⓗ Ⓙ #10
3 ● Ⓑ Ⓒ Ⓓ #13

4 Ⓕ ● Ⓗ Ⓙ #21
5 Ⓐ ● Ⓒ Ⓓ #1

Page 57

1 Ⓐ Ⓑ ● Ⓓ #5
2 Ⓕ Ⓖ ● Ⓙ #20
3 Ⓐ Ⓑ Ⓒ ● #19

4 Ⓕ ● Ⓗ Ⓙ #7
5 ● Ⓑ Ⓒ Ⓓ #1

Page 58

1 Ⓐ Ⓑ ● Ⓓ #9
2 ● Ⓖ Ⓗ Ⓙ #14
3 Ⓐ Ⓑ ● Ⓓ #12

4 Ⓕ Ⓖ ● Ⓙ #15
5 ● Ⓑ Ⓒ Ⓓ #1

Page 59

1 Ⓐ Ⓑ Ⓒ ● #18
2 ● Ⓖ Ⓗ Ⓙ #16
3 Ⓐ Ⓑ ● Ⓓ #17

4 Ⓕ ● Ⓗ Ⓙ #8
5 Ⓐ Ⓑ ● Ⓓ #1

Page 60

1 Ⓐ ● Ⓒ Ⓓ #3
2 ● Ⓖ Ⓗ Ⓙ #2
3 Ⓐ Ⓑ Ⓒ ● #4

4 ● Ⓖ Ⓗ Ⓙ #11
5 ● Ⓑ Ⓒ Ⓓ #1

Answer Key (cont.)

Page 61

1 Ⓐ Ⓑ ⬤ Ⓓ #6
2 Ⓕ Ⓖ Ⓗ ⬤ #21
3 Ⓐ ⬤ Ⓒ Ⓓ #15

4 Ⓕ ⬤ Ⓗ Ⓙ #8
5 Ⓐ ⬤ Ⓒ Ⓓ #1

Page 62

1 Ⓐ Ⓑ ⬤ Ⓓ #12
2 Ⓕ Ⓖ Ⓗ ⬤ #14
3 ⬤ Ⓑ Ⓒ Ⓓ #19

4 ⬤ Ⓖ Ⓗ Ⓙ #7
5 Ⓐ ⬤ Ⓒ Ⓓ #1

Page 63

1 Ⓐ ⬤ Ⓒ Ⓓ #5
2 Ⓕ Ⓖ ⬤ Ⓙ #9
3 Ⓐ ⬤ Ⓒ Ⓓ #17

4 Ⓕ ⬤ Ⓗ Ⓙ #13
5 Ⓐ Ⓑ Ⓒ ⬤ #1

Page 64

1 ⬤ Ⓑ Ⓒ Ⓓ #20
2 Ⓕ Ⓖ ⬤ Ⓙ #18
3 Ⓐ ⬤ Ⓒ Ⓓ #10

4 Ⓕ Ⓖ Ⓗ ⬤ #16
5 ⬤ Ⓑ Ⓒ Ⓓ #1

Page 65

1 ⬤ Ⓑ Ⓒ Ⓓ #3
2 Ⓕ Ⓖ Ⓗ ⬤ #2
3 Ⓐ ⬤ Ⓒ Ⓓ #5

4 Ⓕ ⬤ Ⓗ Ⓙ #20
5 ⬤ Ⓑ Ⓒ Ⓓ #1

Page 66

1 ⬤ Ⓑ Ⓒ Ⓓ #11
2 Ⓕ Ⓖ ⬤ Ⓙ #8
3 ⬤ Ⓑ Ⓒ Ⓓ #13

4 Ⓕ ⬤ Ⓗ Ⓙ #21
5 Ⓐ Ⓑ Ⓒ ⬤ #1

Answer Key (cont.)

Page 67

1 Ⓐ Ⓑ Ⓒ ⬤ #3
2 Ⓕ Ⓖ ⬤ Ⓙ #2
3 Ⓐ ⬤ Ⓒ Ⓓ #5

4 Ⓕ Ⓖ ⬤ Ⓙ #20
5 ⬤ Ⓑ Ⓒ Ⓓ #1

Page 68

1 ⬤ Ⓑ Ⓒ Ⓓ #6
2 Ⓕ Ⓖ Ⓗ ⬤ #4
3 Ⓐ ⬤ Ⓒ Ⓓ #18

4 Ⓕ Ⓖ ⬤ Ⓙ #15
5 ⬤ Ⓑ Ⓒ Ⓓ #1

Page 69

1 ⬤ Ⓑ Ⓒ Ⓓ #17
2 Ⓕ ⬤ Ⓗ Ⓙ #19
3 ⬤ Ⓑ Ⓒ Ⓓ #16

4 Ⓕ ⬤ Ⓗ Ⓙ #10
5 Ⓐ ⬤ Ⓒ Ⓓ #1

Page 70

1 Ⓐ ⬤ Ⓒ Ⓓ #3
2 Ⓕ ⬤ Ⓗ Ⓙ #2
3 Ⓐ Ⓑ Ⓒ ⬤ #4

4 Ⓕ Ⓖ ⬤ Ⓙ #5
5 Ⓐ ⬤ Ⓒ Ⓓ #1

Page 71

1 Ⓐ ⬤ Ⓒ Ⓓ #6
2 Ⓕ Ⓖ ⬤ Ⓙ #7
3 Ⓐ Ⓑ Ⓒ ⬤ #11

4 Ⓕ Ⓖ ⬤ Ⓙ #8
5 ⬤ Ⓑ Ⓒ Ⓓ #1

Page 72

1 Ⓐ Ⓑ ⬤ Ⓓ #20
2 ⬤ Ⓖ Ⓗ Ⓙ #13
3 Ⓐ ⬤ Ⓒ Ⓓ #17

4 Ⓕ Ⓖ Ⓗ ⬤ #15
5 ⬤ Ⓑ Ⓒ Ⓓ #1

Answer Key (cont.)

Page 73

1. Ⓐ ● Ⓒ Ⓓ #19
2. Ⓕ Ⓖ ● Ⓙ #9
3. ● Ⓑ Ⓒ Ⓓ #14
4. Ⓕ Ⓖ Ⓗ ● #12
5. Ⓐ ● Ⓒ Ⓓ #1

Page 74

1. Ⓐ ● Ⓒ Ⓓ #10
2. Ⓕ Ⓖ Ⓗ ● #21
3. ● Ⓑ Ⓒ Ⓓ #16
4. Ⓕ Ⓖ Ⓗ ● #18
5. Ⓐ ● Ⓒ Ⓓ #1

Page 75

A. Ⓐ Ⓑ ● Ⓓ
B. ● Ⓖ Ⓗ Ⓙ
1. ● Ⓑ Ⓒ Ⓓ
2. Ⓕ ● Ⓗ Ⓙ
3. Ⓐ Ⓑ ● Ⓓ
4. Ⓕ Ⓖ Ⓗ ●
5. ● Ⓑ Ⓒ Ⓓ
6. Ⓕ Ⓖ ● Ⓙ

Page 76

A. Ⓐ ● Ⓒ Ⓓ
1. Ⓐ Ⓑ Ⓒ ●
2. ● Ⓖ Ⓗ Ⓙ
3. Ⓐ Ⓑ ● Ⓓ

Page 77

A. Ⓐ ● Ⓒ Ⓓ
B. Ⓕ Ⓖ Ⓗ ●
1. ● Ⓑ Ⓒ Ⓓ
2. Ⓕ Ⓖ ● Ⓙ
3. Ⓐ ● Ⓒ Ⓓ
4. Ⓕ Ⓖ Ⓗ ●
5. Ⓐ ● Ⓒ Ⓓ
6. ● Ⓖ Ⓗ Ⓙ
7. Ⓐ Ⓑ ● Ⓓ
8. ● Ⓖ Ⓗ Ⓙ

Page 78

A. Ⓐ Ⓑ ● Ⓓ
B. ● Ⓖ Ⓗ Ⓙ
1. Ⓐ Ⓑ ● Ⓓ
2. Ⓕ Ⓖ ● Ⓙ
3. ● Ⓑ Ⓒ Ⓓ
4. Ⓕ ● Ⓗ Ⓙ
5. Ⓐ Ⓑ ● Ⓓ
6. ● Ⓖ Ⓗ Ⓙ
7. ● Ⓑ Ⓒ Ⓓ
8. Ⓕ ● Ⓗ Ⓙ
9. Ⓐ Ⓑ ● Ⓓ
10. Ⓕ Ⓖ ● Ⓙ

Answer Key (cont.)

Page 79

A ① ● ③ ④ ⑤   2 ● ② ③ ④ ⑤   5 ① ② ③ ● ⑤   8 ① ② ● ④ ⑤
B ① ② ③ ④ ●   3 ① ② ● ④ ⑤   6 ① ② ● ④ ⑤   9 ● ② ③ ④ ⑤
1 ① ② ③ ● ⑤   4 ① ● ③ ④ ⑤   7 ① ② ③ ④ ●   10 ① ● ③ ④ ⑤

Page 80

A Ⓐ ● Ⓒ Ⓓ   2 Ⓕ Ⓖ ● Ⓙ   5 Ⓐ Ⓑ Ⓒ ●   8 ● Ⓖ Ⓗ Ⓙ
B Ⓕ Ⓖ Ⓗ ●   3 ● Ⓑ Ⓒ Ⓓ   6 Ⓕ Ⓖ ● Ⓙ   9 Ⓐ Ⓑ ● Ⓓ
1 ● Ⓑ Ⓒ Ⓓ   4 Ⓕ ● Ⓗ Ⓙ   7 Ⓐ ● Ⓒ Ⓓ   10 ● Ⓖ Ⓗ Ⓙ

Page 81

A ● Ⓑ Ⓒ Ⓓ   2 Ⓕ Ⓖ Ⓗ ●   5 Ⓐ ● Ⓒ Ⓓ   8 Ⓕ Ⓖ ● Ⓙ
B ● Ⓖ Ⓗ Ⓙ   3 Ⓐ ● Ⓒ Ⓓ   6 Ⓕ ● Ⓗ Ⓙ   9 Ⓐ ● Ⓒ Ⓓ
1 Ⓐ ● Ⓒ Ⓓ   4 ● Ⓖ Ⓗ Ⓙ   7 Ⓐ ● Ⓒ Ⓓ   10 ● Ⓖ Ⓗ Ⓙ

Page 82

A Ⓐ ● Ⓒ Ⓓ   2 Ⓔ ● Ⓖ Ⓗ   5 Ⓐ ● Ⓒ Ⓓ   8 Ⓔ Ⓕ Ⓖ ●
B Ⓔ Ⓕ Ⓖ ●   3 Ⓐ Ⓑ Ⓒ ●   6 Ⓔ Ⓕ ● Ⓗ
1 Ⓐ Ⓑ ● Ⓓ   4 ● Ⓕ Ⓖ Ⓗ   7 Ⓐ Ⓑ ● Ⓓ

Page 83

A Ⓐ ● Ⓒ Ⓓ   2 Ⓔ ● Ⓖ Ⓗ   5 ● Ⓑ Ⓒ Ⓓ   8 Ⓔ Ⓕ ● Ⓗ
B Ⓔ Ⓕ ● Ⓗ   3 Ⓐ Ⓑ ● Ⓓ   6 Ⓔ Ⓕ ● Ⓗ   9 Ⓐ ● Ⓒ Ⓓ
1 ● Ⓑ Ⓒ Ⓓ   4 Ⓔ Ⓕ Ⓖ ●   7 ● Ⓑ Ⓒ Ⓓ   10 Ⓔ Ⓕ ● Ⓗ

Page 84

A Ⓐ ● Ⓒ Ⓓ Ⓔ   2 Ⓕ ● Ⓗ Ⓙ Ⓚ   5 Ⓐ Ⓑ ● Ⓓ Ⓔ   8 ● Ⓖ Ⓗ Ⓙ Ⓚ
B Ⓕ Ⓖ Ⓗ Ⓙ ●   3 Ⓐ Ⓑ Ⓒ Ⓓ ●   6 Ⓕ ● Ⓗ Ⓙ Ⓚ
1 Ⓐ Ⓑ ● Ⓓ Ⓔ   4 Ⓕ Ⓖ Ⓗ ● Ⓚ   7 Ⓐ Ⓑ Ⓒ ● Ⓔ

Answer Key (cont.)

Page 85

	(1)	(2)	(3)	(4)
A		●		
B				●
1			●	
2		●		
3		●		
4		●		
5		●		
6			●	
7			●	
8		●		
9				●
10			●	

Page 86

	A/F	B/G	C/H	D/J
A	A	●	C	D
B	F	G	H	●
1	●	B	C	D
2	F	G	H	●
3	A	B	●	D
4	F	G	H	●
5	●	B	C	D
6	F	●	H	J
7	A	B	C	●
8	F	G	H	●

Page 87

	A/F	B/G	C/H	D/J	E/K
A	A	B	●	D	E
B	F	G	H	J	●
1	A	B	C	●	E
2	F	●	H	J	K
3	A	B	●	D	E
4	F	G	●	J	K
5	A	B	C	D	●
6	●	G	H	J	K
7	A	●	C	D	E
8	F	G	H	●	K

Page 88

	A/F	B/G	C/H	D/J	E/K
A	A	●	C	D	E
B	F	G	H	J	●
1	A	B	●	D	E
2	F	G	H	●	K
3	A	B	C	D	●
4	F	G	H	●	K
5	A	B	●	D	E
6	F	●	H	J	K

Page 89

	(1)	(2)	(3)	(4)
A				●
B	●			
1		●		
2		●		
3				●
4	●			
5			●	
6			●	
7		●		
8			●	
9				●
10	●			

Page 90

	A/F	B/G	C/H	D/J
A	A	●	C	D
B	F	G	H	●
1	A	●	C	D
2	F	G	●	J
3	A	B	●	D
4	●	G	H	J
5	A	●	C	D
6	F	G	●	J
7	●	B	C	D
8	F	G	H	●

Answer Key (cont.)

Page 91

A ⒶⒷ●Ⓓ　　1 ●ⒷⒸⒹ　　3 ⒶⒷ●Ⓓ　　5 ⒶⒷⒸ●
B ⒻⒼⒽ●　　2 ⒻⒼⒽ●　　4 Ⓕ●ⒽⒿ　　6 ⒻⒼ●Ⓙ

Page 92

A ⒶⒷⒸ●　　2 ⒻⒼ●Ⓙ　　5 ⒶⒷⒸ●　　8 ⒻⒼⒽ●
B Ⓕ●ⒽⒿ　　3 ⒶⒷ●Ⓓ　　6 Ⓕ●ⒽⒿ
1 Ⓐ●ⒸⒹ　　4 Ⓕ●ⒽⒿ　　7 Ⓐ●ⒸⒹ

Page 93

A ●②③④　　2 ①●③④　　5 ①②●④　　8 ①②③●
B ①②③●　　3 ●②③④　　6 ●②③④　　9 ①②●④
1 ①●③④　　4 ①●③④　　7 ●②③④　　10 ①②●④

Page 94

A ⒶⒷ●Ⓓ　　1 ⒶⒷⒸ●　　3 ●ⒷⒸⒹ　　5 Ⓐ●ⒸⒹ
B ●ⒻⒼⒽ　　2 Ⓔ●ⒼⒽ　　4 Ⓔ●ⒼⒽ　　6 ⒺⒻ●Ⓗ

Page 95

7 ⒶⒷ●Ⓓ　　9 ⒶⒷ●Ⓓ　　11 ●ⒷⒸⒹ　　13 ●ⒷⒸⒹ
8 ⒺⒻⒼ●　　10 ⒺⒻ●Ⓗ　　12 ●ⒻⒼⒽ　　14 ⒺⒻⒼ●

Page 96

A Ⓐ●ⒸⒹ　　2 Ⓕ●ⒽⒿ　　6 Ⓕ●ⒽⒿ　　10 ●ⒼⒽⒿ
B ⒻⒼ●Ⓙ　　3 ●ⒷⒸⒹ　　7 ⒶⒷⒸ●
C Ⓐ●ⒸⒹ　　4 Ⓕ●ⒽⒿ　　8 Ⓕ●ⒽⒿ
1 Ⓐ●ⒸⒹ　　5 ⒶⒷ●Ⓓ　　9 ⒶⒷ●Ⓓ

Answer Key (cont.)

Page 97   A (A) ● (C) (D)   1 (A) ● (C) (D)   3 (A) (B) ● (D)   5 ● (B) (C) (D)

               B (F) (G) (H) ●   2 (F) ● (H) (J)   4 (F) (G) ● (J)   6 (F) (G) ● (J)

Page 98   A (A) ● (C) (D)   1 (A) (B) ● (D)   2 (F) ● (H) (J)   3 (A) ● (C) (D)

Page 99   A (A) (B) ● (D)   1 (A) (B) (C) ●

               B (F) ● (H) (J)   2 (F) ● (H) (J)

Page 100   A (A) ● (C) (D)   1 (A) ● (C) (D)   2 (F) (G) (H) ●

Pages 101–105 are student-generated writing samples.

Page 106   A ● (B) (C) (D)   1 (A) (B) ● (D)   3 (A) (B) ● (D)   5 ● (B) (C) (D)

               B (F) (G) ● (J)   2 (F) (G) (H) ●   4 (F) (G) ● (J)   6 (F) (G) (H) ●

Answer Key (cont.)

Page 107 A Ⓐ Ⓑ ● Ⓓ   1 Ⓐ Ⓑ Ⓒ ●   3 Ⓐ Ⓑ Ⓒ ●
                                2 ● Ⓖ Ⓗ Ⓙ   4 Ⓕ ● Ⓗ Ⓙ

Page 108 A ● ② ③ ④   1 ① ② ● ④   3 ① ● ③ ④
              B ① ② ● ④   2 ● ② ③ ④   4 ① ② ③ ●

Page 109 A ① ② ● ④   1 ① ② ● ④   3 ① ● ③ ④
              B ① ② ③ ●   2 ● ② ③ ④   4 ① ② ● ④

Page 110 A Ⓐ ● Ⓒ Ⓓ   2 ● Ⓖ Ⓗ Ⓙ   5 Ⓐ ● Ⓒ Ⓓ   8 ● Ⓖ Ⓗ Ⓙ
              B Ⓕ Ⓖ ● Ⓙ   3 Ⓐ ● Ⓒ Ⓓ   6 Ⓕ ● Ⓗ Ⓙ   9 Ⓐ ● Ⓒ Ⓓ
              1 Ⓐ Ⓑ ● Ⓓ   4 Ⓕ Ⓖ Ⓗ ●   7 Ⓐ Ⓑ Ⓒ ●   10 Ⓕ Ⓖ Ⓗ ●

Page 111 A Ⓐ ● Ⓒ Ⓓ   2 ● Ⓖ Ⓗ Ⓙ   4 Ⓕ ● Ⓗ Ⓙ
              1 Ⓐ ● Ⓒ Ⓓ   3 ● Ⓑ Ⓒ Ⓓ   5 Ⓐ ● Ⓒ Ⓓ

Page 112 A Ⓐ Ⓑ ● Ⓓ   1 Ⓐ Ⓑ ● Ⓓ   2 Ⓕ ● Ⓗ Ⓙ   3 ● Ⓑ Ⓒ Ⓓ

Answer Key (cont.)

Page 113

A	1	2	3	●
B	●	2	3	4

1	1	●	3	4
2	1	2	3	●

3	1	2	●	4
4	1	●	3	4

Page 114

A	1	2	●	4
B	●	2	3	4

1	1	●	3	4
2	1	●	3	4

3	1	●	3	4
4	1	2	3	●

Page 115

A	A	B	C	●	E
B	F	G	H	J	●
1	A	B	C	●	E

2	F	G	H	●	K
3	A	●	C	D	E
4	●	G	H	J	K

5	A	B	●	D	E
6	F	G	H	J	●
7	A	B	C	●	E

8	F	●	H	J	K

Page 116

A	A	B	●	D	E
B	F	G	H	J	●
1	A	B	●	D	E

2	F	G	H	●	K
3	A	B	●	D	E
4	F	G	●	J	K

5	A	B	●	D	E
6	F	G	H	●	K
7	A	B	●	D	E

8	F	G	H	J	●

Page 117

A	●	B	C	D	E
B	F	●	H	J	K
1	A	B	●	D	E

2	F	G	H	J	●
3	●	B	C	D	E
4	F	G	●	J	K

5	A	●	C	D	E
6	F	●	H	J	K
7	A	B	C	●	E

8	●	G	H	J	K

Page 118

A	●	B	C	D	E
B	F	●	H	J	K
1	A	●	C	D	E

2	F	G	●	J	K
3	A	B	C	●	E
4	F	G	●	J	K

5	A	B	C	D	●
6	F	●	H	J	K
7	A	B	C	D	●

8	F	G	●	J	K

Answer Key (cont.)

Page 119

A — B	2 — G	5 — B	8 — K	
B — K	3 — C	6 — F		
1 — A	4 — F	7 — B		

Page 120

A — C	2 — H	5 — B	8 — F
B — K	3 — B	6 — K	
1 — A	4 — F	7 — F	

Page 121

A — C	2 — F	5 — A	8 — F
B — J	3 — A	6 — G	
1 — B	4 — G	7 — C	

Page 122

A — A	2 — G	5 — B	8 — F
B — G	3 — D	6 — J	
1 — C	4 — K	7 — B	

Page 123

A — B	2 — J	5 — C	8 — K
B — K	3 — C	6 — H	
1 — C	4 — H	7 — D	

Answer Key (cont.)

Page 124

A. A B ●C D E 2. F G H ●J K 5. A B ●C D E 8. ●F G H J K
B. F G H ●J K 3. A B C ●D E 6. F G ●H J K
1. A ●B C D E 4. F G ●H J K 7. A B C ●D E

Page 125

A. A B ●C D E 2. F G ●H J K 5. A B C ●D E 8. F G ●H J K
B. ●F G H J K 3. A ●B C D E 6. F G H J ●K
1. A ●B C D E 4. F ●G H J K 7. A ●B C D E

Page 126

A. A B C ●D E 2. F G ●H J K 5. A B C ●D E 8. F G ●H J K
B. F G ●H J K 3. A ●B C D E 6. ●F G H J K
1. A B C D ●E 4. F ●G H J K 7. A B ●C D E

Page 127

A. A ●B C D 2. F G H ●J 5. A ●B C D 8. F ●G H J
B. F G ●H J 3. A ●B C D 6. F G ●H J
1. A B ●C D 4. F G H ●J 7. A B ●C D

Page 128

9. A ●B C D   12. F ●G H J   15. A B ●C D
10. F G ●H J 13. ●A B C D   16. F G H ●J
11. A B C ●D 14. F G ●H J

Answer Key (cont.)

Page 129
A: Ⓐ Ⓑ ● Ⓓ B: Ⓕ Ⓖ Ⓗ ●
1: ● Ⓑ Ⓒ Ⓓ 2: Ⓕ ● Ⓗ Ⓙ
3: Ⓐ ● Ⓒ Ⓓ 4: Ⓕ Ⓖ ● Ⓙ
5: Ⓐ ● Ⓒ Ⓓ 6: Ⓕ Ⓖ ● Ⓙ

Page 130
A: Ⓐ Ⓑ ● Ⓓ B: ● Ⓖ Ⓗ Ⓙ
1: ● Ⓑ Ⓒ Ⓓ 2: Ⓕ ● Ⓗ Ⓙ
3: Ⓐ Ⓑ ● Ⓓ 4: ● Ⓖ Ⓗ Ⓙ
5: Ⓐ Ⓑ Ⓒ ● 6: Ⓕ ● Ⓗ Ⓙ

Page 131
A: Ⓐ ● Ⓒ Ⓓ B: Ⓕ Ⓖ ● Ⓙ
1: Ⓐ Ⓑ ● Ⓓ 2: Ⓕ ● Ⓗ Ⓙ 3: Ⓐ ● Ⓒ Ⓓ

Page 132
4: Ⓕ Ⓖ Ⓗ ● 6: Ⓕ Ⓖ Ⓗ ● 8: ● Ⓖ Ⓗ Ⓙ
5: Ⓐ Ⓑ ● Ⓓ 7: Ⓐ Ⓑ ● Ⓓ

Page 133
A: Ⓐ ● Ⓒ Ⓓ B: Ⓕ ● Ⓗ Ⓙ
1: ● Ⓑ Ⓒ Ⓓ 2: Ⓕ Ⓖ ● Ⓙ
3: Ⓐ Ⓑ Ⓒ ● 4: Ⓕ ● Ⓗ Ⓙ

Answer Key (cont.)

Page 134
5 Ⓐ Ⓑ Ⓒ Ⓓ   7 Ⓐ Ⓑ Ⓒ Ⓓ   9 Ⓐ Ⓑ Ⓒ Ⓓ
6 Ⓕ Ⓖ Ⓗ Ⓙ   8 Ⓕ Ⓖ Ⓗ Ⓙ   10 Ⓕ Ⓖ Ⓗ Ⓙ

Page 135
11 Ⓐ Ⓑ Ⓒ Ⓓ   13 Ⓐ Ⓑ Ⓒ Ⓓ
12 Ⓕ Ⓖ Ⓗ Ⓙ   14 Ⓕ Ⓖ Ⓗ Ⓙ

Page 136
A Ⓐ Ⓑ Ⓒ Ⓓ   1 Ⓐ Ⓑ Ⓒ Ⓓ   3 Ⓐ Ⓑ Ⓒ Ⓓ
          2 Ⓕ Ⓖ Ⓗ Ⓙ   4 Ⓕ Ⓖ Ⓗ Ⓙ

Page 137
A Ⓐ Ⓑ Ⓒ Ⓓ   1 Ⓐ Ⓑ Ⓒ Ⓓ   3 Ⓐ Ⓑ Ⓒ Ⓓ   5 Ⓐ Ⓑ Ⓒ Ⓓ
B Ⓕ Ⓖ Ⓗ Ⓙ   2 Ⓕ Ⓖ Ⓗ Ⓙ   4 Ⓕ Ⓖ Ⓗ Ⓙ   6 Ⓕ Ⓖ Ⓗ Ⓙ

Page 138
A Ⓐ Ⓑ Ⓒ Ⓓ   1 Ⓐ Ⓑ Ⓒ Ⓓ   2 Ⓕ Ⓖ Ⓗ Ⓙ

Answer Key (cont.)

Page 139 A Ⓐ Ⓑ Ⓒ ● 1 ● Ⓑ Ⓒ Ⓓ 3 Ⓐ Ⓑ ● Ⓓ
   2 Ⓕ Ⓖ Ⓗ ● 4 Ⓕ Ⓖ ● Ⓙ

Page 140 A Ⓐ Ⓑ ● Ⓓ 1 Ⓐ Ⓑ Ⓒ ● 3 Ⓐ Ⓑ ● Ⓓ 5 Ⓐ Ⓑ ● Ⓓ
   B Ⓕ ● Ⓗ Ⓙ 2 Ⓕ ● Ⓗ Ⓙ 4 Ⓕ Ⓖ ● Ⓙ 6 Ⓕ Ⓖ Ⓗ ●

Page 141 A Ⓐ ● Ⓒ Ⓓ 1 Ⓐ ● Ⓒ Ⓓ 3 Ⓐ Ⓑ Ⓒ ● 5 ● Ⓑ Ⓒ Ⓓ
   B Ⓕ Ⓖ ● Ⓙ 2 Ⓕ Ⓖ Ⓗ ● 4 Ⓕ ● Ⓗ Ⓙ 6 Ⓕ Ⓖ Ⓗ ●

Page 142 A Ⓐ Ⓑ Ⓒ ● 1 ● Ⓑ Ⓒ Ⓓ 3 Ⓐ Ⓑ ● Ⓓ 5 Ⓐ Ⓑ Ⓒ ●
   B ● Ⓖ Ⓗ Ⓙ 2 Ⓕ Ⓖ Ⓗ ● 4 Ⓕ Ⓖ ● Ⓙ 6 Ⓕ ● Ⓗ Ⓙ

Page 143 A Ⓐ Ⓑ ● Ⓓ 1 Ⓐ Ⓑ ● Ⓓ 3 Ⓐ Ⓑ ● Ⓓ
   B Ⓕ Ⓖ ● Ⓙ 2 Ⓕ Ⓖ ● Ⓙ 4 Ⓕ Ⓖ ● Ⓙ